Edwin Cone Bissell

A Practical Introductory Hebrew Grammar

Edwin Cone Bissell

A Practical Introductory Hebrew Grammar

ISBN/EAN: 9783337317171

Printed in Europe, USA, Canada, Australia, Japan

Cover: Foto ©Paul-Georg Meister /pixelio.de

More available books at **www.hansebooks.com**

A PRACTICAL INTRODUCTORY HEBREW GRAMMAR

BY

EDWIN CONE BISSELL

PROFESSOR IN HARTFORD THEOLOGICAL SEMINARY

HARTFORD, CONN.

THE HARTFORD THEOLOGICAL SEMINARY

1891

PREFACE.

This Grammar differs from other primary Hebrew Grammars chiefly in two respects: its compactness of form — attained, it is believed, without loss of important matter — and the facilities it offers for acquiring, during the study of the grammatical principles, a choice Hebrew vocabulary. All words used in the Hebrew Bible over fifty times, the most of those used between twenty-five and fifty times, and not a few of those, of connected roots, used less than twenty-five times are here found, and they are the only Hebrew words employed in the book. Seven hundred of them are made use of in Parts 1 and 2, and three hundred in the additional Exercises (pp. 123–130). It is, of course, to be expected that the student will make special effort to memorize these words as they occur; but the process, it is confidently hoped, will be greatly facilitated by the structure of the Grammar itself. 1. The words are arranged in the several Vocabularies under their respective root-forms. 2. They are very generally accompanied by notes and mnemonics for the purpose of calling special attention to them and fixing them in mind. 3. They are used in the illustrations of principles; in the various tables of inflected forms; and, all of them, in the Exercises for translation. 4. Attention is repeatedly called to them by a careful system of cross references. 5 An alphabetical list is given (pp. 118–120) to serve as a test of the student's acquaintance with the Vocabularies already gone over, as well as for general reference. 6. The Exercises for translating Hebrew into English are purposely placed apart from the Vocabularies in order to encourage independence of them. 7. And, finally, in Ap. ii. (A) about six hundred of the words are associated together in the form of synonyms; and (B) three hundred of similar form or sound are discriminated from one another. Among many advantages of this method, it has been found that, without any considerable increase of the time required to master the principles of the Grammar, the student, while so engaged, has also made a fair beginning in the much neglected departments of Hebrew etymology and synonomy; and, still better, acquired a vocabulary sufficient to enable him to read at sight in the historical books of the Bible. The use of mnemonics is simply incidental to the general plan; but, far-fetched and even ridiculous as some of the suggestions are acknowledged to be, they have proved, after an experience of some years, very effective for their purpose. The only other systematic attempt of the kind with which I am acquainted is that of Stier (*Hebräisches Vocabularium*, Leipz., 1871), who, however, used the system to a very limited extent.

In the arrangement of material, especially of §§ 14–37, I have aimed to be practical rather than strictly scientific. A smaller type has often been made use of for subordinate matter; but very little has been inserted in the body of the work for mere reference.

In the Exercises and in the illustrations of rules, I have sought to confine myself to strictly Biblical expressions. Large use has been made throughout of the inductive principle in the form of presentation.

In treating of the Accents, on the basis of the well-known works of Professor Wickes (Oxford, 1887, 1881), the subject, it is hoped, has been somewhat clarified and simplified. This section, however, might well be omitted until the rest of the Grammar has been learned.

The slight changes made in the nomenclature and classification of the Verb are in harmony with the expressed opinions, if not with the actual practice of some of the best recent grammarians.

The references by numbers, in the Exercises and Word-list, to the Vocabularies, and in the Vocabularies to the appended notes, will be readily understood. The absence of an index will, perhaps, be less keenly felt, in view of the unusually full Table of Contents, which, it is thought, will serve important practical uses both of the student and the teacher.

A chapter, to conclude the work, on the formation of Hebrew words was begun, but subsequently abandoned on reading Strack's notice of the investigations of Professor Barth of Berlin, still in progress, in this department (see *Theol. Literaturblatt*, 1890, Nr. 18). They seem likely to make necessary an entire reconstruction of what has hitherto been thought and written on the subject.

It is doubtless too much to expect that other instructors in Hebrew will always agree with me in what has here been said or purposely left unsaid, especially touching points on which they fail to agree with one another. Those most familiar with recent Hebrew grammatical literature will readily discover that I have been much influenced by the grammars of Gesenius-Kautzsch (25th ed., Leipz., 1889), König (Leipz., 1881) and Strack (3d ed., Berlin, 1890), my large indebtedness to whom I gladly acknowledge.

I wish, also, to give expression to a warm sense of gratitude to numerous colleagues, who, having received advanced sheets of my grammar, have materially aided me with friendly criticisms and valuable suggestions.

EDWIN CONE BISSELL.

HARTFORD, March 2, 1891.

TABLE OF CONTENTS.

§ 1. *The Alphabet:* — of what it consists — final letters — *B^eghadhk^ephath* letters — pronunciation of certain other letters — division of letters according to the organs of speech used in pronouncing them — exercise . . . . pp. 1, 2

§ 2. *The Vowels:* — the three primary — their modifications in tabular form — use of circumflex accent — "vowel letters" and what they severally represent — table of class, character, name, sound, and quantity of the vowels — remark on the character *é* — on means of distinguishing Qâmeç from Qâmeç ḥâṭûph — other ambiguous signs for vowels — where the vowels are written — exceptions — Š^ewâ and the Ḥâṭēphs — vocabulary with notes — exercises . . . . pp. 3–6

§ 3. *The Syllable:* — number in a word — beginning — device if beginning with two consonants — "vocal" Š^ewâ, what and where found — exception to rule for syllable — to that for Š^ewâ — end of a syllable — a final one — an audible consonant and ־ְ at the end of a syllable not final — final Kaph or two audible consonants ending a word — meaning of "audible" — a shut, doubly shut and sharpened syllable — an open syllable — vowel of an open syllable — of a shut syllable — half-open syllables — how distinguished — vowel of a shut final syllable with the tone — of a shut penultimate syllable — a toneless sharpened syllable — the tone — how marked — Methegh what and where found — with the conjunction ו — vocabulary and notes — exercise . . . . pp. 6–9

§ 4. *Other Characters used in the Hebrew text:* — Dâghēš lene — when used — the dot sometimes found in final ה and א — D. l. after a disjunctive accent or at the beginning of a new sentence — D. forte — how distinguished from D. l. — when used with the B^eghadhk^ephath letters — different kinds of D. forte — Raphe — original and present use — Maqqēph — Q^erê and K^ethîbh — further use of the circle — a perpetual Q^erê — special dots (*Puncta extraordinaria*) — end of a verse how marked — vocabulary with notes — exercise . . . . pp. 10–12

§ 5. *The gutturals and quiescent letters:* — the guttural letters — of ־ְ — of ח — in what all are peculiar — D. f. implied — with what letters — when not implied changes required — class of vowels favored — *i* and *u* how changed — vowels short and long with a final guttural — Pathaḥ furtive and the tone or with accretions — gutturals and Š^ewâ — character of the Ḥâṭēph — the vowel preceding a Ḥâṭēph — peculiarity of א — of its losing consonantal force — final א following a silent Š^ewâ — the letter ר — when ו and י are used as consonants — vocabulary with notes — exercise . . . . pp. 12–14

§ 6. *Changes in Vowels:* — causes working to produce them — how far possible — immutable vowels — a tone long vowel in a shut or loosely shut syllable — in a sharpened syllable — vowels of a shut syllable if it be opened — effects of Pause on a short vowel — as to an original or a dropped vowel — on the tone — effect on vowels if the tone be moved forward one syllable — difference in nouns and verbs in this respect — removal of the tone still another syllable — vocabulary with notes — exercise .... pp. 14–16

§ 7. *The Accents:* — table of no., names, form and position of prose accents — derivation of names — accents where found — rule if not on tone syllable — on what their power depends — accents marking highest, high and low tones — meaning of disjunctive and conjunctive — accent closing a verse — general law governing accentual division — object primarily aimed at — main accents where placed — accents as marks of punctuation — accents used to mark the main dichotomy — the minor dichotomy in the Ṣillûq clause — in 'Athnâḥ clause — order of the conjunctives — of an occasional double system of accentuation — form of Pâsēq and its use — poetic accents where found and their use — law governing them in the major dichotomy — in the minor dichotomy .... pp. 16–21

§ 8. *The Personal Pronoun:* — table of forms — the form of אתה — את — הוא — נחני — אנו — original form of 2d pers. sing. and pl. — Dāghēš in המה, הנה — oblique cases of pronoun how indicated — vocabulary with notes — exercise .... p. 22

§ 9. *The Article:* — table of forms — for what original form accounts — Art. before gutturals — in the second syllable from the tone and when not lengthened to Qāmeç — original force of art. — when found with הַר, פַּר, עַם, אֶרֶץ — before a letter having Šᵉwâ — vocabulary with notes — exercise ...... pp. 23, 24

§ 10. *Demonstrative and Relative Pronoun:* — table of dem. pronoun — that for the remote object — Dāghēš in the ל of אלה — other use of זה — זו, זו and זה — אל — the form הלזה *etc.* — position of dem. pronoun — as an adjective — with another adjective — the adjective as predicate — when qualifying — if the subst. be definite — the Rel. pronoun — contracted form — uses — as a sign of relation — a conjunction — vocabulary with notes — exercise .... pp. 24, 25

§ 11. *The Interrogative Pronouns and Particles:* — forms — table showing pointing of מה — use of מי and מה respectively — the Dāghēš following מה — the interrog. pronoun as Genitive — מה before adjectives and verbs — other uses of מי and מה — the interrog. particles — pointing of ה — when used — its relation to אם — when an alternative is suggested — אי without a pronom. suffix — with other adverbs — an interrog. pronoun or particle unnecessary to a question — the D. forte following ה — ה with לא — vocabulary with notes — exercise .... pp. 25–27

§ 12. *The Inseparable Prepositions:* — meaning of ב, ל, כ — their pointing — two Šᵉwâs coming together at the beginning of a syllable — independent form of these prepositions and when used — pointing before יהוה — vocabulary with notes — exercise .... pp. 27, 28

§ 13. *The Preposition* מן *and Wāw Copulative:* — how מן is written — in the case of gutturals following, or ר — with ה and ח — before letters having Šᵉwâ — before י — before יהוה — how the conjunction ו is pointed — before a guttural — the labials or a letter having Šᵉwâ — before the tone syllable, especially with words associated in pairs — before י excepting יהוה — vocabulary with notes — exercise .... pp. 28, 29

§ 14. *The Strong Verb:* — roots of words — how verbs are classified — weak verbs — origin of names of weak verbs — examples — why verbs having gutturals are classified as strong verbs — table of Perfect of strong verb — how formed — origin of the several pronominal fragments — endings not taking the tone — the vowels *a*, *ē*, *ō* in final syllable before affixes beginning with a vowel and having the tone — vocabulary with notes — exercise .... pp. 29–31

§ 15. *The Infinitive and Imperative :* — table of each — what the two Infs. are — vowels of each — Inf. cstr. how used — Inf. abs. — the syllable formed by prefixing ל to Inf. cstr. — ground-form of Imp. — the endings — the Imp. how used — a command in the third person — with a negative — the first vowel in קִטְלִי — lengthened form of Imp. — vocabulary with notes — exercise .. pp. 31–33

§ 16. *The Imperfect and Participles :* — table of the Impf. — why there are prefixes as well as affixes — origin of them — the terms Perf. and Impf. — the former how used — the latter — table of Parts. — whence the Part. pass. — how the Parts. are used — time indicated — original forms and how changed — based on what other form — vocabulary with notes — exercise ...... pp. 33–35

§ 17. *Intransitive verbs :* —principal vowel of a verb — distinction between trans. and intrans. verbs — what the latter indicate — inflection of verbs middle ē — not always taking *a* in the second syllable of Inf. cstr., Imp. and Impf. — inflection of verbs middle ō — forms following the Perf. — the Inf. with a fem. ending — middle *a* verb taking *a* in second syllable of Impf. — vocabulary with notes — exercise .... pp. 35, 36

§ 18. *Lengthened form of the Imperfect and Wāw Consecutive :* — analogy of Imp. followed — formation of Cohortative — tone — where Cohortative is found and its force — the vowel before *ah* — peculiar sequence of Perf. and Impf. in Hebrew — how indicated — original form of this wāw — how joined to the verbs it affects — how preceded — form of Wāw c. with Impf. and the tone — before א of 1st Pers. — before וָ — tone in 1st Pers. sing. — sometimes joined to Cohortative — form of Wāw c. with the Perf. and the tone — uses of projection of tone — vocabulary with notes — exercise .... pp. 36–39

§ 19. *Voices of the Verb :* — ground-form of verb — name Qal — form found in lexicons — how translated — represented as the root of the word — Denominatives — derived stems — "conjugations" or Voices — how formed — whence their usual names — infelicity of nomenclature and how changed — all verbs not found in all voices — vocabulary with notes .... pp. 39, 40

§ 20. *The Niqtal :* — partial table of forms — the voice how formed — original of vowel of 1st syllable — where prefix נ appears — the Inf. cstr. and related parts — use of aspirate הִ — characteristic signs of the Ni. — the tone sometimes retracted — vowel of Impf. 1. sing. — forms of Inf. Abs. on what based — inflection of Ni. and Qal — meaning of Ni. — vocabulary with notes — exercise .... pp. 40–41

§ 21. *The Qiṭṭēl, Quṭṭal and Hithqaṭṭēl :* — most characteristic mark of these voices — the one common to the first two — vowel of 1. syl. of Qi. — original vowel of 2. syl. where appearing and where become ē — original vowel of Inf. abs. — prefix of Parts. here and in following voices — three verbs taking *e* in last syl. of Perf. — where D. forte is dropped from middle radical — further characterization of Qu. — formation of Hithq. — syncopation of הָ — change required if 1st radical be a sibilant — if ת, ד, ט *etc.* — force of Qi. voice — of Qu. — of Hithq. — vocabulary with notes — exercise .... pp. 42, 43

§ 22. *The Hiqṭîl and Hoqṭal :* — partial table of forms — characteristic mark of these voices — original vowels of Hi. Perf. and how changed — Inf. cstr. and related parts — final vowel of Inf. Abs. — the Ho. Part. — shortened forms of the Imp. and Impf. in the Hi. of strong verbs — same with inflectional or other additions — use of the Jussive — analogy of form with that of wāw c. — meaning of Hi. with and without a personal object — meaning of Ho. — vocabulary with notes — exercise .... pp. 44, 45

§ 23. *Guttural Verbs — An Initial Guttural:* — what guttural verbs are — former rules recalled — table of an inflected guttural verb — points of difference from an ordinary strong verb: as to Š^ewâ; a performative letter whether closely or loosely joined to it; the initial guttural, if doubling be called for — the vowel *i* of the Q. Imp. — why some forms of חזק are given — why the Qi. and Qu. are omitted — vocabulary with notes — exercise .... pp. 45–47

§ 24. *Verbs with a Medial Guttural:* — table of forms — additional changes required — why ברך is used in Qi. and derivative voices — the vowel heightened through omission of D. forte — the letter ר before syllables beginning with כ and having the tone — vocabulary with notes — exercise .... pp. 48, 49.

§ 25. *Verbs with a Final Guttural:* — table of forms — characteristics of gutturals most widely exhibited; Pathaḥ furtive; *a* instead of *ō* and of *ē*; a helping vowel in Perf. s. 2. f. of all voices — no special peculiarities in the Qu., Hithq. and Ho. voices — vocabulary with notes — exercise .... pp. 49–51

§ 26. *Nouns. — Gender and Number:* — the two genders — objects regarded as neuter in other languages — form of masc. nouns in the sing. — endings of fem. nouns in sing. — how nouns of common gender are indicated — what the ending ָה often represents — the ending ת in nouns following a consonant — gender of Adjectives — numbers of nouns — ending of masc. pl. — of fem. — of du. — how the last is used — table of forms — how the several endings of the pl. are added to the noun — changes required in changeable vowels — nouns with a fem. ending in sing. having ִים in the pl. — origin of ending וֹת uses of pl. — vocabulary with notes — exercise .... pp. 51–53

§ 27. *Ancient case endings — The Construct State:* — original forms for Nom. and Gen. case — form for Accus. still found — how used and name — how distinguished from fem. ending — when appended to words ending in ָה — Heb. use of prepositions instead of case endings — its mode of representing the Gen. relation — effect on changeable vowels of word in the construct — table of forms — change in terminations of pl. and du. — in ָה of the fem. — in ֶה — other occurrences of the construct — vocabulary with notes — exercise ..... pp. 53–55

§ 28. *The Noun with Pronominal Suffixes:* — table of suffixes for a sing., pl. and du. noun — change of ת to כ in 2d pers. of pronoun — the other fragmentary endings — nouns ending in a consonant and those ending in a vowel — the "connecting" vowel — original form of cstr. in pl. and du. forms — the sing. 1. c. and the pl. 2. f. — the "heavy" suffixes — poetic forms of certain endings — the effect of Pause — table of noun with suffixes — has here an immutable vowel — what the suffixes denote — cstr. form of fem. — fem. of pl. nouns — other endings than those of table — Omission of Dāghēš in the כ of 2. pers. — vocabulary with notes — exercise .... pp. 55–57

§ 29. *First Class of Nouns:* — how nouns with mutable vowels are divided — relation to tone — table of forms — what the first class includes — to what the terminations are added — words beginning or ending with a guttural — feminines of the form גדולה — words of the form עָנִי or עֲנִי — vocabulary with notes — exercise .... pp. 57, 58

§ 30. *Second Class of Nouns:* — what it includes — law of inflection of words of the form of עולם — the Ni. Qu. and Ho. Parts. so inflected — monosyllables with a mutable *ā* — table of forms of אֹיֵב — same as Q. Part. act. — law of inflection — monosyllables in *ē* — words of form חֹזֶה in cstr. and their law of inflection — vocabulary with notes — exercise .... pp. 59, 60

§ 31. *Third Class of Nouns:* — what it includes — table of forms of דָּבָר — when *a* is thinned to *i* — words of the form זָקֵן in cstr. — שָׂדֶה included in this class — peculiar form of some words when additions are taken — table of forms of a fem. of this class ending in ־ָה — to what the endings are added and the law of vocal changes — form of the du. — vocabulary with notes — exercise . . pp. 60–62

§ 32. *Fourth Class of Nouns:* — were originally monosyllabic — their vowels — device for pronouncing — origin of name "Segholate" — change in Segholates of the *a* class — of the *i* and *u* classes — absolute form of words in first two classes — monosyllabic form sometimes retained — table of forms of מֶלֶךְ — law of inflection — the cstr. sing. — characteristic vowel of the inflected forms of words of the *u* (or *o*) class — exceptional pl. forms — how cstr. pl. is actually formed — vocabulary with notes — exercise .... pp. 62, 63

§ 33. *Fourth Class of Nouns* (continued): — table of words with gutturals — helping vowel of Segholates having a guttural for its second or third letter — exception to second part of rule — case of S. of the *u* class — those of the *i* class whose first letter is a guttural — table of feminines formed from masc. S. by the addition of ־ָה and rule of inflection — table of proper fem. S. — what they are and how inflected — double form of some nouns — vocabulary with notes — exercise .... pp. 64–66

§ 34. *Nouns of Peculiar Formation:* — table of such nouns — explanation of their peculiarities: why אַחִים, אָחִיו; ending of אָחוֹת; ה in אֲמָהוֹת pl. of כְּלִי and עִיר — other nouns in preceding vocabularies — vocabulary with notes — exercise .... pp. 66, 67

§ 35. *The Cardinal Numbers:* — vowels of first syllable of word for *one* — the Dāghēš in שְׁתַּיִם — numeral for *one* an adj. — for two — parts of speech and gender of those from 3 to 10 — table of various card. numbers: those from 11 to 19 how formed — the form עַשְׁתֵּי — the two perpetual Q'rēs — num. for 20 — those from 30 to 90 — position of those from 2 to 10 as it respects the noun — use of fem. du. of a cardinal — the ordinals 1 to 10 — above 10 — "fourth" — idiomatic expressions .... pp. 67–69

§ 36. *The Strong Verb with Suffixes:* — those of the Inf. cstr. and Part. excepting 1st Pers. — what the "verbal" suffix always denotes — the nominal — the verbal suffix with the Part. — vowels of the verb how affected by suffixes — the Inf. with the suffixes ךָ, כֶם, כֶן — that of the form קְטֹל — table of the Perf. with suffixes — two ways of expressing the Accus. after a verb — suffixes generally those of the noun — union vowel in the Perf. — exception — in the Impf. and Imp. — changes in the verb before receiving suffixes — changes produced by suffixes — the tone — verbs ending in a vowel — contracted forms — reflexive action how expressed — the Hi. with suffixes — the Qi. and Hithq. — Intrans. verbs how different — vocabulary with notes — exercise .... pp. 69–71

§ 37. *Strong Verb with Suffixes* (continued): — those of the Impf. and Imp. in tabular form — forms ending in a vowel — final *ō* of Impf. before ךָ, כֶם, כֶן — of the Imp. — how union vowel is changed — נ Demonstrative: its origin and how it affects forms — verbs having *a* in last syllable of Impf. and Imp. — the Hi. and Qi. Impf. — vocabulary with notes — exercise............pp. 72, 73

§ 38. *Particles with Suffixes — Adverbs:* — table of forms — in some cases typical, in others, including all — suffixes generally those of noun, but may have

נ demonstrative — include the copula — excepting עוֹד have a cstr. form — other adverbs having some of the nominal suffixes — vocabulary with notes — exercise .... pp. 73, 74

§ 39. *Particles with Suffixes — Prepositions:* — such Prepositions in tabular form — forms of מִן — difference between אֵת *with* and אֵת (אוֹת) with suffixes — עִם like former — like לִ֫י, בִּי — an idiomatic phrase — pleonastic use of לְ — form of אֶל, עַד, עַל in *pl.* and why — in poetry — other Prepositions actually taking a *pl.* form — vocabulary with notes — exercise .... pp. 75, 76

§ 40. *Degrees of Comparison:* — no special forms in Hebrew — how the Compar. degree is expressed — other uses of מִן — various ways in which the idea of superlativeness is expressed — vocabulary with notes — exercise ..... pp. 76, 77

§ 41. *Weak Verbs — Verbs* פ״א: — distinction previously noted — verbs having א as their first radical — table of a פ״א verb in the Impf. — their characteristic — list of these verbs conveniently arranged for remembering — two other verbs occasionally following this analogy — vocabulary and notes — exercise .... pp. 78, 79

§ 42. *Verbs* פ״נ: — the inflected forms of such verb tabulated — נ closing a preform. syllable and having a Šᵉwâ — when assimilation does *not* take place — other verbs of this class having *a* in Q. Impf. and still others, *a* or *ō* — vowel of the sharpened syllable of the Ho. — נ in the Q. of some verbs at the beginning of a syllable with Šᵉwâ — further change in the Inf. cstr. — the verb לקח — נתן in the Q. Perf., Inf. cstr. assimilating its final נ before ת or another נ — the final vowel of Imp. and Impf. — Inf. cstr. inflected as Segholate noun of the *i* class — vocabulary with notes — exercise .... pp. 79–81

§ 43. *Verbs* פ״י: — table of forms — the three classes of פ״י verbs — characteristic of first class — what takes place when the first radical is dropped in Impf. and related forms — when it is retained — the eight verbs regularly dropping first radical — the three retaining י in the Imp. — in verbs originally פ״ו how ו is treated when not initial: as a consonant, as a vowel — the Qi. and Qu. voices — frequent form of Imp. in these verbs — the verb הלך — יכל — the second class of these verbs (originally פ״י) — the analogy they follow — their inflection — how distinguished from verbs פ״נ — third class of verbs (orig., פ״י) characterized (Q. and Hi.) — Ni. and Ho. voices — number of verbs in the class — vocabulary with notes — exercise .... pp. 81–84

§ 44. *Verbs* ע״ו: — table of forms — main irregularity — original and present form of the Q. Perf. — Inf. cstr. and Imp. — Impf. — Part. act. and pass. — Perf. and Part. of intrans. verbs — Ni. Perf. and Part. — Hi. Perf. and Part. — fem. pl. forms of Imp. — change before the affixes beginning with ת and נ — change of tone effects a change of vowels in some parts of Ni. — alternative form in Hi. Impf. and Imp. of נוח — tone in these verbs — intrans. verbs middle *ō* — verbs having *ô* in the Inf. and related forms — peculiarity of the Jussive and wāw c. forms in Q. and Hi. of these verbs — vocabulary with notes — exercise.. pp. 84–86

§ 45. *Verbs* ע״י *and the Intensive Voices:* — table of forms — characteristic change — effect on some forms — how inflected in the Q. — in the other voices — words of this class most used — Q. and Hi. Impf. — probability as to the original middle radical — י as second radical in the Q. Perf. — the intensive voices of these verbs — how the intensive effect is secured — vocabulary with notes — exercise .... pp. 86, 87

§ 46. *Verbs* ע״ע: — table of forms — chief irregularity — effect on the vowels — why ē as stem vowel in Hi. Perf. — vowels of preformatives in open syllables and the original *a* — use of a helping vowel (Perf. ō, Impf. é) — difference from verbs ע״ו — basis of rule for Ho. — device for showing this class of verbs when there is no afformative — Jussive and wāw c. forms — the intensive stems — their names — nouns from verbs ע״ו (ע״י) and ע״ע — vocabulary with notes — exercise .... pp. 88–90

§ 47. *Verbs* ל״ה: — table of forms — what these verbs really are — where the third radical appears — uniform principles of inflection: respecting ending of Perf. 3. s. m. and fem.; the original י — disappearance of ה — ending of Inf. cstrs. — of ground-form of Imp., of Impfs. and Parts. — י before the ending נָה — the Hithq. voice — the Cohortative — vocabulary with notes — exercise . . pp. 90–92

§ 48. *Verbs* ל״ה (continued): — table of apocopated forms — a peculiarity of ל״ה verbs respecting apocopation — forms apocopated and effect: Qi. Imp. — Hi. Imp. — Q. Impf. — Ni. and Qi. Impf. — Hi. Impf. — forms of Q. and Hi. if the first radical be a guttural — the verb ראה — apoc. forms of היה and חיה — other forms of the same — peculiarities of the verb שחה — effect when apocopated — vocabulary with notes — exercise .... pp. 92–94

§ 49. *Verbs* ל״א: — table of forms — origin of peculiarity in the inflection — forms ending in א — Q. Imp. and Impf. — all other forms where א ends a syllable: before affirmatives beginning with a consonant; beginning with a vowel — intransitive verbs — the Hithq. voice — further likeness to verbs ל״ה — vocabulary with notes — exercise .... pp. 94–96

Paradigms, Exercises in Translation, and List of Words: — Table (in full) of the Strong verb קטל, pp. 98, 99. — of the Weak verb קום, pp. 100, 101. — of the Weak verb סבב, p. 102. — exercises in translation (Hebrew into English), pp. 103–117. — list of words found in vocabularies, alphabetically arranged, pp. 118–120. — abstract of notes to vocabularies, pp. 121, 122.

Appendix I. Additional exercises in translation, with vocabulary, pp. 123–130.

Appendix II. (*A*) List of Synonyms. — (*B*) Words (of similar sound or form) to be distinguished, pp. 131–134.

PART I.—CHARACTERS AND SOUNDS.

§ 1. THE ALPHABET.[a]

FORM.	NAME.	EQUIVALENT.	NUMERICAL VALUE.
א	'A̍leph	ʼ	1
ב	Bêth	bh, b	2
ג	Gi̍mel	gh, g	3
ד	Dā̍leth	dh, d	4
ה	Hē	h	5
ו	Wāw	w	6
ז	Zá̍yin	z	7
ח	Ḥêth	ḥ	8
ט	Ṭêth	ṭ	9
י	Yôdh	y	10
כ and ך	Kaph	kh, k	20
ל	Lā̍medh	l	30
מ and ם	Mêm	m	40
נ and ן	Nûn	n	50
ס	Ṣā̍mekh	ṣ	60
ע	'A̍yin	ʻ	70
פ and ף	Pê	ph, p	80
צ and ץ	Çādhê	ç	90
ק	Qôph	q	100
ר	Rêš	r	200
שׂ or שׁ	Sîn or Šîn	s, š (sh)	300
ת	Tāw	th, t	400

[a] REM.—The perpendicular stroke is used everywhere to mark the tone when it is on the penult. Rules for the vowel sounds are given in § 2.

1. The Hebrew alphabet consists of twenty-two consonants, and the language is written from right to left.

2. Five letters have two characters each to represent them, the second being used when the letter is at the end of a word. Such secondary forms are called "final letters." A convenient mnemonic for the letters having final forms is *Kam-n*ᵉ*-phaç* (כַּמְנְפַּץ).

3. Six letters have a two-fold pronunciation, a hard and a soft; the former when a dot is found in them (בּ = b, ב = bh). These letters are commonly known as the *B*ᵉ*-ghadh-k*ᵉ*-phath* (בְּגַדְכְּפַת) letters.

4. The letter ח (ḥ) is pronounced like *ch* in *loch*. א, represented by a smooth breathing, is silent like the *h* in *hour*. ה, at the end of a word, is silent, being used simply as an accompaniment and sign of the preceding vowel. It generally occurs as a final letter in words whose third radical (ו, י, ה) does not appear. When it has consonantal value a dot is placed in it (הּ). The sound of ע, represented by a rough breathing, is scarcely to be distinguished in common usage from that of א.[a] צ (ç) is pronounced much as *ts* would be in the same position. The letter ק has a pronunciation similar to that of כ, but the sound is formed further back in the mouth. The same is true of ט as compared with ת.

5. The Hebrew letters are divided, according to the organs of speech used in pronouncing them, into five classes: Gutturals (ע, ח, ה, א); Palatals (ק, כ, י, ג); Linguals (ת, נ, ל, ט, ד); Dentals or Sibilants (שׁ, שׂ, צ, ס, ז); and Labials (פ, מ, ו, ב).

6. Letters used as prefixes or suffixes in the formation and inflection of words are called "serviles." They are ת, שׁ, שׂ, נ, מ, ל, כ, י, ו, ה, ב, א (mn. אֵיתָן, מֹשֶׁה, וְכָלֵב, *i.e.* "Ethan," "Moses," and (וְ) "Caleb"). The remaining letters are called "radicals."

Exercise.—א, ב, כ, בּ, כּ, ג, נ, גּ, דּ, ר, ד, ך, ה, הּ, ח, ת, תּ, י, ו, ז, ן, ט, מ, ל, ס, ם, פּ, צ, ע, ץ, ף, פּ, שׂ, שׁ; טעם, ירד, אתה, גּם, שׂים, החשך, קום, אח, ספר, תּמם.

d, h, z, r, bh, ḥ, ṭ, k, ṣ, s, š, ʾ, ç, ʿ, ph, q, t; ʾm, lḥn, ʿm, km, rʿ, rç, šwbh, bmdhbr, ʿwph, mṣpdh, ythr, gdhl, ʿyn, ʾrç, kwkhbhym, nws.

---

[a] Originally one of the two sounds of ע approached that of ח; the other that of *g* with a slight *r* sound before it (*ʳg*). The word עַזָּה, *ʿAzzāh*, was transliterated by the LXX. as Γάζα: Gen. x. 19.

§ 2. THE VOWELS.

1. From the three primary vowel sounds, a, i, u (pronounced *ah*, *ee*, *oo*), the remaining vowels arose. Their various modifications, taking place in Hebrew, are shown in the following table. A vowel having no mark above it represents its short sound.

From *a* came	From *i* came	From *u* came
â (= a + a)	î (= i + i or i + y)	û (= u + u or u + w)
ā (lengthened by tone)	ê (= a + i or a + y)	ô (= a + u or a + w)
ô (see next table)	ē (heightened by tone)	ō (heightened by tone)
o (see next table)	e (by deflection or the shortening of ē)	o (by deflection)
i (by thinning)	ĕ (shorter form)	ŏ (shorter form)
ă (shorter form)	ᵉ (shortest form)	ᵉ (shortest form)
ᵉ (shortest form)		

2. Of these vowels those marked with the circumflex accent (â, î, ê, û, ô), being long either by nature or contraction, are no longer changeable. The rest are subject to the changes noted.

3. [1] קָאם *qam*. [2] מה *mah, meh, moh*. [3] לו *lu, lo*, מי *mi, me*. Originally the Hebrew had no characters to represent the vowel sounds. There were four weak consonants, however, which served the purpose to a limited extent (י, ו, ה, א), and are generally known as "vowel letters." א stood for any vowel, but generally represented the *a* sound in the midst of a word.[1] ה at the end of a word stood for any vowel sound except *i* and *u*[2]; while ו represented *u* or *o*, and י *i* or *e* either in the midst or at the end of a word.[3] These characters being found ambiguous and insufficient by later Jewish scholars, a system of vocalization was invented (A.D. 600–800) for the purpose of fixing and preserving the traditional pronunciation. On introducing this change the use of the so-called vowel letters was not discarded, nor the consonantal text disturbed. The new system was simply combined, as far as possible, with the old. A vowel represented both by a vowel letter and one of the new characters was said to be fully, by the latter only, defectively written. The characters adopted, with their names, sounds, and quantity, were as follows (see § 1. R.):—

CLASS.	CHARACTER.	NAME.	SOUND.	QUANTITY.
A	◌ָ	Qâmeç	*a* in father	ā or â
	אָ	"	" "	â
	◌ַ	Påthaḥ	*a* in fat	a
	◌ֲ	Ḥâṭēph-påthaḥ	" " (but shorter)	ă
	◌ְ	Šewâ	*e* in below	ᵉ
I	◌ִ	Ḥîreq	*i* in pin	*i* and (sometimes) î
	◌ִי	"	*i* in ravine	î
	◌ֵ	Çērê	*e* in prey	ē and (sometimes) ê
	◌ֵי	"	" "	ê
	◌ֶ	Seghôl	*e* in met	e
	◌ֶי	"	*e* in there	é
	◌ֱ	Ḥâṭēph-seghôl	*e* in met (but shorter)	ĕ
	◌ְ	Šewâ	*e* in below	ᵉ
U	וּ	Šûreq	*u* in true	û and (rarely) u
	◌ֻ	Qibbûç	*u* in put	u and (often) û
	◌ֹ	Ḥôlem	*o* in note	ō and (often) ô
	וֹ	"	" "	ô and (rarely) ō
	◌ָ	Qâmeç-ḥâṭûph	*o* in on	o
	◌ֳ	Ḥâṭēph-qâmeç	" " (but shorter)	ŏ
	◌ְ	Šewâ	*e* in below	ᵉ

REM. 1. — The character é will be used for ◌ֶי only. By consulting the former table it will be observed that it is represented as coming from *a* (others say, *ay*). It is found in such combinations as גְּלֶינָה *gᵉ-lé-nāh*, דְּבָרֶיךָ *dᵉ-bhā-ré-khā*. The Seghôl in the word יִגְלֶה (= יִגְלַי) *yigh-leh*, is really equivalent to it; but it will be found sufficient for practical purposes to represent all other forms of Seghôl by *e*, including two other forms from *a*, — as that in the first syllable of מֶלֶךְ (from מַלְךְ) *me-lek*, and of יֶדְכֶם *yedh-khem*, compounded of יַד and כֶם, — as well as the form from *i* or ē.

REM. 2. — The character ◌ָ, it will be seen, stands both for Qâmeç and Qâmeç-ḥâṭûph. Many times they are distinguishable only after one has become familiar with the derivation of words. In general, it may be said that the sign ◌ָ = o only when the vowel concerned was originally o. The following rules cover most of the cases of its occurrence. The sign ◌ָ = o (1) in a toneless closed syllable (חָכְמָה *ḥokh-māh*); (2) before a guttural with ◌ֳ, or before another *o* (הָעֳמַד *ho-'ŏ-madh*, הָעָמְדוּ *ho-'om-dhû*) excepting the article; (3) in the two abnormal plural forms קֳדָשִׁים (*qo-dhā-šîm*), שָׁרָשִׁים (*šo-rā-šîm*). In No. 3 ָ (o) is used for ֳ (ŏ), for which, in turn, ְ (ᵉ) might have been expected. There is some degree of ambiguity, it will be noticed, attaching to several other characters (ֹו ָ, וֹ, וּ, ָ); but it will practically disappear when the laws of the syllable come to be understood.

4. [1] כִּי *kî*. [2] אוֹ *'ô*, חֹק *ḥōq*, צֹאן *çôn*. [3] ו = wō, not ō. [4] יְהוָֹה *Yᵉ-hô-wāh*. [5] יְהוָֹה. [6] שֹׂנֵא *sô-nē'*. [7] שֹׁדֵד *šô-dhēdh*, תָּפְשׂ *tā-phōs*. The vowel signs, except in a few cases, are written directly under the consonants to which they belong and after which they are pronounced.[1] Šûreq is always found in the bosom of ו (וּ). The same is true of Qāmeç or Šᵉwâ with a final Kaph (ךְ, ךָ). Ḥôlem when accompanied by ו, as a vowel letter, should be found over its right side; when without ו, it is placed over the left of the letter with which it is pronounced, or over the right of the following letter.[2] When ו is a consonant and Ḥôlem is used with it, it should be placed over its left side.[3] The character וֹ will be ō-w if the preceding consonant have no other vowel and ו—being used as a consonant—have a vowel under it.[4] In some texts, when ו is a consonant and Ḥôlem is used just before it, it is placed over the left of the preceding letter to which it really belongs.[5] With the letters שׂ, שׁ, a defectively written Ḥôlem may coincide with the dot ("diacritical point") of these letters respectively. It is then dropped, the one point answering both purposes.[6] When the vowel in this form is used in connection with these letters and does not coincide with the diacritical point, it is placed over the right or left limb, as may be required.[7] Still another exception will be found to the rule that vowels are placed under the consonants after which they are pronounced in Pâthaḥ furtive (§ 5).

5. [1] אֲדֹנָי *'Ă-dhô-nāy*, אֱלֹהִים *'Ĕ-lô-hîm*, חֳלִי *ḥŏ-lî*. The sign ְ (simple Šᵉwâ), it will be observed, is common to the three principal vowel sounds. Each class of vowels has also a Ḥāṭēph, otherwise known as "composite Šᵉwâ," being compounded of a simple Šᵉwâ and one of the vowels ָ, ַ, ֶ. The Ḥāṭēphs are chiefly used, instead of simple Šᵉwâ, with guttural letters.[a]

---

[a] The Ḥāṭēphs (ֳ, ֲ only) are found with other letters than gutturals: (1) when the same consonant is written twice in the midst of a word, and the first would naturally receive a vocal Šᵉwâ; (2) sometimes with ב and ר after long vowels and just before the tone; (3) with the sibilants directly after the conjunction וּ; (4) occasionally after *i*, *a*, *o* (Baer, Gen. xxxii. 18) under a sibilant, liquid or ק. Ḥāṭēph-qāmeç, when used with other letters than gutturals, is chiefly found with the sibilants or the emphatic consonants ט, ק.

especially in the first and second syllables before the tone, to give them a more distinct vocal sound and facilitate their pronunciation.[1]

אָדוֹן 'ā-dhôn, *m.* lord. אֲדֹנָי 'Ă-dhō-nāy, Lord.
אוֹ[1] *adv.* or.
אֱלוֹהַּ 'Ĕ-lô-ah, *m.* God; *pl.* אֱלֹהִים 'Ĕ-lô-hîm.
אִם (interrog. and optat. particle) if, or; כִּי *conj.* that, when, because. כִּי־אִם but, unless, except.
אֵת[2] (אֶת־) *prep.* with; also sign of definite accus.
חוּץ[3] *adv.* without, on the street.
חָלָה[4] *ḥā-lāh.* be weak, sick. חֳלִי † [a] *ḥŏ-lī*, *m.* sickness.
חֹק[5] *m.* statute; *pl.* חֻקִּים *ḥuq-qîm.* חֻקָּה *ḥuq-qāh*, *f.* statute.
כֹּל[6] (כָּל־ kol) *m.* every, all, whole; *adv.* wholly.
מְאֹד[7] *m^{e}-'ōdh*, *m.* force; *adv.* very, exceedingly.
צֹאן[8] *f.* flock (of sheep or goats).
שָׂנֵא[9] *sā-nē'*, hate. שִׂנְאָה † *sin'-āh*, hate.
שָׁדַד[10] *šā-dhadh*, be strong, to desolate. שֹׁד * *m.* force, violence.
תָּפַשׂ[11] *tā-phas*, seize, hold, set (in), overlay with.

[1] Its sound is that of the first letter of *or*. [2] Its last letter is equivalent to the last two of *with*. [3] Pronounced nearly like the *pl.* of *coot*. [4] Suggests *cholera*, from χολή. [5] Has nearly the sound of Coke, the famous English jurist. [6] Corresponds partly in pronunciation with *whole*. [7] Approaches in sound and sense *my oath*. [8] Sheep are not found in the frigid *zone*. [9] Begins with a *hissing* letter. [10] Is the root of שַׁדַּי *Šad-day*, a title of God: Gen. xvii. 1. [11] Associate with *topaz* often *set in* gold.

Exercise. — 'ĕ-meth, bath, bēn, dām, d^{e}-mûth, hû', ḥă-lôm, ṭôbh, ḥōq, ḥuq-qîm, ḥēq, dôr, šîr, yēš, yôm, kaph, min, 'im, çûr, yo-'ŏ-madh, lé-khā.

REM. — In this exercise the circumflex accent represents a fully written vowel in Hebrew.

---

§ 3. THE SYLLABLE.

1. [1]חוּץ, אֶלֶף *'e-leph.* [2]מְאֹד *m^{e}-'ōdh.* [3]יְאֹר *y^{e}-'ōr,* חֲלוֹם *ḥă-lôm.* A Hebrew word has as many syllables as there are full vowels, the Š^{e}wâs and Pathaḥ furtive (§ 5) not being regarded as such.[1] Every syllable begins with a consonant, and may begin with two.[2] If a syllable begin with two consonants, the first will have under it a simple or composite Š^{e}wâ — the latter with gutturals — to aid in the pronunciation.[3] Simple Š^{e}wâ in this place is said to be "vocal"

---

[a] The sign * attached to a word indicates that it is used less than fifty times, the sign † that it is used less than twenty-five times, in the Bible.

to distinguish it from silent Š^ewâ, which is found at the end of a syllable only and is not sounded. Vocal Š^ewâ is always found and only found under the first of two consonants—other than a guttural —that begin a syllable.

Rem. 1.—The conjunction ו when pointed with a dot in its bosom (וּ) is the sole exception to the rule that every syllable begins with a consonant.

Rem. 2.—An exception to the rule for vocal Š^ewâ is the numeral שְׁתֵּי two (for אֶשְׁתֵּי), Gen. iv. 19, where the Š^ewâ is silent.

2. [1] כִּי, אִם. [2] מֶלֶךְ *malk*. [3] שִׂמְחָה *sim-ḥāh*, שָׁמַעְנוּ *šā-ma'-nû*. [4] שָׂמַךְ *sā-makh*, דַּלְתְּ *dalt* (original form of דֶּלֶת *de-leth*). [5] רֵאשִׁית *rê-'šîth* (contracted from רְאֵשִׁית *r^e-'ē-šîth*). A syllable may end either with a vowel or a consonant.[1] Only a final syllable can end with two consonants, and the last one, if sounded, must be a strong letter (one of the *B^e-ghadh-k^e-phath* or ק, ט).[2] An audible vowelless consonant, and generally צ, ending a syllable—other than the final—is provided with a silent Š^ewâ.[3] The same is true of final Kaph and of each of two audible consonants ending a word.[4 a] "Audible" consonants are so named to distinguish them from the vowel letters (י, ו, ה, א) which, as already noted, generally become silent after homogeneous vowel sounds.[5]

3. [1] יָד *yādh*, שִׂמְחָה *sim-ḥāh*, שִׁנַּיִם *šin-na-yim*. [2] נָא, פֹּה, אוֹ. אֶלֶף *'e-leph*, [3] מַיִם *ma-yim*, סָמַךְ *sā-makh*. [4] אִמְרָה *'im-rāh*, חָכָם *ḥā-khām*. A syllable ending in a consonant is said to be shut; doubly shut if that consonant be immediately followed by another consonant in the same word; sharpened, if these two consonants are the same letter repeated (seldom), or the same letter doubled by a dot in it, known as Dāghēš forte (§ 4).[1] A syllable ending in a vowel—as also ה, and א except in certain verbs whose first root letter it is—is said to be open.[2] The vowel of an open syllable must be long unless it have the tone, and a toneless syllable with a long vowel is open.[3 b] The vowel of a shut syllable must

---

[a] There are a few instances where a silent Š^ewâ stands under a *single* final consonant; but they are mostly those where one of the original consonants has been dropped: אַתְּ for אַנְתְּ. In Baer's text the final ת of the 2d *sing. fem. perf.* of verbs whose last root letter is א or ה has it.

[b] The only open syllables having short vowels, even with the tone, are those which were originally doubly closed and have been opened by means of a short helping vowel (דֶּלֶת *de-leth*, from an original דַּלְתְּ *dalt*) and the verbal suffix ־ַנִי *a-nî*.

be short unless it have the tone, and a toneless syllable with a short vowel is shut.[4]

4. [1] יְדְכֶם *yedh-khem* (your hand), נַעֲרָה *na-'ă-rāh*. Besides open and shut syllables, there is what is known as the half-open, or intermediate, syllable.[a] It has a short, toneless vowel, and its final consonant a Š^ewâ, simple or composite. This Šewâ is neither silent nor vocal, though approaching the latter, and is called medial. It need not be confounded with vocal Šewâ, since the syllable which it (partly) closes has a short, toneless vowel. And when followed by the *Beghadhkephath* letters, it need not be confounded with a silent Šewâ, since the dot (Dāghēš lene, § **4. 1**) which is found in these letters when following a silent Šewâ is omitted after a medial one.[1]

REM. — A shut final syllable, with the tone, may have any vowel (*ĭ* is found only in מִן, אִם, עִם, and certain apocopated verbal forms); a shut penultimate syllable, with the tone, has only *a*, *e*, and *ā*, *ē*, *ō*. In a toneless sharpened syllable only the vowels *a*, *i*, *u* can stand.

5. [1] בַּ֫יִת. The principal tone in Hebrew words must be on one of the last two syllables, and is generally found on the last syllable.[b] In this book, as heretofore, whenever the tone syllable is not final it will be indicated by a perpendicular line over the penult.[1]

6. [1] שָׂ֫מְחָה she rejoiced. [2] עֵֽינֵיכֶם your eyes. [3] חָֽכְמָה she was wise, חָכְמָה wisdom. [4] הָֽחֳלִי the sickness. Méthegh (meaning *bridle*) is a small perpendicular line placed beneath a word, usually on the left of a vowel, to indicate a kind of lighter, secondary tone.[1] It is found (1) with the second syllable before the tone, if open; or on the third or fourth open syllable, if the second be shut[2]; (2) with a long vowel just before a pretonic vocal Šewâ (useful for distinguishing Qāmeç from Qāmeç-ḥāṭûph *in this*

---

[a] Half-open syllables arise from the dropping of vowels through inflectional and other changes; the preference of gutturals for the Ḥāṭēphs; the omission of Dāghēš forte, as with the article and ו copulative; and the composition of words with particles or fragments of words affixed or prefixed, though not ל with the infinitive.

[b] Words taking the tone on the penult are for the most part: (1) those whose last syllable has simply a helping vowel; (2) those having the local ending ָה, meaning *towards* or *into* a place; (3) those having certain light verbal and nominal suffixes; (4) those whose tone has been changed through the influence of ו consecutive (§ **18**) or the Pause (§ **6**); (5) those in which the tone syllable, if final, would be immediately followed by another tone syllable.

position)[3]; with any vowel before composite Šᵉwâ[4]; and (3) in numerous other cases when it is desired to indicate the distinct pronunciation of a vowel sound. The conjunction וְ *and* is not subject to the first and second of these rules.

אֶלֶף[1] *m.* ox; *pl.* thousand.

בַּיִת[2] (*cstr.* בֵּית) *m.* house; *pl.* בָּתִּים *bâttîm.*[a]

גָּמַל[3] recompense, perfect. גָּמָל *c.* camel.

דֶּלֶת *f.* door (which swings).

חָכַם[4] be wise. חָכָם *adj.* wise. חָכְמָה[4] *f.* wisdom.

חֲלוֹם[5] *m.* dream.

יְאֹר[6] *m.* river, (mostly) the Nile.

יָדָה stretch, throw out, praise. יָד *f.* hand (shut). תּוֹדָה* *f.* praise.

כַּף *f.* hand (open), palm, sole (of foot); *du.* כַּפַּיִם.

מַיִם (*cstr.* מֵי) *m.* water.

נָא *part.* come! now! pray!

סָמַךְ*[7] support, *intrans.* lean.

עַיִן (*cstr.* עֵין) *f.* eye, fountain; *du.* עֵינַיִם; *pl.* עֲיָנוֹת.

פֶּה (*cstr.* פִּי) *m.* mouth; *pl.* פִּים, פִּיּוֹת.

רֹאשׁ *m.* head; *pl.* רָאשִׁים (for רְאָשִׁים). רִאשׁוֹן *adj.* foremost, former. רֵאשִׁית *f.* beginning, first, former.

שָׂמַח[7] rejoice. שִׂמְחָה *f.* joy.

שֵׁן *c.* tooth; *du.* שִׁנַּיִם.

[1] The letter א has the form of a bullock's head, especially in Phœnician. Mn. "*cattle* on a *thousand* hills": Ps. l. 10. [2] Good mnemonics for this and most of the other words of this list will be the respective letters of the alphabet ש, ר, פ, ע, ס, מ, כ, י, ד, ג, ב. The form of the letter as well as its sound is to be especially noted in *each case.* [3] The camel was so called because so complete and perfect an animal. [4] The wisdom literature of the Bible is often called the *ḥokhmāh* literature. [5] Suggests, though somewhat remotely, *hal-lucination.* [6] Suggests *yᵉ oar.* [7] Put here because it sounds like סָמַךְ; joy supports.

Exercise. — ʿim, ʾēth, lô, ḥûç yhôwāh, ʾĔlôhîm, ḥālāh, kathábhtā, yarōnnû, yēšt, mᵉʾôdh, wayyarʾ, maçâʾthā, dibbēr, ḥuqqîm, simḥāh, šébhaʿ, ʿalékhā, náʿar, naʿărāh, šamáyim, dābhrāh, kullô, taphas, malkhêhem, ûlyamîm, šādhadh, haʾadhām, ʿênêkhem, ʾabhrahām, sānēʾ, kanphêhem.

Rem. — The quantity of a vowel is not always given where, from foregoing principles, it should be known. The exercise will be useful also for placing the Šᵉwâs and Methegh, and distinguishing the half-open or medial syllable. The same letter repeated indicates a sharpened syllable.

---

[a] The Dāghēš forte in the second letter of בָּתִּים is *characteristic* (§ **4.** 2) and exceptional. Others would write the word *bâtîm*, making the Dāghēš a Dāghēš lene, which, however, would be equally abnormal (§ **4.** 1).

§ 4. OTHER CHARACTERS USED WITH THE HEBREW TEXT.

1. [1]בְּגַדְכְּפַת. [2]חָכְמָה wisdom, חָכְמָהּ her wisdom. *Dāghēš lene* is the name given to a point already referred to (§ 1), which is put in the *Bghadhkphath* letters to harden them.[a] It is used whenever these letters do not immediately follow a vowel, a vocal or composite Šᵉwâ, or a half-open syllable; in short, the least vowel sound.[1] The dot sometimes found in final הּ (§ 1. 4), a few times also with אּ (Gen. xliii. 26; Lev. xxiii. 17; Job xxxiii. 21; Ezra viii. 18), giving them consonantal power, is properly a Dāghēš lene, although it is commonly called Mappîq.[2]

Rem. — In the case of a disjunctive accent on the preceding word (§ 7), or any other sufficient pause just before them, like the end of a chapter, section, or verse, these letters cannot be said to follow immediately a vowel sound.

2. [1]Except בָּתִּים (§ 3. foot-note). [2]כִּכָּר *kikkār*, not *kikhkhār*. *Dāghēš forte* is a dot of the same kind placed in letters — the *Bᵉghadhkᵉphath* included — which are to be doubled in pronunciation.[b] It is easily distinguished from Dāghēš lene in that it mostly immediately follows a full, though a short, vowel.[1] When it is used with the *Bᵉghadhkᵉphath* letters, it hardens as well as doubles them.[2]

Rem. — Dāghēš forte is called *compensative* when it doubles the same consonant or assimilates two that are unlike; *characteristic* when it characterizes a grammatical form, whether the doubling be original or inflectional; *conjunctive* when it is placed in the first letter of a word for the purpose of joining it to the last vowel of a preceding word; *emphatic* when it is used to give strength to the tone syllable (mostly the penult); *firmative* when it is used with liquids to prevent a too slight pronunciation of the preceding vowel; *separative* when it is used in a letter having a vocal Šᵉwâ in order to render the latter more audible. Cases will be noted under each head as they may occur.

3. [1]לַמַּיִם *to waters*, not לְמַיִם, with a Dāghēš forte *firmative* (see preceding note). *Raphe* (רָפֶה soft) is a horizontal line placed over a letter. It was originally intended for every letter destitute

---

[a] In Baer's text the rule is usually followed that a Dāghēš lene should be put in every consonant after a guttural with a silent Šᵉwâ, as also in one which, beginning a word, is the same as that with which the word next preceding ends. The principle, however, has not been generally accepted.

[b] Dāghēš forte is omitted from a final vowelless consonant (except נָתַתְּ, אַתְּ); often from certain consonants — mostly קּ, נּ, מּ, לּ, יּ, וּ, and the sibilants — in the middle of a word with only a vocal Šᵉwâ under them; from the gutturals (generally including ר), in some of which the Dāghēš is then implied (possible in א, ע, frequent in ח, ה), or compensation takes place by heightening the preceding vowel (§ 5).

of the kind of hardness indicated by a Dāghēš (or Mappîq). At present, however, it is principally used to show that the dot has been *intentionally* omitted.[1]

4. [1]כִּי־אִם, אֶת־, כָּל־, מִן־. *Maqqēph* is a horizontal line placed between words, closely related in sense, in order to make them one word as it respects pronunciation and tone.[1]

5. [1]בְּרֵאשִׁית in (the) beginning. *Qᵉrê* and *Kᵉthîbh*. In the usual Hebrew text attention is called to different readings by means of a small circle placed over a word.[1] The suggested reading is found at the bottom of the page. The *vowels* of the word placed there, however, are used with the *original word* still found in the text. This original word is called the *Kᵉthîbh*, i.e., what is written. The word at the bottom of the page, the *Qᵉrê*, i.e., what is (suggested to be) read. The circle is also used to call attention to any critical remarks made in the margin. In the case of a few words of very frequent occurrence, the word in the margin — whose vowels have been used with a word in the text — has been omitted. This is called a perpetual Qᵉrê.[a]

6. [1]בֵּינֶיךָ between thee. The second י is superfluous. Special dots (*Puncta extraordinaria*) are found above certain words in fifteen passages (ten in the Pent., as in Gen. xvi. 5).[1] In some cases they indicate that the letter or letters of a word over which they stand are to be omitted; in others, their meaning is no longer clear.

7. The end of a verse is marked in the Hebrew Bible by two dots (׃) called *Sôph Pāsûq* (i.e., end of the verse).

כִּכָּר[1] *f.* circuit, plain, talent, loaf.
כָּסָה[2] cover. כִּסֵּה (or כִּסֵּא) *m.* stool, throne.
כָּתַב[3] write.
קָרָא[4] call, read, proclaim.
קָרָה[5] (and קָרָא) meet. קִרְיָה* *f.* city.
רָפָא[6] soften, mitigate, heal.
רָפָה*[7] sink down, (causative) let sink, let go.
שַׂק *m.* sackcloth.

[1] R. כרר (כר) to go around. The meanings of the noun are all closely related to this idea. It suggests *car*. [2] Suggests *case*, *in-case*. The throne

---

[a] The examples of perpetual Qᵉrê are (1) הוא (in Pent. only), for which היא is read (as in Gen. ii. 12); (2) יהוה, for which אֲדֹנָי is read, unless the two words are found together, when the vowels of אֱלֹהִים are given to the former as far as applicable (as in Gen. ii. 4); (3) נַעַר (in Pent. only as feminine), for which נַעֲרָה is read (as in Gen. xxiv. 14); (4) יְרוּשָׁלַם, for which יְרוּשָׁלַיִם is read (as in Josh. x. 1); (5) יִשָּׂשכָר, for which יִשָּׂכָר is read (as in Gen. xxx. 18); and apparently (6) the numerals שְׁנֵים, שְׁתֵּים, for which שְׁנֵי and שְׁתֵּי are respectively read (as in Ex. xxviii. 21).

was so called probably from its canopy. [3] Mn. *Kthîbh*. [4] Mn. *Qrê*. [5] To be associated with the preceding, whose form it often takes. [6] Mn. *Raphe*. [7] Mn. "*Rephaim*" (*rphā'îm, ir. pl.* of רָפָה), the stretched out, lifeless (in Sheol).

Exercise. — báyit, kap, peh, gamāl, kōl, kol, 'ādôn, ḥakām, 'ēt, 'ak, mišpāṭ, btôk, ḥelqkā, yēšt, mamléket, ykattēb, tdabbēr, mdubbār, šabbāt, wayyinnāgpû, lipnê, ḥiṭṭāh, lamáyim.

Rem. — The pupil is expected to determine for himself, in this exercise, the quantity of some of the vowels, where Šᵉwā is required, and whether a *Bᵉghadhkᵉphath* letter should be hard or aspirated.

---

§ 5. THE GUTTURALS AND QUIESCENT LETTERS.

1. [1] הַחֹשֶׁךְ (for הַחֹּשֶׁךְ) the darkness. [2] הָאֹלֶף not הַאֹּלֶף, בֵּרֵךְ not בִּרֵּךְ, בֹּרַךְ not בֻּרַּךְ. Of the guttural letters (ע, ח, ה, א), ע represents a sound similar to that of א, but firmer; and so ח with respect to ה. The last two letters are stronger gutturals than the former two. All are peculiar, first, in that they cannot be doubled by receiving a Dāghēš forte. It may be implied, however, i.e., simply left out without producing any change in the word. This occurs often with ח, ה, less often with ע, and sometimes with א.[1] When Dāghēš forte would naturally be called for in these letters and it *is not implied*, there is compensation made for the omission. The short vowel preceding the guttural is heightened (a to ā, i to ē, u to ō). In other words, such vowels come to stand in an open, instead of a sharpened, syllable, and are accordingly changed to the corresponding tone long vowel.[2]

2. [1] Not נִעְמַד, הָעְמַד but נֶעֱמַד, הָעֳמַד (*ho'ŏmadh*). [2] Not שָׂמֵח but שָׂמֵחַ, not אֱלוֹהּ but אֱלוֹהַּ. A second peculiarity of the gutturals (ע, ח, ה) is that they prefer the *a* class of vowels about them and require ◌ַ or ◌ָ when final. Hence (a), before these gutturals not final, *i* and *u* are generally changed to *e* and *o*, and, less frequently, after them.[1] (b) Any short vowel but ◌ַ with these gutturals when final is changed to ◌ַ. And (c) after any long vowel with a final guttural except ◌ָ the vowel ◌ַ steals in (Pathaḥ furtive), to be sounded before the guttural. Such Pathaḥ cannot take the tone, and, of course, disappears when additions are made to the word.[2]

3. [1]חֲלוֹם; נֶעֱמַד not נֶעְמַד. [2]Not בְּחֲלוֹם but בַּחֲלוֹם in a dream. A third peculiarity of gutturals is that they require in place of a simple Šᵉwâ (vocal) a composite one, chiefly Pathaḥ. They may take a simple Šᵉwâ silent; but here too, in many cases, a Ḥāṭēph is preferred. If a Ḥāṭēph be taken in place of a silent Šᵉwâ, it will be homogeneous with the preceding short vowel (ֲ corresponding to ַ, ֱ to ֶ, ֳ to ָ, i.e., *o*), and the syllable in which it stands will be half open.[1] On the same principle, if a letter preceding a Ḥāṭēph is to be supplied with a vowel, it will take a short one corresponding with the Ḥāṭēph.[2] From this fact is derived the rule found in some grammars that a guttural letter points itself and the letter next preceding, and *vice versa*. For the pointing of a consonant before a guttural with *o*, see § **2**. 3. R. 2.

4. [1]אֵם. [2]נָא. [3]לֶאֱכֹל to eat. [4]יָצָאתִי or יָצָתִי I have gone forth. The letter א has consonantal power (and is treated as a guttural) only at the beginning of a syllable.[1] At the end of a syllable[2] (except in certain verbs whose first letter is a guttural and when protected by a Ḥāṭēph in a half-open syllable[3]) it coalesces with the vowel next preceding, making it long and the syllable an open one. Occasionally the א in such cases disappears entirely.[4]

REM. 1. — א may also lose its power as a consonant when following another consonant with vocal Šᵉwâ or a Ḥāṭēph, merging them in its own or a homogeneous long vowel, in which it then itself quiesces after that consonant (רָאשִׁים *heads* for רְאָשִׁים, לֵאמֹר for לֶאֱמֹר or לְאֱמֹר, לֵאלֹהִים for לֶאֱלֹהִים, בַּאדֹנָי for בַּאֲדֹנָי).

REM. 2. — A final א following a letter having silent Šᵉwâ is said to be *otiant*, and is ignored in pronunciation (חֵטְא ḥēṭ').

5. [1]הָרֹאשׁ not הַרֹאשׁ the head; בֵּרְכָה she blessed. The letter ר approaches the gutturals in some of its peculiarities. It takes Dāghēš forte only exceptionally, compensation being almost exclusively by heightening the preceding vowel; prefers the vowel *a* about it, especially before it; and sometimes takes a Ḥāṭēph pathaḥ instead of a simple vocal Šᵉwâ.[1]

6. [1]וָו *wāw;* צֹאנָיו *çô'nâ(y)w* his flocks, צֹאנַי *çô'na-y* my flocks; גּוֹי *gô-y* nation; זִו *Ziw* one of the Hebrew months; חָלוּי ḥālû-y, *pass. part.* of חָלָה. It has already been noted (§ **2**) that ו and י ordinarily lose their value as consonants at the end of a syllable, after homogeneous vowel sounds (ו becoming וּ and וֹ, י becoming ִי, ֵי, ֶי), and that with the heterogeneous *a* vowel they often unite to form diphthongal long vowels (ו with *a* becoming ô, י with

a becoming ê). Occasionally, however, these characters retain at the end of a syllable their consonantal power after *a*, as they always do after other heterogeneous vowels.[1]

אָמַר speak. אֵמֶר (i)[1] *m.* word. אִמְרָה *f.* word.
גָּאַל[2] redeem.
חָטָא sin. חֵטְא*[3] (*cstr.* חֵטְא, *pl.* חֲטָאִים) *m.* sin. חַטָּאת *f.* sin.

חֹשֶׁךְ[4] *m.* darkness.
יָצָא[5] go forth, rise (of the sun). מוֹצָא *m.* going-forth, utterance.
עָמַד[6] stand, stand out, remain, stand still. עַמּוּד *m.* pillar.

[1] From the same root *Emir* (or Ameer), i.e. speaker, commander. [2] *Cf.* Gaol. [3] May be associated with *hate.* [4] *Cf.* שָׁכַח forget, i.e., have *darkness* of memory. [5] *Yachts* — go forth. [6] Might link its second meaning with its second syllable.

Exercise. — אְמֹר, גַּיְא, עְמַדְתֶּם, מָצָאתָ, כְּאֲרִי, הַחשֶׁךְ, בֵּרֵךְ, שֶׁבֶע, שָׁלוּח, הִשְׂמִיח, שָׂמֹח, שְׂמֶח, כְּחֲלוֹם, חֲלוֹם, נַעֲמַד, הָעְמְדָה (§ 2. R. 2) הָעְמַד, יֶעֱמַד, נִעְמַד, נֶעֱמַד, בְּרֵךְ, אְדֹנָי, אֱלֹהִים.

Rem. — In this exercise each word requires correction. Initial א in the pretone prefers ֲ; at a distance from the tone, generally ֱ (though not in אלהים).

---

§ 6. CHANGES IN VOWELS.

1. The several causes working to produce vowel changes are changes in the character of a syllable; the contact of a vowel with a different consonant or another vowel; the shortening or lengthening of a word and the consequent shifting of the tone. These causes do not act independently of one another, but one change is likely to carry with it one or more of the others.

2. [1] הָרֹאשׁ for הַרֹאשׁ. [2] הַחֹשֶׁךְ. [3] שִׂמְחָה, חֻקִּים. Vowel changes in Hebrew are possible within the limits already stated (§ 2), the vowels represented by â, ê, î, û, ô, being immutable under any circumstances. They are generally distinguishable by being fully written. Other immutable vowels are: (a) such as are made long by way of compensation before a guttural or ר;[1] (b) a short vowel before a guttural in which Dăghēš forte is implied;[2] and (c) a short vowel in a doubly closed or sharpened syllable;[3] the rule, in each of these cases, holding good as long as the conditions are unaltered.

3. [1] יָד but יֶדְכֶם; כֹּל but כָּל־; שֵׁן but (generally) שֶׁן־. [2] חֹק but חֻקִּים. In addition to the principles already given under the head of the syllable (§ **3**. 3. 4), it may be said that a vowel which has been made long by the tone, whether in an open or a shut syllable, will be changed to its own short form, or deflected to some homogeneous short vowel, if that syllable becomes a toneless shut, or loosely shut, syllable (*ā* becoming *a* or *e*, *ē* becoming *e* or *i*, sometimes *a*; *ō* becoming *o*, and rarely *u*).[1] If the change be to a sharpened syllable, there is a corresponding reduction of the vowel (*ē* to *i*, and *ō* generally to *u*).[2]

4. [1] דְּבַר *cstr.* of דָּבָר, but *pl.*, דְּבָרִים; אֱמֹר from אֱמֹר; קֹדֶשׁ from קָדְשׁ; מֶלֶךְ from מַלְךְ; בֹּרַךְ, בֵּרַךְ, instead of בֻּרַּךְ he was blessed, בִּרֵּךְ he blessed. [2] יֵצֵא not יַצֵּא. If a shut syllable become open by the loss of its final consonant (including the gutturals and ר, § **5**. 1. 5), either by its being joined to the following syllable,[1] or, being a quiescent letter (י, ו, א), by losing its consonantal quality and coalescing with the preceding vowel, its vowel is lengthened—or deflected—(*a* to *ā*, *è*, *i* and *e* to *ē*, *u* and *o* to *ō*).[2]

REM.—The effect may here be noted which is produced on vowels by what is known as the Pause; i.e., some one of the heavy disjunctive accents (§ **7**) which, for rhythmical and liturgical purposes, was put at the end of a sentence or main division of it. A vowel under such an accent is said to be *in Pause*. The effect is to *heighten a short vowel to its corresponding tone long* (ַ, however, sometimes becomes ֶ, and *vice versa*); *restore an original vowel* (ְ, ֻ, sometimes becoming ָ Qâmeç); *or a dropped vowel* (ְ before ךָ becoming ֶ); giving it, in each case, the form required by the tone; and, frequently, *to shift the tone*, mostly from the ultimate to the penultimate syllable, but sometimes the reverse.

5. [1] גָּמָל, *cstr.* גְּמַל, *pl.* גְּמַלִּים; בְּרָכָה, *cstr.* בִּרְכַּת; אֲמַרְתֶּם ye have spoken. If the tone of a word be carried forward one syllable or become weakened (by the construct state or otherwise), a changeable vowel standing before it will be volatilized (become vocal or medial Šᵉwâ) or be dropped (leaving silent Šᵉwâ), according to the nature of the syllable that may result.[1]

REM.—There is an important distinction between nouns and verbs in this respect. Verbs generally volatilize *a*, *ē*, *ō*, in the *last* syllable, when the tone is moved forward a place; nouns, *ā* and *ē* in the penultimate syllable (עָמְדָה she stood, from עָמַד; but דְּבָרִים words, from דָּבָר).

6. [1] דִּבְרֵיכֶם your words, גְּמַלֵּיהֶם their camels. If the tone be carried forward two places, of two changeable vowels coming before it, the one nearest to it will be dropped; while the other, now standing in a (loosely) shut syllable at a distance from it, will be correspondingly shortened or thinned (*ā* often being changed to *i*).[1]

בָּרַךְ[1] kneel, bless. בְּרָכָה *f.* blessing. דִּבֶּר[2] speak. דָּבָר *m.* word. מִדְבָּר *m.* place of pasturage, wilderness, desert. דֶּבֶר *m.* pestilence.

קָדַשׁ[3] be apart, holy. קָדוֹשׁ (and קָדֹשׁ) *adj.* holy. קֹדֶשׁ *m.* holiness. מִקְדָּשׁ *m.* sanctuary.

[1] *Pass. part.* is בָּרוּךְ = "Baruch," (blessed) scribe of Jeremiah. [2] Mn. "Deborah" (דְּבוֹרָה) bee. R. means *drive, pour forth* (as words from the mouth); hence מִדְבָּר a *drive* or *range* (for cattle), like the Germ. *Trift* from *treiben*. [3] Mn. Qādhēš ("Kadesh"). There is an apparent play on the word in Num. xx. 1, 13, when Israel, being in "Kadesh," Jehovah is said to have been "sanctified" (יִקָּדֵשׁ *Kadeshed*) in them.

---

§ 7. THE ACCENTS.

A.—THE PROSE ACCENTS.

	THE DISJUNCTIVES.		THE CONJUNCTIVES.	
No.	Form and Position.	Name.	Form and Position.	Name.
1	דָּבָֽר	Sillûq	דָּבָ֣ר	Mûnâḥ
2	דָּבָ֑ר	'Athnâḥ	דָּבָ֤ר	M^{e}huppākh
3	דָּבָ֒ר	Ṣ^{e}ghôltā........	דָּבָ֥ר	Mêr^{e}khā
4	דָּבָ֓ר׀	Šalšéleth	דָּבָ֦ר	Double Mêr^{e}khā
5	דָּבָ֕ר	Great Zâqēph ...	דָּבָ֧ר	Dargā
6	דָּבָ֔ר	Little Zâqēph ...	דָּבָ֨ר	'Azlā
7	דָּבָ֖ר	Ṭiphḥā	דָּבָ֩ר	Little T^{e}lîšā
8	דָּבָ֗ר	R^{e}bhîa'	דָּבָ֪ר	Galgal
9	דָּבָ֮ר	Zarqā	תַּ֖עֲשֶֽׂה	Mây^{e}lā (always with Ṣillûq or 'Athnâḥ). It is properly a Ṭiphḥā, but in *this place* it has the above name.
10	דָּבָ֙ר	Pašṭā		
11	דָּ֚בָר	Y^{e}thîbh		
12	דָּבָ֛ר	T^{e}bhîr		
13	דָּבָ֜ר	Géreš		
14	דָּבָ֞ר	Double Géreš		
15	דָּבָ֡ר	Pâzēr		
16	דָּבָ֟ר	Great Pâzēr		
17	דָּ֠בָר	Great T^{e}lîšā		
18	דָּבָ֣ר׀	L^{e}gharmēh		

1. The names of the accents are, in some cases, Aramaic; in others, Hebrew. They are based on their form, position, pausal or musical value.

2. Each word, or the last word of a series connected by Maqqēph, has an accent. As a rule, it is found on the tone syllable. When this is not the case, the principle requires that it should be repeated on the tone syllable; but, in most texts, this is carried out only as it respects Pašṭā.

3. The usual division of the accents into "emperors," "kings," "dukes," etc., is inexact, since the power of each accent varies greatly according to its position in the verse. The accents marking the *highest tones* in cantillation were those of the Disjunctives numbered (4), 13–16; those marking the next higher tones were 8, 9, (3), 12, 18; those marking low, sustained tones were 1, 2, 5–7.

4. The names of the two general classes of accents suggest their third principal use: to indicate where there were to be pauses in the recitation, or cantillation, and where there was to be none. The Disjunctive accents, accordingly, have reference to what precedes them; the Conjunctive, to what follows.

Final.	First Word.	Second Word.	Third Word.	Fourth Word.	Fifth Word.	Sixth Word.

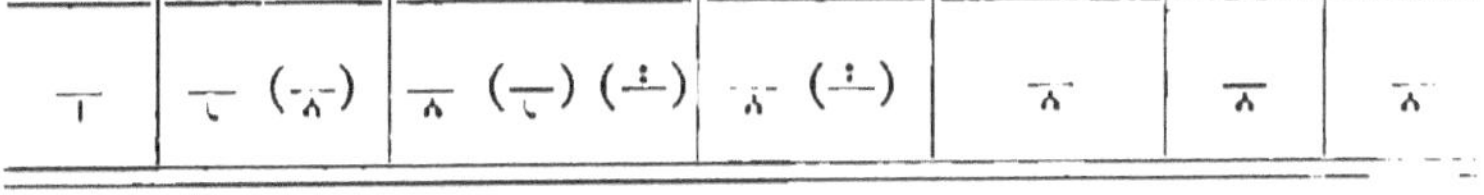

5. *The Main Division.* Every verse closes with the accent Ṣillûq, and this accent is used nowhere else. It is followed, as we have seen (§ **4.** 7), by two dots resembling the colon, called Ṣôph Pāṣûq. The great law governing the accentual subdivisions of the verse, i.e., the use of the remaining Disjunctives, is that of dichotomy. If the verse is long enough to allow it, it is divided into two parts, usually by 'Athnâḥ; and, if the same condition holds respecting them, each of these parts, in turn, is divided into two parts, and so on, as long as the words of the verse hold out. These parts are not, necessarily, of equal length. The primary object aimed at in the division was musical effect in the public recitation of the Scriptures, combined with the desire so to mark the several parts of the verse as to bring out its thought to the best advantage. The general principle of the divisions seems to have been to put the main ones after the more important statements, or after words or clauses seeming to call for special emphasis. In this way, not

infrequently, the logical and syntactical connection is given a subordinate place. Moreover, by this plan of division it was often needful, as has been noted, to mark pauses of equal value by accents of unequal pausal value. Hence we are not able to say that a certain accent always implies a pause equivalent to the comma, the semicolon, and so on. Words and clauses receive one accent rather than another simply because of their position in the verse.

6. The law governing the main dichotomy of the verse as represented in the table was as follows. The main dichotomy, if falling in the first word before Ṣillûq, is generally marked by Ṭiphḥâ, but it may be 'Athnâḥ; if on the second word, it is more likely to be 'Athnâḥ; but may be either Ṭiphḥâ or Zâqēph; if on the third word, it will generally be 'Athnâḥ, though Zâqēph is possible; if on the fourth or any preceding word, it will be invariably 'Athnâḥ.

Clause.	Final.	First Word.	Second Word.	Third Word.	Fourth Word.	Fifth Word.	Sixth Word.
Ṣillûq	◌ֽ	◌֖	◌֖ (◌֔)	◌֔	◌֔	◌֔	
'Athnâḥ	◌֑	◌֖	◌֖ (◌֔)	◌֔ (◌֖)	◌֔ (◌֒)	◌֒ (◌֔)	◌֒ (◌֔)

7. *The First Minor Division.* The main division of the verse having been thus effected, the next question concerned the division of each of these halves, i.e., the Ṣillûq clause and the 'Athnâḥ clause, which remained. The principle is set forth in the table. In the Ṣillûq clause, if the first minor dichotomy fall on the first word from it, it will be marked by Ṭiphḥâ; if on the second, by Ṭiphḥâ or Zâqēph; if on the third, or any preceding word, by Zâqēph only. In the 'Athnâḥ clause, if the first minor dichotomy fall on the first word before it, it will be Ṭiphḥâ; if on the second, the same or Zâqēph; and so on, as shown; the more remote the position in a given accentual clause the heavier the accent, and the more remote *the same* accent the greater its disjunctive power.

Rem. — The general principle governing the use of the Disjunctive prose accents having thus been shown, it seems unnecessary to pursue the subject further in this Grammar. Let it suffice to say that each of the Disjunctives may have a clause of its own which is entitled to subdivision under the rules of a continuous dichotomy.

Clause.	Disj.	First Conj.	Second Conj.
Ṣillûq	◌ֽ	◌֥	
'Athnâḥ	◌֑	◌֣	◌֣
Zâqēph	◌֔	◌֣	◌֣
Seghôltā	◌֒	◌֣	◌֣
Ṭiphḥā	◌֖	◌֥ (◌֥)	◌֧

8. *Order of the Conjunctives.* The Conjunctives have influence, severally, only within the limited space between two Disjunctives, and, as already remarked, it is in the direction of the one that follows. In general, it is only closely connected words (a noun and its genitive, or adjective, etc.) that are joined together by a Conjunctive accent. The table shows which Conjunctives are found with the principal Disjunctives; and in case there is more than one required, what one is found in the second place. With Ṣillûq there will never be found any other Conjunctive than Mêrekhā; with 'Athnâḥ, Mûnâḥ. So with all the remaining Disjunctives there is a uniform law respecting the Conjunctives that shall precede them in the sentence.

Rem. — A double system of accentuation is found in certain passages: as in Gen. xxxv. 22^{b}, where the object is a more rapid reading of the words so accentuated; and in the Decalogue (Ex. xx. 2–17; Deut. v. 6–18), where the object is to reduce the twelve verses to ten, i.e., to the number of the commandments. There are also, occasionally, single words which have two (alternative) accents (Lev. x. 4; 2 Kings xvii. 13; Ezek. xlviii. 10; Zeph. ii. 15).

9. [1] וַיֹּ֫אמֶר ׀. *The Use of Pâsēq.* Pâṣēq (= cutting off) is a short perpendicular line found between words.[1] It is of two kinds, the ordinary and extraordinary. The former is used before *any* Disjunctive, to separate, to some extent, words otherwise bound together; the latter, only before *certain* Disjunctives, to provide a means of marking a minor dichotomy where the usual accents fail to do so (Gen. i. 5, 8; xviii. 15; Deut. ix. 4; xxv. 19; 2 Sam. xxiv. 13; 1 Kings xxi. 2). Of the ordinary Pâṣēqs there are the following classes: (1) that distinguishing words as to sense (Gen. xviii. 15); (2) as to emphasis (Ex. xv. 18); (3) that found between words repeated (Gen. xxii. 11); (4) that separating words, one of which ends in the same letter with which the following one begins (Cant. iv. 12).

B.—THE POETIC ACCENTS.

	THE DISJUNCTIVES.		THE CONJUNCTIVES.	
No.	Form and Position.	Name.	Form and Position.	Name.
1	דָּבָֽר	Șillûq	דָּבָ֥ר	Mûrᵉkhā
2	דָּבָ֥֫ר	'Ôle-wᵉyôrēdh ..	דָּבָ֖ר	Ṭarḥā
3	דָּבָ֑ר	'Athnâḥ	דָּבָ֨ר	'Azlā
4	דָּבָ֗ר	Rᵉbhîa' (great)..	דָּבָ֣ר	Mûnâḥ
5	דָּבָ֗ר	Rᵉbhîa' (little) ..	דָּבָ֬ר	'Illûy
6	דָּ֝בָ֗ר	Rᵉbhîa' mughrāš	דָּבָ֤ר	Mᵉhuppākh
7	דָּבָ֮ר	Çinnôr	דָּבָ֪ר	Galgal
8	דָּבָ֭ר	Dᵉḥî	דָּבָ֓ר	Šalšéleth (little)
9	דָּבָ֡ר	Pâzēr	דָּבָ֘ר	Çinnôrîth (pretonic)
10	דָּבָ֓ר ׀	Šalšéleth		
11	דָּבָ֨ר ׀	'Azlā		
12	דָּבָ֤ר ׀	Mᵉhuppākh lᵉgharmēh		

1. The use of Poetic Accents is confined to the Books of Job, Psalms, and Proverbs. They serve much the same purpose in poetry as the Prose Accents do in prose. The verse is divided on the principle of a continuous dichotomy; though here, the dichotomy, naturally, is not carried as far.

2. יְהוָ֤ה אֲדֹנֵ֗ינוּ מָֽה־אַדִּ֣יר שִׁ֭מְךָ בְּכָל־הָאָ֑רֶץ אֲשֶׁ֥ר־תְּנָ֥ה
הוֹדְךָ֗ עַל־הַשָּׁמָֽיִם׃ Ps. viii. 2. The rule for the main dichotomy in poetry is as follows: (1) If it be on any one of the first three words from Șillûq, it will be marked by 'Athnâḥ; (2) if on the fourth or fifth words, by 'Athnâḥ or 'Ôle-wᵉyôrēdh; (3) if on any previous word, by the latter only.

3. וְֽהָיָ֗ה כְּעֵץ֮ שָׁת֪וּל עַֽל־פַּלְגֵ֫י־מָ֥יִם אֲשֶׁ֤ר פִּרְי֨וֹ ׀
יִתֵּ֬ן בְּעִתּ֗וֹ וְעָלֵ֥הוּ לֹֽא יִבּ֑וֹל וְכֹ֖ל אֲשֶׁר־יַעֲשֶׂ֣ה יַצְלִֽיחַ׃
Ps. i. 3. The principles governing the consecution of accents in the minor dichotomy it will be sufficient to illustrate in the clause closed by Șillûq. If 'Ôle-wᵉyôrēdh has been used to divide the verse

into its two halves, then 'Athnâḥ may be expected to mark the second division. If 'Athnâḥ has been used for this purpose (see example under 2), Rᵉbhîa' mughrâš will mark the second division, or, in some few cases, Šalšéleth. If there is another division called for between Rᵉbhîa' mughrâš and Ṣillûq, it will be marked by Mᵉhuppākh lᵉgharmēh.

PART II. — WORDS AND FORMS.

§ 8. THE PERSONAL PRONOUN.

1.

I	אֲנִי, אָנֹכִי	we	נַחְנוּ, אֲנַחְנוּ
thou	אַתָּה, *f.* אַתְּ	you	אַתֶּם, *f.* אַתֵּן, אַתֵּנָה
he	הוּא, she הִיא	they	הֵם, הֵמָּה, *f.* הֵן, הֵנָּה

Rem. — 1. The form אַתָּה is found five times without ה. 2. אַתְּ appears seven times (*K'thîbh*) as אַתִּי. 3. הוּא is used for הִיא — eleven times excepted — throughout the Pentateuch. 4. נַחְנוּ occurs but six times in the Bible; a still shorter form אֲנוּ but once. 5. The *2d pers. sing.* and *pl.* was originally written with נ after the א; hence the Dāghēš forte *compensative* in תּ (§ 4. 2. R.). The full original forms in the *pl.* were אַנְתּוּם, אַנְתּוּן. 6. The Dāghēš in הֵנָּה, הֵמָּה is a D. forte *firmative* (§ 4. 2. R.).

2. The Personal Pronoun in this form — excepting הֵן, which is used solely with prefixes — is found only in the *Nom.* case. The oblique cases are indicated by abbreviations of the same appended as suffixes to verbs, nouns, and particles.

אָב[1] (*cstr.* אֲבִי, *pl.* אָבוֹת) *m.* father.
אָבַד[2] be lost, perish.
אוֹר*[3] be clear, bright. אוֹר *m.* light, מָאוֹר *m.* luminary.
חָרֵב*[4] be dry, desolate. חֶרֶב *f.* sword. חֹרֶב† *m.* dryness, desolation. חָרְבָּה* *f. ibid.*

עָבַד[5] serve, minister. עֶבֶד *m.* servant. עֲבֹדָה *f.* service, work.
עוֹר[6] *m.* skin.
עָפָר *m.* dust. (אֵפֶר† *m.* ashes.)
קָבַץ[7] collect.

[1] Mn. and derivative "Abba" (Rom. viii. 15). [2] Mn. and deriv. "Abaddon," the Destroyer. [3] Suggests *ore*. [4] Mn. "Horeb" with its *bald* summit. חָרֵב is from an allied root (*stripped* even to brightness and sharpness). [5] Mn. "Obed" (עֹבֵד servant). [6] Associate with, and discriminate from, אוֹר. The *skin* of Moses' face *shone*. [7] Mn. and deriv. the name of the vowel (ָ), i.e., a *collection* of dots.

§ 9. THE ARTICLE.

הַקּוֹל [1]	Before ordinary consonants...	הַ·
הַחֹדֶשׁ [2]	Before ח, ה (rarely ע)	הַ
הַהֵיכָל [2]		
הָאִישׁ [3]	Before א, ר (generally ע) ...	הָ
הָרֹאשׁ [3]		
הָעָם [3]		
הָעֶרֶב [3]		
הֶעָמָל [4]	Before עָ, הָ without the tone	הֶ
הֶהָמוֹן [4]		
הֶחָכָם [5]	Before חָ, חֳ	הֶ
הֶחֳלִי [5]		

The original form of the Article was הַל. This accounts for the accompanying D. forte which, placed in a following consonant, marks the assimilation of a letter (§ **4**. 2. R.).[1] Before gutturals, which do not admit of doubling, the Article undergoes certain changes, whose law has been already indicated (§ **5**. 1). D. forte may be implied; then it is simply omitted, and the vowel of the Article remains unchanged.[2] Or there may be compensation made for the omission, the vowel of the Article being lengthened.[3] In the second syllable from the tone, however,[4] and in all other cases where the vowel of the article is not lengthened to ָ, it is deflected to ֶ, D. forte being implied.[5]

Rem. 1. — The Article in Hebrew had originally the force of a demonstrative pronoun, and still retains it in some expressions. הַיּוֹם this day, *or* to-day.

Rem. 2. — With the Article the vowels of הַר, פַּר, עַם, and the first vowel of אֶרֶץ, are changed to ָ. הָאָרֶץ, הָהָר.

Rem. 3. — When the consonant following the Article is not supported by a full vowel, its D. forte is frequently omitted. הַיְאֹר.

אִישׁ *m.* man; *pl.* אֲנָשִׁים; *cstr.* אַנְשֵׁי. אִשָּׁה *f.* woman, wife; *cstr.* אֵשֶׁת; *pl.* נָשִׁים.

אֶרֶץ *f.* earth, land.

הָמָה *[1] sound, roar. הָמוֹן *m.* noise, multitude, abundance.

הַר[2] *m.* mountain.

חָדָשׁ* new. חֹדֶשׁ[3] *m.* new moon, month.

יָכֹל[4] be capacious, able. הֵיכָל *m.* temple; palace.

עַם[5] *m.* people, nation. עִם with.

עָמָל[6] *m.* toil, travail.

עֶרֶב[7] *m.* evening.

פָּרָה*[8] be fruitful, bear. פַּר bullock (*f.* פָּרָה). פְּרִי *m.* fruit.

קָהַל*[9] call, convene. קָהָל *m.* convocation. קוֹל *m.* voice, cry, sound.

[1] Mimetic; *cf.* hum. [2] R. הרר = *horrere*, be stiff, rigid. Mn. "Hor" (הֹר). [3] To be associated with, but discriminated from, קֹדֶשׁ (§ 6). The seventh Jewish *month* was especially the *holy* month. [4] The origin of היכל is probably an Assyr. word for *great house*. [5] R. עמם = bind together. Hence the *prep.* meaning *with*. [6] Mn. "Moil," to which it is in idea akin. [7] Allied Assyrian word is *Êrêbu; cf. Erebus*. [8] Mn. "Ephraim" (אֶפְרַיִם double fruitfulness): Gen. xli. 52; or with פְּרִי there may be associated *berry, pear*. [9] Mn. קֹהֶלֶת "Qōheleth," the *Preacher* of Ecclesiastes (i. 1). קוֹל is from a kindred root (קוּל).

Exercise. — The statute.[2] The flock.[2] The house.[3] The mouth.[3] The tooth.[3] The eye.[3] The sin.[5] The darkness.[5] The talent.[4] The wisdom.[3] The wise.[3] Thou (art) the man. She (is) the woman. I (am) God (*pl.*).[2] We (are) the people. The Nile (River).[3] The earth. The bullock. The cow. The toil. They (are) a multitude. The dust.[8] The skin.[8] The sword.[8]

---

§ 10. DEMONSTRATIVE AND RELATIVE PRONOUNS.

1. *The Demonstrative Pronoun.* זֶה this, *f.* זֹאת, *pl. c.* אֵלֶּה. הוּא that, *f.* הִיא, *pl. c.* הֵם, הֵמָּה, *f.* הֵן, הֵנָּה.

Rem. — 1. It will be noticed that for the demonstrative pronoun of the remote object the 3d pers. of the personal pronoun is used. 2. The Dāghēš in the ל of אֵלֶּה is D. forte *firmative* (§ 4. 2. **R.**). 3. זֶה is sometimes used adverbially = here, now. 4. זוֹ and זוּ are each used once, and זֹה several times for זֹאת; אֵל is found nine times for אֵלֶּה, though but once outside the Pentateuch. 5. A form הַלָּזֶה (*f.* הַלֵּזוּ, *c.* הַלָּז) for the remote object = *that one yonder*, occurs a few times.

2. [1]זֶה הַיּוֹם this is the day. [2]הַיּוֹם הַהוּא that day. [3]הַיּוֹם הַגָּדוֹל הַהוּא that great day. [4]גָּדוֹל הַיּוֹם great is the day. [5]הַיּוֹם הַגָּדוֹל the great day. The demonstrative pronoun, when used as such, is placed at the head of the sentence.[1] It may be used as an adjective; then, like other adjectives, it follows the substantive, and both usually take the article.[2] If another adjective be used, the demonstrative adjective is placed after it, and each word is usually made definite by the article.[3] An adjective, when a

predicate, ordinarily precedes the substantive, and is without the article.[4] When it qualifies a substantive, as remarked, it follows it; and if the latter be definite, the adjective is made so.[5]

3. *The Relative Pronoun.* אֲשֶׁר who, which, what.

Rem. — In place of the ordinary form of the relative there is not infrequently found, though mostly in the later biblical books, ·שֶׁ, ·שַׁ, or שֶׁ, the א of the original word, as most suppose, having fallen away, while the ר has been assimilated. זוּ is also used as a relative fourteen times (1. R. 4).

4. [1]בָּהּ in it, בָּהּ . . . אֲשֶׁר in which; שָׁם there, שָׁם . . . אֲשֶׁר where. The relative pronoun is indeclinable, and used for all genders, numbers, and cases. Often it serves as a sign of relation, giving a relative signification to a pronoun or adverb that follows at a greater or less distance.[1] It may also be used as a conjunction in the sense of *that, when, because,* (with כַּ) *according as.*

גָּדַל be, become great. גָּדוֹל great. מִגְדָּל[1] *m.* tower.
טוֹב* be good. טוֹב[2] good. טוּב* *m.* goodness. יָטַב be good, well.
יוֹם[3] *m.* day; *pl.* יָמִים. יוֹמָם daily, by day.

רוּם be high. רָם[4] high, exalted. מָרוֹם *m.* height, high place. תְּרוּמָה *f.* (heave) offering, tribute.
שֵׁם[5] *m.* name, fame (R. שָׁמָה be high); *pl.* שֵׁמוֹת. שָׁמַיִם heavens.
שָׁם there.

[1] Mn. "Migdol." [2] Mn. "Tobias" (טוֹבִיָּה Jehovah is good), the apocryphal hero. [3] The word "Yom" for *day* has become somewhat familiar through discussions over Gen. i. [4] Mn. "Abram" (=אַבְרָם high father). [5] Mn. "Shem" (שֵׁם), the *name* of a son of Noah.

Exercise. — This day. These (are) the statutes.[2] These statutes. A people[9] great and (וְ) high. Thou (art) a great God.[2] A good name. This high mountain.[9] That land.[9] All[2] which he had made (עָשָׂה). This people.[9]

§ 11. THE INTERROGATIVE PRONOUNS AND PARTICLES.

1. *The Interrogative Pronouns.* מִי who? מָה which? what?

·מַה	Before ordinary consonants (usually with Maqqēph).
מַה	With D. forte implied before ח and (rarely) ה.
מָה	Always before א and ר, generally before ה without Qāmeç.
מָה	With disjunctive accents (§ 7).
מֶה	Before ע, ח, ה.
מֶה (or מָה)	Before ordinary consonants when without Maqqēph and at a distance from the principal accent of the clause.

2. [1]מִי אַתָּה who art thou? [2]מַה־זֹּאת what is this? The interrogative מִי is used for persons,[1] מָה for things.[2] It will be noticed that the pointing of the latter is much like that of the Article. The D. forte sometimes following it may be regarded as *conjunctive* (§ **4**. 2. R.).

Rem. 1. — The interrogative pronouns are sometimes used in the Genitive, in which case they follow the word they limit. חֲמוֹר מִי whose ass?

Rem. 2. — מַה before adjectives and verbs may have an adverbial and exclamatory force. How! Wherefore! מַה־טּוֹב how good!

Rem. 3. — מִי and מָה are sometimes used as indefinite pronouns: *whoever* (any one who), *whatever.*

3. *Interrogative Particles.* הֲ, אִם if whether, אֵי where.

הֲ	Before ordinary consonants.
הַ·	Before ordinary consonants with Šᵉwâ (sometimes ·הֲ).
הַ	Before gutturals (D. forte implied).
הֶ	Before gutturals with Qāmeç.

4. [1]הֲזֶה is this? [2]הַאַתָּה זֶה בְּנִי whether thou here (art) my son (§ **10**. R. 3). [3]אִם־אֶחְיֶה מֵחֳלִי זֶה whether I shall recover (live) from this sickness. [4]אֵי הֶבֶל where is Abel? [5]אֵי־זֶה which? who? The inseparable particle הֲ is generally used in direct,[1] but sometimes in indirect questions.[2] אִם introduces indirect, very seldom direct, questions.[3] In questions where an alternative is suggested (whether — or), הֲ pretty uniformly precedes, followed by אִם in the next, or the second clause. אֵי when found without a pronominal suffix, always takes the form אֵי.[4] Used with other adverbs or pronouns, it simply gives them an interrogative sense.[5]

Rem. — 1. There may be a question asked without the use of an interrogative pronoun or particle. 2. When a D. forte is used with הַ interrogative (see table) it is a D. f. *separative* (§ **4**. 2. R.). 3. Combined with the negative לֹא not (הֲלֹא), הֲ requires the answer *yes* (= *nonne* in Latin).

אֱנוֹשׁ *m.* man.

בָּנָה[1] build. בֵּן (*cstr.* בֶּן־ or בִּן־; *pl.* בָּנִים) son. בַּת (*pl.* בָּנוֹת) daughter.

הָיָה[2] be, become.

חָיָה live. חַי (*pl.* חַיִּים) life. חַיָּה *f.* life, (wild) beast.

חֲמוֹר[3] *m.* ass.

כָּבֵד be heavy, rich, glorious. כָּבֵד *adj.* same meaning. כָּבוֹד[4] *m.* glory, wealth.

לֹא (or לוֹא) *not.*

לָמָּה[5] (or לָמָה) *wherefore.*

[1] The family is *built up* through children: Gen. xvi. 2. בַּת written fully would be בַּנְתְּ; hence the *pl.* [2] This is to be discriminated from the following, which has the stronger ח; so *living* compared with *being*. [3] Mn. "Hamor," name of a prince: Gen. xxxiii. 19. Homer compares Ajax to an ass (Il. xi. 557). [4] Mn. "Ichabod" (אִי כָבוֹד, 1 Sam. iv. 21), inglorious. [5] לָמָּה = מָה and לְ = to what, for what, *wherefore*. The form לָמָּה (and לָמֶה) occurs mostly before gutturals.

Exercise. — Who (is) that man? Who (art) thou (*f*)? Whose daughter (art) thou? How good! What (are) these? Wherefore (is) this? Wherefore have I (is there to me = לִי) life (*pl.*)? A son honoreth (יְכַבֵּד) a father.[8] Is it not this? What (is) man? Is the people[9] strong (חָזָק Order: Is strong, etc.)?

§ 12. THE INSEPARABLE PREPOSITIONS.

1. בְּ in (among), by (for *or* through), with; לְ to, unto, belonging to, at, for; כְּ as, like, according to. The pointing of these prepositions, when combined with other words, is as follows: —

בְּסֵפֶר	Before a vowel, Šᵉwâ.
כִּפְרִי	Before a Šᵉwâ, Ḥîreq.
כַּאֲרִי	Before a composite Šᵉwâ, the corresponding short vowel.
כַּבְּהֵמָה	Before the Article, takes its vowel, and ה is syncopated.
בָּאֵלֶּה	In the pretone often Qâmeç.
בַּמָּה	בְּ and כְּ with מָה, Pāthaḥ with Dāghēš; but כָּמָה, בָּמָה in Pause (§ 6. 4. R.) and before א.

Rem. 1. — When, by processes of inflection or composition, two Šᵉwâs come together at the beginning of a syllable, a new (half open) syllable arises, whose vowel is Ḥîreq (כִּפְרִי as fruit).

Rem. 2.—These several prepositions have independent forms (בְּמוֹ, כְּמוֹ, לְמוֹ, מוֹ = מָה), but, excepting כְּמוֹ, they are only used in poetry.

Rem. 3.—Before יְהֹוָה, which generally has the vowels of אֲדֹנָי (§ **4.** 5. n.), these prepositions take the pointing required by the Ḥăṭēph of the latter (Pāthaḥ), and the following Šᵉwâ disappears (לַיהֹוָה, לַאדֹנָי). *Cf.* § **5. 4.** r. 1.

אָרוֹן[1] *c.* ark (of testimony).
אֲרִי[2] *m.* lion.
בְּהֵמָה[3] *f.* beast, (domestic) cattle.
דָּרַךְ[4] tread, walk. דֶּרֶךְ *c.* way, walk.
כֹּהֵן[5] *m.* priest.

כֶּסֶף[6] *m.* silver, money.
סָפַר[7] write, count, recount. סֵפֶר (i) *m.* book, letter. מִסְפָּר *m.* number.
שָׁאַל[8] ask. שְׁאוֹל "Sheol."

[1] May be associated with אַהֲרֹן "Aaron" who kept it. [2] Mn. "Ariel" (אֲרִיאֵל lion of God). [3] Mn., its *pl.*, "Behemoth" (בְּהֵמוֹת Job xl. 15 = the hippopotamus). [4] *Cf.* *T(d)rack*. [5] Origin of the names "Kohen," "Cohen," etc. [6] R. כסף means split, cut; so כֶּסֶף properly *a piece* (of money). [7] May be associated with *cipher*. [8] The word שְׁאוֹל is by some derived from this r., and so would mean the place that is always demanding. More likely its r. is שׁעל, the derivative meaning the *sunken* place.

Exercise.—To the number. To the woman.[9] By wisdom.[3] Among cattle. In the palace.[9] In a dream.[3] In the dream. In the land.[9] Like an ass.[11] As the dust.[8] According to all.[2] According to the number. Like (the) people,[9] so (= like the) priest. On (in) that day.[10] For (בְּ) silver. In Jehovah.

---

§ 13. THE PREPOSITION מִן AND WĀW COPULATIVE.

1. מִן ; מִחוּץ[4]. מֵאִישׁ[3] (מֵהָעֵץ). מִקֶּדֶם[2]. מִן־הָעֵץ[1]. from, out of. מִן is generally found independently written with words having the article, and often in poetry.[1] In other cases it is wont to coalesce with the word to which it is prefixed, the final ן being assimilated (§ **4.** 2. r.).[2] In the case of gutturals—including the article when מִן is not connected with it by Maqqēph—and ר, in which a Dāghēš cannot stand, there is compensation made for the omission of Dāghēš by heightening the vowel.[3] With ח and ה, however, D. forte is sometimes implied (§ **5.** 1).[4]

Rem. 1.—In letters having Šᵉwâ the D. forte may be omitted (§ **9.** r. 3). מִפְּרִי of fruit.

Rem. 2.—If the word with which מִן coalesces begins with יְ, it unites with the latter to form מִי : מִיהוּדָה from Judah; but מֵיְהֹוָה, the word אֲדֹנָי being implied. § **5.** 4. r. 1.

2. [1]וְהָאָרֶץ· [2]וָחֳלִי· [3]וּמֶלֶךְ, וּלְכֹל· [4]יוֹם וָלַיְלָה; וְ and (but, or, etc.). The conjunction ו as copulative is ordinarily pointed with Š^ewâ; but before a guttural with a Ḥăṭēph, with the corresponding short vowel;[2] before the labials or another simple Š^ewâ, with a dot in its bosom;[3] immediately before the tone syllable, especially when connecting words associated in pairs, and at the end of a clause, with Qāmeç.[4]

REM. — Placed before words beginning with יְ, ו unites with the latter to form וִי (וִיהוּדָה and Judah); excepting with יְהוָה, where it becomes וַ, in harmony with principles already noticed.

מָלַךְ reign, become king. מֶלֶךְ[1] (*f.* מַלְכָּה). מַלְכוּת *f.* מַמְלָכָה (or מַמְלֶכֶת) *f.* kingdom.
עֵץ[2] (*f.* עֵצָה) tree, wood.
צָדַק be just, righteous. צַדִּיק righteous. צֶדֶק[1] (i) *m.* righteousness.
צְדָקָה *f.* righteousness.
קָדַם*[3] be before. קָדִים *m.* east wind. קֶדֶם *adv.* before; *m.* the east. קֵדְמָה* eastward.

[1] Mn. "Melchizedek" (מַלְכִּי־צֶדֶק Gen. xiv. 18). [2] The *pl.* is used for sticks of wood, timber, etc. [3] Mn. Κάδμος, who is said to have brought the original Greek alphabet from the *east*.

Exercise. — From the house.[3] From the land.[9] From 'Ădhônāy. From a tree. From without.[2] From Jerusalem (יְרוּשָׁלַםִ). From a kingdom. And I. Bread (לֶחֶם) and water. And righteousness (*f.*). And cattle.[12] The heavens[10] and the earth.

---

§ 14. THE STRONG VERB.

1. [1]קָטַל. The roots from which Hebrew words in their present form are derived consist almost invariably of three (unpointed) consonants;[1] although there are a few words having four or five (quadriliterals, quinqueliterals).[a]

2. [1]נָגַשׁ· [2]שָׁדַד· [3]אָמַר· [4]רוּם (בִּין)· [5]יָשַׁב· [6]מָצָא; גָּלָה. Verbs are classified as strong or weak according to the nature of the radicals they contain. Weak verbs are such as have one or more of the following letters as radicals: נ,[1] י, ו, ה, א; or repeat

---

[a] Words composed of more than three root letters have been generally formed from pre-existing triliterals; just as many triliteral roots may be referred to original biliterals.

the second radical letter as a third.[2] The names given to the different kinds of weak verbs are derived from the verb פָּעַל (to do), which was formerly used in inflection. A verb whose first letter is נ is called a פ״נ,[1] the נ standing in the place of פ in פָּעַל. A verb whose first letter is א is called a פ״א.[3] One whose middle letter is ו or י, an ע״ו or ע״י.[4] One whose second and third root letters are the same is called an ע״ע.[2] The verb יָשַׁב, accordingly, is a פ״י;[5] while מָצָא and גָּלָה are named, respectively, ל״א[6] and ל״ה.[6]

Rem. — In this Grammar verbs having gutturals as radicals are classified as strong verbs. They require, it is true, as compared with other strong verbs, certain changes in vocalization; but they do not, like the weak verbs, call for changes in the consonants themselves which make up the root.

3. *The Perfect.*

Sing.	Plur.	Sing.	Plur.
3. *m.*	3. *c.* . . . . . וּ	3. *m.* קָטַל he killed	3 *c.* . . . . . קָֽטְלוּ they killed
3. *f.* . . . ָה		3. *f.* קָֽטְלָה she killed	2. *m.* קְטַלְתֶּם ye killed
2. *m.* . . . . תָּ	2. *m.* . . . תֶּם	2. *m.* קָטַלְתָּ thou killedst	2. *f.* קְטַלְתֶּן ye killed
2. *f.* . . . . תְּ	2. *f.* . . . . . תֶּן	2. *f.* קָטַלְתְּ thou killedst	1. *c.* . . . קָטַלְנוּ we killed
1. *c.* . . . תִּי	1. *c.* . . . . . נוּ	1. *c.* קָטַלְתִּי I killed	

The so-called Perfect of the strong verb is formed by appending to the simple stem the above shortened forms of the Personal Pronoun (§ **8**).

Rem. 1. — The immediate origin of most of these pronominal fragments is obvious. The ending ָה is for ַת (§ **1**. 4), which letter, indeed, the verb always takes when other suffixes are added, and sometimes without them. The ending תִּי is, most likely, for כִי in אָנֹכִי. The ending וּ seems to have been at one time וּן (still found Deut. viii. 3, 16; Isa. xxvi. 16), and originally *ûna*, an old plural ending of masculine nouns. The ending נוּ is from נַחְנוּ.

Rem. 2. — It will be noticed that the endings תָּ, תִּי, and נוּ do not take the tone; in all other cases, however, the tone is on the final syllable.

Rem. 3. — As it respects vocal changes, certain earlier statements should be here recalled. *The vowels a, ē, ō, in the final syllable of the verb, are volatilized immediately before affixes beginning with a vowel, and having the tone* (§ **6**. 5. R.). A few cases, to be hereafter noted, are excepted from this rule.

בִּין[1] distinguish, perceive, understand. בֵּין between. בִּינָה* *f.* understanding. תְּבוּנָה* *f.* same.
גָּלָה[2] strip, uncover, reveal. גּוֹלָה* *f.* captivity, captives.
יָשַׁב[3] sit, dwell, be enthroned. מוֹשָׁב* *m.* seat, dwelling.

מָצָא[4] find.
נָגַשׁ[5] draw near.
קָטַל kill (poetic).
שָׁבַר break (mn. *shiver*); as denom. of שֶׁבֶר sell grain. שֶׁבֶר* (שֵׁבֶר) breach, destruction, grain.

[1] *Distinguish between* בִּין and בֵּין, on the one hand, and בֵּין and בֵּן[11], on the other. [2] A derivative is גָּלְיַת "Goliath," meaning the polished, brilliant (*cf.* חֶרֶב § 8). [3] An allied root of שָׁבַת (be firm, rest) with its natural mn. "Sabbath." [4] Associate with יָצָא (§ 5) in the order מָצָא, יָצָא he went forth, he found. [5] Belongs to a class of verbs beginning with נג, having the meaning hit, push, strike, etc.

Exercise. — I wrote.[4] Which he wrote. He wrote in the book.[12] They have trodden.[12] He reigned[13] in Jerusalem (יְרוּשָׁלַםִ). I have broken Moab (מוֹאָב). She has ruled. Ye have ruled. Thou hast counted.[12]

REM. — Pers. pr. as subjects of verbs are only to be expressed when italicized.

---

§ 15. THE INFINITIVES AND IMPERATIVE.

1. *Infinitives.* *Imperative.*

Infinitives			Imperative		
Inf. construct	קְטֹל	to kill	*Sing.* 2. *m.*	קְטֹל	kill thou
Inf. absolute	קָטוֹל	killing	2. *f.*	קִטְלִי	kill thou
			Plur. 2. *m.*	קִטְלוּ	kill ye
			2. *f.*	קְטֹלְנָה	kill ye

The two Infinitives are, strictly speaking, verbal nouns, and independent of one another. The *Inf. cstr.* has a changeable vowel; the *Inf. abs.* is unchangeable in form, the *ô* in the last syllable coming not from ָ, but being an obscured *â*.

2. [1]בִּשְׁמוֹר הָאִישׁ when the man kept. [2]חָדַל לִסְפֹּר he ceased to count. [3]פָּקֹד פָּקַדְתִּי visiting I (= I surely) visited. The respective names of the Infinitives describe fairly well their uses. The *Inf. cstr.* is used in *construction* with prefixed preposi-

tions (לְ, בְּ, כְּ, מִן),[1] as well as with pronominal suffixes; it may govern substantives or be governed by them, or by verbs.[2] The *Inf. abs.* serves to emphasize the abstract idea of its root without limitation by subject or object. Used before a verb in a finite form, it usually emphasizes *the fact* of the action expressed by it;[3] used after one, it has the same effect, or, more often, expresses the idea of *continuance.*

Rem. — The syllable formed by the prefixing of a preposition to the *Inf. construct* is generally half open; but to this rule לְ is a special exception (§ **3. 4.** foot-note).

3. קְטֹל from an original קְטֻל. It should be noted that the ground-form of the Imperative (and *Impf.*, § **16**) is the same as the *Inf. cstr.*

Rem. — Of the pronominal endings, ִי is from אַתִּי (= אַתְּ, § **8.** 1. r. 2); וּ = וּן (perhaps from *ûna*, § **14.** 3. r. 1); נָה is from הֵנָּה (§ **8**).

4. [1]יִקְטֹל let him kill. [2]אַל־תִּקְטֹל (never אַל־קְטֹל) do not kill. The *Imp.* is used in the second person only. When a command is given in the third person, the Imperfect (§ **16**) is used;[1] as also in the second person when a negative is required (prohibition).[2]

Rem. 1. — In explanation of the vowel of the first syllable of קִטְלִי, קִטְלוּ, see § 12. r. 1.

Rem. 2. — The form קְטֹל may appear in the lengthened form קָטְלָה, *āh* (ָה) being added, and the original Ḥôlem (ō), placed under the word, becoming in a shut, toneless syllable Qāmeç-ḥāṭûph (o, § **2.** 3. r. 2). This lengthened form is sometimes called the emphatic Imperative. As a matter of fact, it more often softens the command, making it an entreaty or an expression of strong desire.

אַל not (with Jussive, etc.).

דָּרַשׁ[1] seek.

חָדַל[2] leave off, cease.

מָשַׁל[3] rule. מָשָׁל *m.* similitude, proverb.

פָּקַד[4] visit (judicially), muster, appoint. פְּקֻדָּה* *f.* visitation, charge.

פִּקּוּדִים† precepts.

קָבַר[5] bury. קֶבֶר (1) *m.* grave, sepulchre.

שָׁמַר[6] keep, observe. מִשְׁמֶרֶת *f.* post, watch, ordinance.

[1] Mn. "Midrash" (מִדְרָשׁ), explanation, a commentary on the Talmud. [2] Associate with חָלַל[40] *begin.* [3] R. = place in order (*marshal*); hence the meaning of the noun. [4] R. = open wide (the eyes). *Cf.* פֶּקַח ("Pekah") blossom. [5] Mn. *Cover* (by accommodation), the r. meaning *heap up.* [6] It may be associated with שָׁבַר (break, keep).

Exercise. — To bury. Bury thou. To rule over (בְּ) the day.¹⁰ To keep the way.¹² The man⁹ (asking) *asked* (verbs first).¹² To (לְ) seek Jehovah. Inquire of (seek) Jehovah. He left off counting (to count).¹² I surely visited (= visiting, I v.). Thou hast visited the earth.⁹

§ 16. THE IMPERFECT AND PARTICIPLES.

1. *The Imperfect.*

SING.	PLUR.	SING.		PLUR.	
3. m. ... יִ	3. m. ... וּ ... יִ	3. m. יִקְטֹל	he will kill	3. m. יִקְטְלוּ	they will kill
3. f. ... תִּ	3. f. נָה ... תִּ	3. f. תִּקְטֹל	she will kill	3. f. תִּקְטֹלְנָה	they will kill
2. m. ... תִּ	2. m. וּ ... תִּ	2. m. תִּקְטֹל	thou wilt kill	2. m. תִּקְטְלוּ	ye will kill
2. f. ִי ... תִּ	2. f. נָה ... תִּ	2. f. תִּקְטְלִי	thou wilt kill	2. f. תִּקְטֹלְנָה	ye will kill
1. c. ... אֶ	1. c. ... נ	1. c. אֶקְטֹל	I will kill	1. c. נִקְטֹל	we will kill

It will be observed that the *Impf.* has generally affixes only in the *pl.*; but takes prefixes — of single consonants — throughout. The former are due to the circumstance that the prefixes do not always suffice to indicate the gender and number. The reason why the *Impf.* takes prefixes, while the *Perf.* has only affixes, lies largely in the fact that, in the one case, the emphasis is laid more on the act; in the other, on the one acting.

REM. — The origin of the several prefixes and affixes it is not possible to fix with certainty in every instance. Those of the 1st *Pers.* are, respectively, from אֲנִי, נַחְנוּ. The ת prefixed to the 2d *Pers.* is from אַתָּה, אַתֶּם, etc.; and the affix נָה from הֵנָּה, אַתֵּנָה. The other affixes of the 2d *Pers.* (י, ו) have been explained (§ 14. 4. R. 1). Of the prefixes of the 3d *pers.*, ת may be supposed to be the original feminine ending of the noun. The prefix י, it has been suggested, represents an original *ya* (still found in Arabic). In most cases the vowel has been thinned to ִ, but with א (§ 5. R. under Exercise) deflected to ֶ.

2. The terms *Perf.*, *Impf.*, as applied to the Hebrew verb (notwithstanding the translations appended in the tables above), do not, properly speaking, represent tenses. The former refers to what is *completed*, especially in the past, but also in the present or future; the latter to what is *incomplete*, especially to something about to be entered upon, though also to what has been already

entered upon. The *Perf.* is employed in prophecies and asseverations, where the event is looked upon as certain; the *Impf.*, in speaking of what is possible, may or ought to be. Either may be used of what is customary and of general truths, according to the point of view.

3. *The Participles.*

Part. active	קֹטֵל	killing
Part. passive	קָטוּל	killed

The simple stem of the verb alone (Qal; see § **19**) has two participles; and even here, the *Part. pass.* appears to be the remnant of a lost passive verbal form of this stem (still used in Arabic).

4. The Participles may be used either as nouns (verbal) or adjectives; take prefixes (the Article and prepositions) and suffixes to indicate gender and number, or (pronominal, to indicate) the relation of government or dependence with respect to some person or thing.

5. The Participles mostly indicate present time; but may refer to the future, especially to something just about to take place; or to the past, in a context descriptive of a past event.

REM. — The original form of the *Part. act.* was qâṭil. The â has been obscured to ô, and *i* heightened to ē. In the *Part. pass.*, on the other hand (orig., qaṭûl), it is the vowel of the second syllable that is unchangeable; while the first, being tone long, is changeable. The *Part.* is based on the *Perf.* of the verb, as the *Imp.* and *Impf.* on the *Inf. cstr.*

גָּרַשׁ*[1] drive out. מִגְרָשׁ[2] *m.* common, precincts, suburbs.

מָלַט[3] escape.

סָגַר[4] cover, close up, shut.

פָּלַט*[3] escape. פָּלִיט† *m.* one escaped. פְּלֵיטָה* *f.* escape, deliverance.

צָפַן* cover, keep, lay up. צָפוֹן[5] *c.* North.

קָצַף*[6] be angry. קֶצֶף* (i) *m.* anger.

קָשַׁר*[7] bind, conspire.

שָׁבַת[8] rest, cease. שַׁבָּת *f.* Sabbath.

[1] *Cf.* Sansc. *gras* (Eng. *grass*), devour. [2] Properly a *drive* (for cattle). *Cf.* מִדְבָּר from דָּבַר (§ **6**). [3] R. = make smooth (and *escape*). The next word but one = divide, break through (and *escape*); *cf. plat.* [4] Same r. letters as Span. *seguro* (Eng. *secure*). [5] So called as the covered, dark region. [6] R. קץ = cut, break. This word means break loose, break out in anger. [7] R. קש = be fast, hard, stiff. [8] Mn. "Sabbath." *Cf.* יָשַׁב, § **14**.

Exercise.—*I* am driving out (*Part.*). They drive out (*Impf.*). And[13] the door[3] he shut. Yᵉhôwāh will shut (verb first). Shut ye the door. He will be angry. *I* am angry (*Part. act.*). The goodness[10] which thou hast laid up. They will conspire. And it (הוּא) was shut (*Part. pass.*). And ye shall describe[4] (write) the land.[9]

---

§ 17. INTRANSITIVE VERBS.

1. [1]קָטַל. [2]כָּבֵד; קָטֹן. The principal vowel of the verb is that of the second syllable. On that is generally based the distinction between verbs transitive and intransitive. The verbs already treated have *a* (ַ) in that position, and are commonly called middle *a* verbs.[1] There are others which have *ē* (ֵ)[2] or *ō* (ֹ)[2] in the second syllable, and are called middle *ē* or middle *ō* verbs. The latter classes are generally intransitive, or, as others name them, stative, verbs. They indicate, for the most part, some state or condition of the subject.

2. [1]כְּבַד. [2]כְּבַד (with ָה paragogic, כִּבְדָה; § **15**. 4. R. 2). [3]יִכְבַּד. Verbs middle *ē* are inflected in the *Perf.* and *Inf. abs.* like verbs middle *a* (see table of Strong Verbs). In the *Inf. cstr.*,[1] *Imp.*,[2] and *Impf.*,[3] they are generally said to take *a* (ַ) in the second syllable. As a matter of fact, most of the *Inf. cstrs.* of middle *ē* verbs end in *ō*.[a]

3. [1]קָטֹנְתָּ. [2]קָֽטְנָה. [3]קְטָנְתֶּם. Verbs middle *ō* retain *ō*, under the tone, throughout the *Perf.*;[1] but in an open syllable without the tone it becomes Šᵉwâ (§ **14**. 3. R. 3);[2] and in a shut syllable without the tone, Qāmeç-ḥāṭûph (§ **2**. R. 2).[3] In the forms following the *Perf.*, verbs middle *ē* and middle *ō* conform to the same law of vocalization, excepting the Participles (Qal; see § **19**), which take the form of the *Perf.* (3. *s. m.*).[b]

---

[a] The middle *ē* verbs, strong and weak, most used are the following: זָקֵן, חָפֵץ, טָהֵר, טָמֵא, יָבֵשׁ, יָרֵא, כָּבֵד, מָלֵא (trans. or intrans.), מֵת, נָבֵל, צָמֵא, שָׂנֵא, שָׁפֵל. In addition, there is a considerable number of verbs which in the ground-form are either middle *ē* or *a*, but which are always middle *ē* in Pause (§ **6**. 4. R.), and take *ē* as a pretonic vowel before a suffix, in all cases without change of sense.

[b] The following are the more common middle *ō* verbs: אוֹר, בּוֹשׁ, טוֹב, יָכֹל, קָטֹן.

Rem. 1. — Both forms of the *Inf. cstr.*, קְטֹל, כְּבַד, may take a feminine ending (קִטְלָה, כִּבְדָה), and may then be used either as proper infinitives or substantives. These forms are mostly found in the intransitive verbs.

Rem. 2. — There are about thirty middle *a* verbs which take *a* also in the second syllable of the *Impf.* (Qal); and about twenty that may have either *a* or *ō*.

בּוֹשׁ be ashamed. בֹּשֶׁת*[1] *f.* shame.
זָקֵן†[2] be old. זָקֵן old.
יָרֵא[3] be afraid. יָרֵא fearing. יִרְאָה* *f.* fear.
מָלֵא[4] be full. מָלֵא full. מְלֹא* *m.* fulness.
נָבֵל*[5] be (lax) foolish, wither, fade.

נָבָל† foolish. נְבָלָה† *f.* folly.
נֵבֶל* (i) *m.* psaltery. נְבֵלָה* *f.* corpse.
קָטֹן† be small, young. קָטֹן small.
קָטָן[6] small.
שָׁפֵל* be low, humbled. שְׁפֵלָה[7] *f.* plain, valley.

[1] Mn. "Ishbosheth" (אִישׁ־בֹּשֶׁת, 2 Sam. ii. 8). [2] The connection between being old and "cane" (קָן) is not remote. Note also form of first letter. [3] י and ו are interchangeable in certain פ״י verbs; and וָרֵא approaches, in sense and sound, "wary." [4] Mn. "Millo" (הַמִּלּוֹא = the Filling, fortification, a part of ancient Jerusalem, 1 Kings ix. 15). [5] Mn. "Nabal" (נָבָל fool, 1 Sam. xxv. 25), originally so called from unresponsiveness, like the unstrung cord of a viol. Note the same general idea in the other words. [6] Mn. "Joktan" (יָקְטָן, Gen. x. 25), a descendant of Shem. Was he smaller or simply younger? [7] "Shephelah" = the Lowlands, one of the districts of southern Palestine.

Exercise. — Abraham (אַבְרָהָם) was old (see R. 1). Abraham was very[2] rich.[11] Thou hast acted foolishly (been foolish). And the leaf (עָלֶה) has faded. I am small. This (*f.*) will be small (R. 2). He will be humbled. Thou art humbled (Perf.). They were not[11] able.[9] She was not able. I was able. Jehovah shall be glorious.[11] *I* fear (Part.) God.

Rem. 1.—With a finite verb (a verbal sentence), the order of words in a sentence is usually: (negative) verb, subject, object. In a nominal sentence (substantive or pronoun) with its predicate (substantive, adjective, or participle), the order is: subject, predicate. An adverb limiting an adjective follows it.

Rem. 2. — In this Exercise the *Impfs.* are in *a*.

---

§ 18. LENGTHENED FORM OF THE IMPERFECT AND WĀW CONSECUTIVE.

1. [1] אֶקְטְלָה I *will* kill, let me (I would like to) kill; נִקְטְלָה let us kill. It has been seen (§ **15**. 4. R. 2; § **17**. 2) that the *Imp.*

besides its ordinary form has also a lengthened one, generally expressive of strong desire, entreaty. Following this analogy, there is also a lengthened form of the *Impf.* called the Cohortative. It is formed in the same way as the lengthened *Imp.* by appending *āh* (ָה) to the ordinary form.[1] This paragogic ָה takes the tone like ּ and ִי. With few exceptions, it is found only with the 1*st Pers.* (*s.* and *pl.*), but occurs in all classes of verbs, and in all Imperfects excepting, naturally, the Passives. It indicates the special direction of the will toward the act, and carries the idea of purpose, wish, or exhortation (*pl.*).[1]

Rem. — That the vowel originally under the tone is volatilized before *āh*, the latter attracting the tone to itself, is in harmony with a law already considered (§ **6.** 5. n.; § **14.** 3. n. 3).

2. *Wāw consecutive.* [1] "In those days Hezekiah was sick (*Perf.*) ... and (Wāw consecutive) there came (*Impf.*) to him Isaiah ... and (Wāw consec.) said (*Impf.*)": 2 Kings xx. 1. [2] "Lest he put forth (*Impf.*) his hand and (Wāw consec.) take (*Perf.*) ... and (Wāw consec.) live (*Perf.*) forever": Gen. iii. 22. It has been observed (§ **16.** 2) that the *Perf.* and *Impf.* of the Hebrew verb are not limited to the expression of time past and future respectively. They have also a still more marked peculiarity in their relation of sequence to one another. In a narrative of past events, for example, only the first of the verbs is ordinarily put in the *Perf.* Those that follow are in the *Impf.*, the narrative being looked upon as continuous from that point.[1] On the other hand, if a series of events be regarded as taking place in the future, the verb introducing the narrative will be put in the *Impf.;* while those that follow will be in the *Perf.*, the matter described being looked upon by the narrator as completed (in the future).[2] This peculiar consecution of the *Perf.* and *Impf.* is indicated by what is known as Wāw consecutive; that is, by a ו so pointed as generally to denote when joined to a *Perf.* or *Impf.* that it sustains this peculiar relation to the verb next preceding.

Rem. 1. — The original form of Wāw consec. was *wa* (וַ).

Rem. 2. — Wāw consec. is always joined *to the verbs successively* which it is expected to affect, the same being placed at the head of the connected clauses. If this order is broken (in prose), a new start has to be made.

Rem. 3. — It is not necessary, though usual, that Wāw consec. should be preceded by a verb in the *Perf.* or *Impf.* An *Imp.* or *Part.*, or some statement or *implication* of past or future time, may suffice to begin the series. For example, a number of books of the Bible begin with the *Impf.* and Wāw consec., implying the existence of the book or books preceding.

3. [1] וַיִּקְטֹל and he killed. [2] וַיֹּאמֶר and he said (יֹאמַר = *Impf.* of אָמַר). With the *Impf.*, Wāw consec. has its original form (וַ); and on account of its close connection with its word, the letter following, if not a guttural, has D. forte.[1] Still further, *wa* being a syllable prefixed, it attracts the tone toward it, from the final to the penultimate syllable — *if the latter be an open syllable*, and the tone is not already on it — with a corresponding change (shortening) of the final vowel (§ **3.** 3).[2]

Rem. 1. — Before א of the *1st Pers.*, which does not admit a D. forte, Wāw consec. becomes וָ (§ **5.** 1). וָאֶקְטֹל.

Rem. 2. — Before the prefix יְ, the pointing is וַ, and D. forte is omitted (§ **4.** 2. footnote; § **9.** R. 3). וַיְקַטֵּל.

Rem. 3. — The *1st Pers. s.* retains the tone on the final syllable. וָאֹמַר.

Rem. 4. — Wāw consec. is not infrequently — mostly, however, in the later books — joined to the Cohortative form וָאֶשְׁמְרָה and I kept. Its usual demand for a shortened form of the *Impf.*, when such a form is possible, will be specially noted hereafter.

4. [1] וְקָטַלְ and he will kill; וְהָיָה and it will (be) come to pass. [2] וְעָמַדְתָּ and thou shalt stand. With the *Perf.*, Wāw consec. takes the pointing of Wāw copulative (§ **13**) under the same circumstances,[1] and the tone is often *thrown forward* upon the final syllable, if it be not already there.[2] The projection of the tone serves to distinguish Wāw consec. from Wāw copulative. It also well indicates the force of the former with the *Perf.*, the thought being thrown forward by it into the future, in harmony with the verb that precedes.[a]

זָבַח[1] slaughter, (especially for) sacrifice. זֶבַח (i) *m.* slaughtering, sacrifice. מִזְבֵּחַ *m.* altar.

זָכַר[2] remember. זָכָר *m.* male.

טָבַח† slaughter, (especially for) eating. טַבָּח* guard (executioner). טֶבַח† *m.* slaughter.

לָמַד[3] learn, (in some forms) teach.

קָרַב draw near. קֶרֶב (i) *m.* midst. קָרְבָּן[4] *m.* gift, sacrifice. קָרוֹב near, neighbor.

שָׁמַע[5] hear. שְׁמוּעָה* *f.* report.

[1] *Cf.* טָבַח. [2] Mn. "Zechariah" (זְכַרְיָהוּ Jehovah has remembered). זָכָר distinguishes the male (sexually) as נְקֵבָה the female. [3] Mn. "Talmud" (תַּלְמוּד) = that which is taught. [4] Mn. "Corban" (Mk. vii. 11). [5] Mn. "Ishmael" (יִשְׁמָעֵאל God heareth).

---

[a] The shifting of the tone never occurs in Pause (§ **6.** 4. R.); with the *1st Pers. pl.*; when another tone syllable would immediately follow; or in certain other forms of the Strong and Weak verbs to be noted when they occur.

Exercise.—Let us draw near. O keep[15] this (§ **15.** 4. R. 2). O hear! (*Impf.* = יִשְׁמַע, § **17.** 2). Let us hear. And (w.c.) ye shall sacrifice. And (w.c.) I remembered. They shall hear and (w.c.) shall keep. And (w.c.) thou shalt stand.[5] He heard and (w.c.) kept. I have heard and (w.c.) will remember. In (בְּ) the midst. And (w.c.) God remembered Noah (אֶת־נֹחַ, § **2.** vocab.).

---

§ 19. VOICES OF THE VERB.

1. [1]קָטַל. The *Perf.* 3. *s. m.* of the verb, as inflected above (§ **14**), is one of its simplest forms, and is accordingly taken as a ground-form.[1] *Cf.* § **16.** 5. R. For the same reason this stem throughout is called the Qal (i.e., light) stem.

Rem. 1.—The Hebrew verb is found in lexicons and generally cited in grammars under this form, excepting verbs ע״ו and ע״י (§ **14.** 2) whose *Inf. cstr.* is given. מָלַךְ rule; but קוּם to rise up.

Rem. 2.—For convenience this form of the verb is translated in vocabularies as though it were an *Inf. cstr.* קָטַל kill, *or* to kill; lit., he has killed.

Rem. 3.—This same form of the Q. (theoretically, when stripped of its vowels) is generally used to represent the root of Hebrew words of three letters (§ **14.** 1); though a nominal root of the same form may exist alongside of it (דבר = דָּבָר or דִּבֶּר); and there is a class of verbs called Denominatives, which is derived directly from nouns, themselves primitive or derivative. אָהַל live in a tent, from אֹהֶל[33] tent.

2.

פָּעַל	Qal	קָטַל	Qal
נִפְעַל	Niph'al	נִקְטַל	Niqṭal
פִּעֵל	Pi'ēl	קִטֵּל	Qiṭṭēl
פֻּעַל	Pu'al	קֻטַּל	Quṭṭal
הִתְפַּעֵל	Hithpa'ēl	הִתְקַטֵּל	Hithqaṭṭēl
הִפְעִיל	Hiph'îl	הִקְטִיל	Hiqṭîl
הָפְעַל	Hoph'al	הָקְטַל	Hoqṭal

Besides the primitive stem of the verb (Qal), there are several others based upon it and used to express various modifications of the verbal idea. These different formations have generally received the name "Conjugations"; but they are less incorrectly named

Voices. The derived stems (or voices) are formed from the Q. stem by means of prefixes, certain vowel changes, and the repetition of the second or third radical letter. The several Voices of the Hebrew verb (excepting Qal) have commonly received their names from the forms they took with the verb פָּעַל, which was formerly used as a paradigm (§ **14.** 2). But since that verb has been rejected as a paradigm, because poorly adapted to the purpose, and קָטַל has been generally substituted for it, it seems more practical to use the latter as the basis of designation. Familiarity with the old names, however, will be found necessary in using the lexicon and other grammars; hence both are given. Few verbs appear in all the Voices; some are found only in a single one.

בָּגַד* deceive, deal treacherously.
  בֶּגֶד[1] (i) *m.* a garment.
לָכַד take (prey, a city, etc.), choose out.
לָקַח[2] take.
קוּם[3] rise up, (Hi.) establish. קוֹמָה *f.* height. מָקוֹם *c.* place.

קָלַל[4] be light, hold light, curse.
  קְלָלָה* *f.* curse.
שָׁכַב[5] settle, lie down. מִשְׁכָּב *m.* lying down, bed.
שָׁכַם rise up (early). שְׁכֶם† *m.* shoulder.

[1] The connection between noun and verb seems to be the same as between *robe* and *rob*, the garment being the thing oftenest stolen. [2] This and the preceding word are to be carefully distinguished in form and sense. [3] Mn. *ταλειθά κούμ* = "Damsel, Arise!" Mk. v. 41. [4] Mn. Qal. [5] This word and the next should be associated. The root of each means to bow, that of שָׁכַם to let down the shoulder (used of the camel, etc.) for the (early) morning burden.

---

§ 20. THE NIQṬAL (*Niph'al*).

Perf. ...נִקְטַל	*Inf. cstr.* ...הִקָּטֵל	*Imp.* ...הִקָּטֵל
Part. ...נִקְטָל	*Inf. abs.* ...הִקָּטֹל (or נִקְטֹל)	*Impf.*...יִקָּטֵל

1. This Voice is formed by prefixing נ to the primitive stem. Throughout the Strong verb its original vowel *a* has been thinned to *i*. The prefix נ actually appears only in the Perf., Part., and one form of the Inf. abs. In the Inf. cstr. and *related parts*, the syllable *in*—*hin* for distinctness—is used, whose *n* is then assimilated to the first radical (§ **4.** 2. R.). The aspirate הַ is used with it,

except in the Impf., which has prefixes of its own, where הַ is syncopated.

Rem. 1. — The characteristic sign of the Ni. is for the Perf. and Part. a prefixed נ; for the remaining parts a D. forte (compensative) in the first radical.

Rem. 2. — The tone in the Inf., Imp., and Impf. is generally retracted (ֵ in the last syllable becoming ֶ) when a syllable having the tone follows it immediately. הִשָּׁמֶר נָא take heed now.

Rem. 3. — The Impf. 1. s. may take ֶ as well as ִ with א (§ 5. R. under Exercise). אֶקָּטֵל.

Rem. 4. — The second form of the *Inf. abs.* is based on the *Perf.* as the first follows the *Inf. cstr.*

Rem. 5. — The inflection of the Ni., on the basis of these typical forms, is quite analogous to that of Qal.

2. [1]שָׁמַר keep; נִשְׁמַר keep oneself, take heed. [2]קָבַר bury; נִקְבַּר be buried. In meaning the Ni. is either reflexive[1] (occasionally reciprocal), or — what is now more common — passive[2] of the Qal.

בְּרִית[1] *f.* covenant.
גָּנַב*[2] steal.
כָּפַר[3] cover, atone. כְּפִיר *m.* a young lion. כֹּפֶר† *m.* bribe. כַּפֹּרֶת* *f.* (cover of the ark) mercy-seat.
כָּרַת[1] cut, cut off.
מָכַר[4] sell.

פָּרַץ break, break in. פֶּרֶץ*[5] (i) *m.* a breach.
פָּרַשׂ[6] break, spread, scatter.
פָּרָשׁ *m.* rider, riding-horse.
שָׁלֵם be whole, well, at peace. שָׁלוֹם *m.* peace. שֶׁלֶם[7] *m.* (mostly *pl.*) peace-offering.
שָׁמַד[8] smite, destroy.

[1] R. = cut (like that of כָּרַת), so, separate, decide. בְּרִית and כָּרַת ("cut a covenant") are often found together. [2] Note 2d syl., *nab.* [3] *Cf.* קָבַר.[15] Mn. "cover." The young lion was so called on account of his luxuriant main. The bribe covered the eyes. [4] *Cf.* Lat. *mercator*, merchant. [5] Mn. "Perez" — Uzzah, 2 Sam. vi. 8. [6] Mn. "Pharisee" = the separated. The roots פָּרַשׂ and פָּרַשׁ are allied in sense (the idea of the rider being of one who springs forward, breaks away). [7] Mn. "Salaam" (= peace), a form of salutation in the East. [8] *Cf.* the root-letters with the consonants of "smite."

Exercise. — And if (אִם־[2]) it shall be stolen (Ni.). And (w.c.) that soul (נֶפֶשׁ *f.*) shall be cut off. And he (w.c.) shall be sold. The land (*f.*)[9] shall not be sold. And thou (w.c.) shalt spread abroad. In peace. They shall be scattered. And I (w.c.) shall be destroyed. Ye shall be utterly (Ni. Inf. abs.; § **15**. 2) destroyed. To be destroyed. I will be sanctified[6] (Ni.). I *will* be honored[11] (Ni. Cohort.). He was shut in.[16] Shut thyself in (Ni.).

§ 21. THE QIṬṬĒL (*Pi'ēl*), QUṬṬAL (*Pu'al*), AND HITHQAṬṬĒL (*Hithpa'ēl*).

Perf.	קִטֵּל	קֻטַּל	הִתְקַטֵּל
Inf. cstr.	קַטֵּל		הִתְקַטֵּל
Inf. abs.	קַטֵּל (קַטֹּל)	קֻטֹּל	הִתְקַטֵּל
Imp.	קַטֵּל		הִתְקַטֵּל
Impf.	יְקַטֵּל	יְקֻטַּל	יִתְקַטֵּל
Part.	מְקַטֵּל	מְקֻטָּל	מִתְקַטֵּל

1. The most characteristic mark of these Voices is the doubling of the middle radical throughout; another, common to the first two, is the Šᵉwâ (originally a vowel) under the preformatives. The vowel in the first syllable of Qi. (orig. *a*, as in Q., Ni.) has been thinned in the Perf. to *i*, though appearing in all the other forms of this Voice and everywhere in Hithq. The *original* vowel of the second syllable (*a*) appears in all forms of the Perf. having affixes beginning with a consonant (see table below); elsewhere in the Qi. and Hithq. it has been thinned to *i*, and then, under the influence of the tone, heightened to *ē* (§ **2**. table). In the Inf. abs., *ô* of the final syllable is from an original *â* (as in Q.).

Rem. 1. — The prefix מְ in the Participles of these and the following Voices is connected with the Interrogative Pronoun. מִי (*one who* ——).

Rem. 2. — Three verbs, when not in Pause, take *e* instead of *ē* in the Perf. 3. *s. m.* כִּפֶּר. כִּבֶּס, דִּבֶּר.

Rem. 3. — The D. forte in the middle radical of verbs of these Voices may be dropped when such letter is not supported by a full vowel (§ **4**. 2. foot-note).

2. The Qu. is still further characterized by a so-called "dark vowel" *u* (rarely *o*) in the first syllable. It lacks the Inf. cstr. (except Ps. cxxxii. 1) and the Imp.

3. The Hithq. is formed directly from the Qi. by restoring the original vowel of its first syllable and prefixing the syllable Hith. In the *Impf.* and *Part.*, which are provided with other prefixes, the weak ה of the prefix הִתְ is syncopated after such prefixes.

Rem. — If the first radical is a sibilant (§ **1**. 5), the ת of the prefix changes places with it, for euphonic reasons (as הִשְׁתַּמֵּר for הִתְשַׁמֵּר). If, further, that sibilant is צ, the ת not only changes places with it, but is itself changed to ט (as הִצְטַדֵּק for הִתְצַדֵּק). If, again, the stem begin with the Linguals

ת, ד, or ט (occasionally נ, כ; שׁ, ר, ז, once each), the ת of the prefix is assimilated to it, the same being indicated by D. forte *compensative* (as הִטַּהֵר for הִתְטַהֵר purify oneself).

4. [1]שִׁבֵּר shiver (Q. break). [2]סִפֵּר recount, relate (Q. count); רִדֵּף persecute (Q. follow); קִבֵּר bury many (Q. bury). [3]לִמֵּד teach (Q. learn). [4]גֻּנַּב be stolen. The Qi. Voice as related to the Q. mostly carries the idea of *intensity*,[1] including that of repetition;[2] occasionally that of causation.[3] The Qu. is the Passive of Qi. (sometimes of the Q.).[4]

5. [1]הִתְקַדֵּשׁ sanctify oneself. [2]הִתְרָאָה look at one another. [3]הִתְפַּתַּח (§ 5. 2) open for oneself. [4]הִתְחַלָּה feign oneself sick. [5]יִשְׁתַּכְּחוּ they will be forgotten. The Hithq. Voice holds nearly the same relation to the Qi. that the Ni. does to the Q. It is (1) chiefly reflexive (intensive);[1] but, also, (2) reciprocal;[2] (3) medial (do for oneself);[3] (4) has the idea of giving oneself out as something;[4] and (5) rarely has a Passive signification.[5]

טָהֵר[1] be clean. טָהוֹר clean.
טָמֵא be unclean. טָמֵא *m.* unclean.
טֻמְאָה* *f.* uncleanness.
כָּבַס[2] tread, wash. כֶּבֶשׂ[3] *m.* lamb.
סָתַר[4] cover, hide. סֵתֶר* (i) *m.* hiding-place, covert, secrecy.

פָּתַח[5] open. פֶּתַח (i) *m.* door.
רָדַף[6] follow.
שָׁכַח[7] forget.
שָׁכַן[8] settle down, dwell. מִשְׁכָּן Tabernacle.

[1] Assoc. with following (clean, unclean), which also begins with ט. [2] *Washing* was done by *treading*. Fix in mind as one of the three exceptions named above. [3] R. allied to that of כבס. [4] Qi. Part. = מְסַתֵּר, with which compare *mystery*. [5] Mn. Pāthaḥ. *Cf.* דֶּלֶת, § 3. [6] Mimetic. Repeated, the word sounds like the hoof-beat. [7] Same radicals חָשַׁךְ[5] (here darkness of memory). [8] Mn. "Shekinah," connected with the Tabernacle.

Exercise. — Thou hast spoken.[6] He has spoken. Wash thou. Let him wash. And he (w.c.) washed. Is not (§ **11.** 4. R. 3) David (דָּוִד) hiding himself (Hithq. *Part.*)? I will cause to dwell (Cohort.). On (in)[12] the Sabbath.[16] The heavens[10] recount[12] (*Part.*) the glory of God (כְּבוֹד־אֵל). How[11] shall we justify ourselves?[13] Sanctify yourselves.[6] To sanctify. (The one) sanctified. He made atonement.[20] Atonement was made (Qu.).

Rem. — Only the Voices treated in the present section are to be used in this Exercise.

§ 22. THE HIQṬÎL (*Hiph'il*) AND HOQṬAL (*Hoph'al*).

	Hi.		*Hi.*		*Ho.*
Perf.	הִקְטִיל	*Impf.*	יַקְטִיל	*Perf.*	הָקְטַל
Inf. cstr.	הַקְטִיל	(Jussive)	יַקְטֵל	*Inf. abs.*	הָקְטֵל
Inf. abs.	הַקְטֵל	(Jussive)	תַּקְטֵל	*Impf.*	יָקְטַל
Imp.	הַקְטֵל	*Part.*	מַקְטִיל	*Part.*	מָקְטָל

1. The characteristic mark of the Hi. and Ho. Voices in the Perf. is a prefixed הַ; in the Inf. and related forms (including the Part.) of the Hi. it is the vowel *a*, of the Ho. the dark vowel *o* (or *u*) under the preformative letter. Both the vowels in the Hi. Perf. were originally *a*. The first has been uniformly thinned to *i*; the second (as *Inf. cstr., etc.,* following verbs ע״וּ) becomes *î*, except before consonantal suffixes, and takes the tone. In the Inf. cstr. and related parts (also the Part.), an original *i* of the second syllable has been lengthened to *î*, except in the ground-form of the Imp. and in the Jussive (see 2), where the normal heightening of *i* to *ē* under the tone has taken place.[a]

REM. 1. — It will be noted that the final vowel of the *Inf. abs.* in these Voices is *ē* (like the dominant Inf. abs. Qi.).

REM. 2. — The Ho. Part., like *the other two Pass. Part.*, has *ā* in the last syllable.

2. [1] הַקְטִילָה· [2] הַקְטִילִי· [3] וַיַּקְטֵל· It has been seen (§ **15**. 4. R. 2; § **17**. 2; § **18**. 1) that both the Imp. and Impf. may have lengthened forms with an accompanying change of sense. Ordinary forms of the Imp. and Impf. may also be shortened. In the Strong Verb this takes place only in the Hi. Voice; namely, in the ground-form of the Imp. and in the Impf. (chiefly 2. and 3. *s.*). The shortened form of the Imp. maintains itself only when *without augment at the end.* In the case of the lengthened Imp.,[1] and with inflectional and other additions,[2] it assumes its normal state. The Impf. Jussive is used to express a command, wish, or (with אַל) a prohibition. Such forms have arisen from a natural effort to speak the word quickly. Connected with this is a tendency to draw back the tone from the final syllable. And inasmuch as the same tendency was

[a] The form תַּקְטֵלְנָה (Impf. 2. and 3. *f. pl.*), although found in the table below, does not occur; but the Imp. 2. *f. pl.* follows this analogy. הַקְטֵלְנָה·

observed with *Wāw consec.* of the Impf., we often find the two forms agreeing orthographically.[3]

3. [1]הִקְדִּישׁ sanctify (Q. be holy); הִצְדִּיק declare righteous (Q. be righteous). [2]הִגְבִּיר show one's self strong (Q. be strong). [3]הָשְׁלַךְ is (has been) cast away (Hi. to cast away). In sense the Hi. is (much oftener than Qi.) a causative Voice. With a personal object it is indirectly causative; i.e., such person is caused to do or be the thing denoted by the verb.[1] Without a personal object it is directly causative; i.e., the thing itself denoted by the verb becomes the object.[2] The Ho. is *Pass.* of the Hi., sometimes of the Q.[3]

גְּבוּל *m.* coast, border (see following).
גָּבַר[1] be strong, prevail. גִּבּוֹר *m.* hero. גְּבוּרָה *f.* strength. גֶּבֶר (*cstr.* גְּבַר) *m.* man (poetic).
דָּבַק cleave, follow closely, hard.
כָּשַׁל[2] stumble.

לָבַשׁ[3] clothe. לְבוּשׁ *m.* clothing.
נָפַל fall. Mn. "*Nephilim*": Gen. vi. 4.
שָׁלַח[4] send, stretch forth. שֻׁלְחָן *m.* table.
שָׁלַךְ[5] (Hi. and Ho.) cast down, away, out.

[1] One of a series of words beginning with גב which mean *be rounded out, gibbous.* This word = be high: so *strong*: the preceding, be high, and so marking a boundary. [2] Sometimes associated with נָפַל "stumble and fall." [3] A pupil suggests *lavish* (i.e., in clothing) as mnemonic. [4] Mn. "Siloam" (Σιλωάμ, John ix. 7, "by interpretation Sent"). [5] To be associated with preceding; the one = throw *out*; the other, throw *down*.

Exercise. — All the coast of Yisrā'ēl. The waters[3] prevailed (Q.) exceedingly.[2] And he (w.c.) shall make strong a covenant.[20] And he (w.c.) followed hard (Hi.). They stumbled and fell. Ye have caused to stumble. And he (w.c.) shall cleave. He cast away. To cast away. I was cast away. Cast not (אַל) away (§ **15**. 4). And she (w.c.) cast down. And *thou* art cast out. The head[3] shall be (*Part.*) cast out. He sent. They sent. He put forth the hand.[3] And he (w.c.) shall fall. She fell.

---

§ 23. GUTTURAL VERBS. — AN INITIAL GUTTURAL.

1. Guttural Verbs are those having gutturals (including ר, ה) among their radical letters. א is regarded as a guttural only when used as a consonant (not when a vowel-letter, and so quiescent). For the peculiarities of ה and ר, see § **1**. 4, § **5**. 5, respectively. The

latter section might now be reviewed with profit, since it contains the general principles distinguishing, in their inflection, the guttural from other Strong verbs.

	Q.ᵃ		Ni.	Hi.	Ho.
Perf. s. 3. m.....	עָמַד		נֶעֱמַד	הֶעֱמִיד	הָעֳמַד
3. f.....	עָמְדָה		נֶעֶמְדָה	הֶעֱמִידָה	הָעָמְדָה
2. m.....	עָמַ֫דְתָּ		נֶעֱמַ֫דְתָּ	הֶעֱמַ֫דְתָּ	הָעֳמַ֫דְתָּ
pl. 2. m.....	עֲמַדְתֶּם		נֶעֱמַדְתֶּם	הֶעֱמַדְתֶּם	הָעֳמַדְתֶּם
Inf. cstr........	עֲמֹד		הֵעָמֵד	הַעֲמִיד	wanting
Inf. abs........	עָמוֹד		נַעֲמוֹד	הַעֲמֵד	הָעֳמֵד
Imp. s. m........	עֲמֹד	חֲזַק	הֵעָמֵד	הַעֲמֵד	wanting
f........	עִמְדִי	חִזְקִי	הֵעָמְדִי	הַעֲמִ֫ידִי	
pl. f........	עֲמֹ֫דְנָה	חֲזַ֫קְנָה	הֵעָמַ֫דְנָה	הַעֲמֵ֫דְנָה	
Impf. s. 3. m.....	יַעֲמֹד	יֶחֱזַק	יֵעָמֵד	יַעֲמִיד	יָעֳמַד
2. f....	תַּעַמְדִי	תֶּחֱזְקִי	תֵּעָמְדִי	תַּעֲמִ֫ידִי	תָּעָמְדִי
1. c....	אֶעֱמֹד	אֶחֱזַק	אֵעָמֵד	אַעֲמִיד	אָעֳמַד
pl. 3. f.....	תַּעֲמֹ֫דְנָה	תֶּחֱזַ֫קְנָה	תֵּעָמַ֫דְנָה	תַּעֲמֵ֫דְנָה	תָּעֳמַ֫דְנָה
Part. act........	עֹמֵד		נֶעֱמָד	מַעֲמִיד	
Part. pass.......	עָמוּד				מָעֳמָד

2. יֶחְדְּלוּ[1]. The following are the chief points of difference between the verb whose typical forms are given in the table and the ordinary Strong verb: (1) An initial guttural requiring Šewâ takes a Ḥāṭēph. (2) With a preformative letter the guttural is either closely joined to it (mostly ה), forming a shut syllable,[1] or it is loosely joined, forming a half-open syllable (§ **3. 4**). In the latter case, which is by far the more common, if the second radical has a

---

ᵃ Typical forms only are given in this and a few subsequent tables. The remaining ones can easily be supplied by the student on the basis of קָטַל, following the analogy of the typical forms.

vowel, the guttural will take a Ḥāṭēph corresponding to the short vowel of the preformative; if the vowel of the second radical is volatilized the guttural will take a short vowel corresponding to that of the preformative (Q. Impf. *2. f. s.*, *3. m.*, *2. m. pl.*, etc.). The vocalization is further disturbed (changed from the *a* class of vowels) only when an original *a* thinned to *i* (§ **5.** 2) lies at the basis of the form (Perf. Ni., Hi., etc.). (3) When the initial guttural would, if an ordinary letter, be doubled, compensation is made for the doubling by heightening the preceding vowel (Ni. Inf., Imp., Impf.).

Rem. 1. — The vowel *i* of the Q. Imp. 2. *s. f.* is explained elsewhere (§ **12.** R. 1).
Rem. 2. — Some forms of חֲזַק are given (Q. Imp., Impf.) as an example of a verb whose Imp. and related parts take *a*.
Rem. 3. — The Qi. and Qu. Voices are omitted as offering no irregularities.

אֶבֶן[1] *f.* stone.
אָסַף[2] collect, assemble.
אָמַן[3] be faithful, true, (Hi.) believe. אֱמוּנָה *f.* faithfulness. אֱמֶת (= אמנת) *f.* truth.
חָזַק[4] be strong, (Hi.) lay hold of. חָזָק strong.
חָדַל[5] cease, leave off.
לֵב (לֵבָב)[6] *m.* heart; *pl.* לִבּוֹת.
עָבַר[7] pass over, along. עֵ֫בֶר *m.* passage (ford), place of passage, the beyond. עֶבְרָה* *f.* (overflow of) anger.
עָזַב[8] leave, forsake.
עָזַר help. עֵ֫זֶר* (*e*) (עֶזְרָה *f.*) help.

[1] Mn. "Ebenezer" (= אֶ֫בֶן, עֵ֫זֶר), 1 Sam. iv. 1. [2] Asaph (אָסָף) was a *collector* of psalms: 1 Ch. vi. 24. [3] Mn. and deriv. "Amen." [4] Mn. "Hezekiah" (חִזְקִיָּה, strength of Jehovah). [5] Discrim. from עָזַב (see § 15). [6] The heart, too, needs *lav*-ing. [7] Origin of the word "Hebrew," as those coming over the Jordan or Euphrates. [8] Used by our Lord (in Aramaic form) on the cross (לָמָּה עֲזַבְתָּ, *cf.* Ps. xxii. 2): Matt. xxvii. 46.

Exercise. — They were not able[9] to stand.[5] 'Abhrāhām believed in (בְּ) Jehovah. Forsake not wisdom.[3] The people[9] had not assembled themselves (Ni. Perf.). Be strong. And (w.c.) the men[9] laid hold. The land (*f.*)[9] shall be forsaken (Ni.). Jehovah hath helped. She left off speaking (Qi. Inf.).[6] Pass along (*pl.*). He made pass over. He stood[5] before (לִפְנֵי) Jehovah. I have served.[8] Holding in service (Hi. Part.). I am (Ni. Perf.) helped. To be helped.

§ 24. VERBS WITH A MEDIAL GUTTURAL.

	Q.	*Ni.*	*Qi.*	*Qu.*	*Hithq.*
Perf. s. 3. m......	שָׁחַט	נִשְׁחַט	בֵּרַךְ	בֹּרַךְ	הִתְבָּרֵךְ
3. f.	שָׁחֲטָה	נִשְׁחֲטָה	בֵּֽרְכָה	בֹּֽרְכָה	הִתְבָּֽרְכָה
2. m......	שָׁחַ֫טְתָּ	נִשְׁחַ֫טְתָּ	בֵּרַ֫כְתָּ	בֹּרַ֫כְתָּ	הִתְבָּרַ֫כְתָּ
pl. 2. m......	שְׁחַטְתֶּם	נִשְׁחַטְתֶּם	בֵּרַכְתֶּם	בֹּרַכְתֶּם	הִתְבָּרַכְתֶּם
Inf. cstr..........	שְׁחֹט	הִשָּׁחֵט	בָּרֵךְ	wanting	הִתְבָּרֵךְ
Inf. abs.	שָׁחוֹט	נִשְׁחוֹט	—		—
Imp. s. m.........	שְׁחַט	הִשָּׁחֵט	בָּרֵךְ	wanting	הִתְבָּרֵךְ
f.	שַׁחֲטִי	הִשָּׁחֲטִי	בָּֽרְכִי		הִתְבָּֽרְכִי
pl. f.	שְׁחַ֫טְנָה	הִשָּׁחַ֫טְנָה	בָּרַ֫כְנָה		הִתְבָּרַ֫כְנָה
Impf. s. 3. m.	יִשְׁחַט	יִשָּׁחֵט	יְבָרֵךְ	יְבֹרַךְ	יִתְבָּרֵךְ
2. f.	תִּשְׁחֲטִי	תִּשָּׁחֲטִי	תְּבָֽרְכִי	תְּבֹֽרְכִי	תִּתְבָּֽרְכִי
1. c.	אֶשְׁחַט	אֶשָּׁחֵט	אֲבָרֵךְ	אֲבֹרַךְ	אֶתְבָּרַךְ
pl. 3. f.....	תִּשְׁחַ֫טְנָה	תִּשָּׁחַ֫טְנח	תְּבָרַ֫כְנָה	תְּבֹרַ֫כְנָה	תִּתְבָּרַ֫כְנָה
Part. act.	שֹׁחֵט	נִשְׁחָט	מְבָרֵךְ		מִתְבָּרֵךְ
Part. pass........	שָׁחוּט			מְבֹרָךְ	

1. The following changes from verbs non-guttural, in addition to those referred to in the preceding section, are worthy of notice: (1) The original ַ has been restored, through the influence of the guttural, in the first syllable of the Q. Imp., in the forms ending in ִי and ָה. (2) By the same influence, ַ is introduced in the last syllable of the Q. Imp. and Impf. This change is no more general elsewhere, because a guttural has less influence on a following than on a preceding vowel.

Rem. 1.—The change to the verb ברך in the last three Voices is because ר alone in this position (except Ezek. xvi. 4) requires compensation for an omitted D. forte by heightening the preceding vowel. The other gutturals (ע, ח, ה, and sometimes א) permit D. forte to be simply implied (§ 5. 1). שָׁחַת, (Qi.) שִׁחֵת.

REM. 2.—The vowel heightened through the omission of D. forte is unchangeable.

REM. 3.—The letter ר takes a composite in place of simple Šᵉwâ in forms of the Qi. and related Voices before syllables beginning with כ, and having the tone.

זָעַק[1] (and צָעַק) cry out.
כְּרוּב *m.* Cherub.
כֶּרֶם[2] *c.* vineyard.
לָחַם[3] (Q.) eat, fight; (Ni.) fight.
 לֶחֶם *m.* bread. מִלְחָמָה *f.* war.
שָׂרַף burn. Mn. "Seraph."

שָׁחַט[4] slay (espec.) for sacrifice.
שָׁחַת[4] corrupt, destroy. שַׁחַת † *f.* corruption, destruction.
שָׁקַט*[5] be quiet, rest.
שֵׁרֵת (Qi.) serve, minister, (Qi. Part.) מְשָׁרֵת[6] servant, minister.

[1] Mimetic. [2] With servile letter ל = כַּרְמֶל, i.e., vineyard-like. [3] Mn. "Bethlehem" (= בֵּית, לֶחֶם). [4] R. שח = be low; שָׁחַח, שָׁחָה[49] sink; שָׁחַט lay low, שָׁחַת destroy. [5] Discrim. from שׁחט. [6] Syn. of עָבַד. The latter is more slavish, the former voluntary, noble service.

Exercise.—They cried unto (אֶל־) Jehovah. David (דָּוִד) blessed (Qi.) Jehovah. To strengthen (Qi.).[23] Whom (אֲשֶׁר) thou blessest (Qi. Impf.) he shall be blest (Qu. Part.). Pass not[15] now[3] along.[23] Ask (*f.*).[12] Fight ye (Ni. *m.*). And (w.c.) the earth (*f.*) was corrupt (Ni.). To destroy (Hi.). Destroy thou (Hi. *m.*). *I* am destroying (Hi. *Part.*). He slew the lamb.[21] And thou (w.c.) shalt burn the city (עִיר). To serve. They shall minister. I will cut off (Hi.).[20] They have cut off. To cleanse (Qi.).[21]

---

§ 25. VERBS WITH A FINAL GUTTURAL.

	Q.	*Ni.*	*Qi.*	*Hi.*
Perf. s. 3. *m.*	שָׁלַח	נִשְׁלַח	שִׁלַּח	הִשְׁלִיחַ
3. *f.*	שָׁלְחָה	נִשְׁלְחָה	שִׁלְּחָה	הִשְׁלִיחָה
2. *f.*	שָׁלַחַתְּ	נִשְׁלַחַתְּ	שִׁלַּחַתְּ	הִשְׁלַחַתְּ
pl. 2. *m.*	שְׁלַחְתֶּם	נִשְׁלַחְתֶּם	שִׁלַּחְתֶּם	הִשְׁלַחְתֶּם
Inf. cstr.	שְׁלֹחַ	הִשָּׁלַח	שַׁלַּח	הַשְׁלִיחַ
Inf. abs.	שָׁלוֹחַ	נִשְׁלֹחַ	שַׁלֵּחַ	הַשְׁלֵחַ
Imp. s. m.	שְׁלַח	הִשָּׁלַח	שַׁלַּח	הַשְׁלַח
f.	שִׁלְחִי	הִשָּׁלְחִי	שַׁלְּחִי	הַשְׁלִיחִי
pl. f.	שְׁלַחְנָה	הִשָּׁלַחְנָה	שַׁלַּחְנָה	הַשְׁלַחְנָה

	Q.	*Ni.*	*Qi.*	*Hi.*
Impf. s. 3. *m.*	יִשְׁלַח	יִשָּׁלַח	יְשַׁלַּח	יַשְׁלִיחַ
2. *f.*	תִּשְׁלְחִי	תִּשָּׁלְחִי	תְּשַׁלְּחִי	תַּשְׁלִיחִי
1. *c.*	אֶשְׁלַח	אֶשָּׁלַח	אֲשַׁלַּח	אַשְׁלִיחַ
pl. 3. *f.*	תִּשְׁלַחְנָה	תִּשָּׁלַחְנָה	תְּשַׁלַּחְנָה	תַּשְׁלַחְנָה
Part. act.	שֹׁלֵחַ	נִשְׁלָח	מְשַׁלֵּחַ	מַשְׁלִיחַ
Part. pass.	שָׁלוּחַ			

1. The characteristic of gutturals most widely exhibited in the present class of verbs is that of Pathaḥ furtive, required under a final guttural immediately after a heterogeneous long vowel (§ **5**. 2; *cf.* Q. Inf. cstr., abs., Part. act. and pass.; Ni. Inf. abs.; Qi. Inf. abs., Part.; Hi. Perf., Inf. cstr. and abs., Impf., Part.). Again, in some cases where *ō* would otherwise be expected (final syl. of Q. Imp., Impf.), we find *a*, largely through the influence of the final guttural. Still further, in final syllables where *ē* would be expected in non-guttural Strong verbs (Ni. Inf. cstr., Imp., Impf.; Qi. Perf., Inf. cstr., Imp., Impf.; Hi. Imp.), *a* is ordinarily to be found, though under the influence of the tone it may become *ē*. Finally, in the Perf. *s.* 2. *f.* of all Voices, the guttural, for euphonic reasons, takes in place of a silent Šᵉwâ a helping Pathaḥ, though the following ת retains its usual pointing (§ **3**. 2. foot-note; § **4**. 1). Like Pathaḥ furtive, this helping vowel cannot have the tone, and disappears when the verb takes suffixes.

2. [1] שֻׁלַּח, יְשֻׁלַּח, מְשֻׁלָּח. [2] הִשְׁתַּלַּח (Inf. cstr. the same), יִשְׁתַּלַּח, מִשְׁתַּלֵּחַ. [3] הָשְׁלַח, (Inf. abs.) הָשְׁלֵחַ, יָשְׁלַח, מָשְׁלָח. The Qu.[1] (Inf. and Imp. wanting), Hith.[2] (Inf. abs. wanting), and Ho.[3] (Inf. cstr. and Imp. wanting) Voices have no special peculiarities.

בְּאֵר [1] *f.* well, spring.
בָּקַע [2] split, divide. בִּקְעָה † *f.* valley.
בָּרַח [3] flee. בְּרִיחַ * *m.* bolt, bar.
מָשַׁח anoint. מָשִׁיחַ [4] anointed, Messiah.
פָּגַע * [5] meet, press, light upon.
פָּשַׁע * [6] transgress. פֶּשַׁע (i) *m.* transgression.
שָׂבַע [7] be satisfied.
שָׁבַע (Ni., Hi.) swear. שֶׁבַע *m.* (שִׁבְעָה *f.*) seven. שְׁבוּעָה * *f.* oath.
תָּקַע [8] smite, blow (a blast).

[1] Mn. with שֶׁבַע "Beersheba": Gen. xxi. 32. [2] The "Beka" (בֶּקַע) was

the split, i.e., half Shekel. [3] Discrim. from בָּרַךְ. [4] Mn. "Messiah." [5] *Cf.* πάγω, *pango*, *pact*, etc. [6] Many a "Pasha" transgresses. [7] Discrim. from the following. [8] Mn. "Tekoa" (תְּקוֹעַ, 2 Sam. xiv. 2), properly the place where tent-pins were (often) driven in, i.e., a favorite tenting-ground.

Exercise. — To (לְ) flee. Flee. He made flee. (One) making flee. (One) splitting wood (עֵצִים). It (Ni. *f.*) shall be split. They shall be split (Qu.). They shall be cleft (Hithq., cleave themselves). And thou (w.c.) shalt anoint as (לְ) king.[13] He caused to light upon. Transgressor (Q. Part.). They transgressed. And (w.c.) Moab (מוֹאָב) transgressed against (בְּ) Israel. Thou art satisfied. Ye shall be satisfied (with) bread.[24] The oath which I swore (Ni.) to (לְ) 'Abhrāhām. Blow the trumpet (שׁוֹפָר) in Tekoa. If[2] ye shall hearken[18] diligently (§ **15. 2**).

---

§ 26. NOUNS. — GENDER AND NUMBER.

1. [1] דָּבָר. [2] מַלְכוּת; בְּרִית. The Hebrew has but two genders, a masculine and a feminine. Objects regarded as neuter in other languages it treats as *masc.* or *fem.*, more frequently the latter. *Masc.* nouns have in the *sing.* no peculiarity of form distinguishing them as such;[1] the endings ָה (with the tone) and ת (after a vowel), mark the *fem. sing.*[2]

Rem. 1. — There are not a few words which are used as either *masc.* or *fem.* Such are marked here c.; i.e., common.

Rem. 2. — The ending ָה, as already noted (§ **1. 4**), often represents an original ַת, which, as will be hereafter seen, needs to be restored in certain forms of the noun and verb. שִׁירָה = שִׁירַת.

Rem. 3. — The ending ת may mark the *fem.* in nouns also after a consonant, if a helping vowel (ֶ, or ַ with a guttural) be used in pronouncing it. שַׁחַת for שַׁחְתְּ; מַמְלֶכֶת for מַמְלַכְתְּ.

Rem. 4. — Adjectives, as it respects Gender and Number, follow the analogy of nouns.

2. [1] שְׁנַיִם. [2] יְאֹרִים. [3] תּוֹדוֹת. [4] יָדַיִם. [5] יוֹמַיִם. Nouns are used in the *sing.*, *pl.*, and (more rarely) *dual* numbers; adjectives, excepting the numeral for *two*,[1] in the *sing.* and *pl.* only. The ending of the *masc. pl.* is generally ִים (or ִם);[2] of the *fem. pl.*

וֹת (or תֹ)[3]; of the *du.* ־ַיִם.[4] The *du.* is mostly used with things occurring in pairs, like certain members of the body, or things which may be conceived of as in pairs.[5]

	SING.	PLUR.	SING.	PLUR.	DU.
Masc.	טוֹב	טוֹבִים	סוּס	סוּסִים	סוּסַיִם
Fem.	טוֹבָה	טוֹבוֹת	סוּסָה	סוּסוֹת	סוּסָתַיִם

3. The endings ־ִים and ־ַיִם are added directly to the *masc. sing.* But before adding the latter to the *fem. sing.* with ־ָה, this ending is restored to its original form ־ַת, the vowel becoming ָ in an open syllable (§ **3**. 3). The ending וֹת is added directly to the *sing.* of nouns not already ending in ־ָה; but in the case of those so ending, the latter is simply changed to the former for the *pl.*

REM. 1.—The changes required in the *changeable* vowels of a word to which syllables attracting the tone to themselves are added will be noted hereafter. For the present, the principle is illustrated by words with unchangeable vowels.

REM. 2.—There are many nouns having a *fem.* ending in the *sing.* which take ־ִים in the *pl.*; and, on the other hand, *masc.* nouns sometimes take וֹת in the *pl.*

REM. 3.—The *pl.* ending וֹת is an obscured âth (*cf.* Q. Inf. abs.), and is unchangeable. That it is here, however, a strengthened form of the original *sing.* ending *ath* is doubtful.

REM. 4.—The *pl.* in Hebrew is used to indicate a variety of relations besides plurality; especially those expressed in other languages by abstract nouns. חַיִּים (*pl.* of חַי) = life; קָדוֹשִׁים most holy: Hos. xii. 1.

דָּם *m.* blood; related to אָדוֹם red.

מַר* (*f.* מָרָה) bitter. Mn. "Marah": Ex. xv. 23.

סוּס (*f.* סוּסָה) horse.

צוּר wind, press, besiege. צוּר *m.* rock. צַוָּאר* *m.* neck. מָצוֹר* *m.* siege, fortress. Mn. "Tyre" (צוֹר).

צָרַר bind together, shut in, oppress.

צַר (*f.* צָרָה) enemy, oppressor. Mn. "Tsar."

שַׂר (*f.* שָׂרָה) prince. Mn. "Sarah": Gen. xvii. 15.

שִׁיר sing. שִׁיר[1] (*f.* שִׁירָה) song.

שָׁקָה[2] (Qu., Hi.) give to drink.

שָׁתָה (Q., Ni.) drink. מִשְׁתֶּה *m.* banquet.

[1] The heading of a number of Psalms. [2] This verb and the next are defective, but mutually supplementary, as will be noted (*cf.* the root-letters). The p. n. "Rabshakeh" (2 Ki. xviii. 17) is usually derived from it (רַב־שָׁקֵה), i.e., chief cup-bearer; probably it is the Assyr. *Rab-sak*, chief captain.

Exercise. — Bullock.[9] Cow. Cows. These (are) the good cows. Two mares. The princes. The waters[3] were[a] bitter. These mountains[9] are very high.[10] Enemies (*m.*). A new[9] song (*m.*). He took[10] asses.[11] He did not drink from[13] the waters. Wisdom[3] is good. And[13] with (בְּ) horses. Righteousnesses[13] (*f.*). Oaths[25] (*f.*). Two talents.[4] Ye shall keep[15] the Sabbaths (־וֹת).[16] Bela' reigned[13] in 'Ĕdôm. Heroes[22] like[12] those.

[a] Rem. — Not infrequently the subject and predicate in clauses of this nature are united by the 3d pers. (*sing.* or *pl. masc.* or *fem.*) of the Pers. Pronoun serving as copula (These are, were = אֵלֶּה הֵנָּה). When the copula is to be expressed, the word representing it will *not* be inclosed in parentheses.

---

§ 27. ANCIENT CASE ENDINGS. — THE CONSTRUCT STATE.

1. [1]חַיְתוֹ for חַיַּת: Gen. i. 24; מְתוּשָׁאֵל (מְתוּ = מַת): Gen. iv. 18; בְּנִי for בֶּן־: Gen. xlix. 11. It would appear that, originally, the Hebrew had endings to represent, respectively, the *Nom.* and *Gen.* case. The one was ו (וֹ or וּ), the other ־ִי. In rare instances these endings still remain;[1] but their power as case endings has entirely ceased.

2. [1]־ָה. [2]הָהָרָה towards the mountain; הַשָּׁמַיְמָה towards the heavens. Another old case ending, however, representing the Accusative, generally toneless, has, to some extent, maintained itself as well in fact as in form.[1] It is appended to substantives mostly to denote direction (*whither*, more rarely *where*), and has accordingly received the name ־ָה *locative.*[2]

Rem. 1. — ־ָה locative being without the tone may be easily distinguished from the *fem.* ending of nouns; and, for the same reason, it does not usually disturb the vocalization of a word to which it is appended. שָׁמָּה thither.

Rem. 2. — When appended to a word having a like fem. ending, the latter reverts to its original form ־ַת. עֶזְרָה help; עֶזְרָתָה help!

3. [1]סוּס הַמֶּלֶךְ the horse of the king. The relations expressed in other languages by case endings are expressed in Hebrew mostly by Prepositions. But in addition to what has been said above of the Accus., it has also a method of representing the close relation ordinarily indicated by the *Gen.* (subjective and objective), the Adj., etc. One noun (the one to be limited) is put before another

(the one limiting) so as to express with it one idea.[1] The former word is said to be in the *construct* state with the latter, which is in the *absolute* state.

4. דְּבַר הַמֶּלֶךְ[1] the word of the king. כֹּל[2] but כָּל־. Furthermore, since the emphasis of this compound expression is on the final word while the first one is hastened over, *changeable* vowels in the first word will be either dropped, volatilized, thinned, or shortened;[1] the effect being the same as though the tone were removed one place beyond it[2] (§ **3.** 3. 4. n; § **6.** 5).

Abs.	סוּס,	סוּסָה,	סוּסִים,	סוּסַיִם,	סוּסָתַיִם,	מַחֲנֶה.
Cstr.	סוּס,	סוּסַת,	סוּסֵי,	סוּסֵי,	סוּסְתֵי,	מַחֲנֵה

5. The changes taking place in other (changeable) vowels of nouns put in the construct state will be further illustrated hereafter (§ **29**); those required in the *terminations* of such constructs should be stated here. The terminations of the *pl. masc.* and *du.* (־ִים, ־ַיִם) become ־ֵי (orig., ־ַי); the ־ָה of *fem.* nouns reverts to its original form ־ַת; while nouns ending in ־ֶה change the same to ־ֵה.

Rem. — The construct may also be found before words governed by Prepositions, before clauses beginning with a Relative pronoun, and in many other cases where a close connection of thought is indicated. הָרֵי בַגִּלְבֹּעַ mountains in (of) Gilboa. מְקוֹם אֲשֶׁר the place in which.

אָחַז[1] seize, possess. אֲחֻזָּה *f.* possession.
חָנָה[2] bend, settle, encamp. חֲנִית*[3] *f.* spear. מַחֲנֶה[2] *c.* encampment.
מִנְחָה *f.* gift, (meal) offering, *Minḥāh.*
נֵר[4] (R. נוּר) *m.* lamp, light. מְנוֹרָה* *f.* candlestick.

צִפּוֹר[5] *c.* bird (chirper).
שָׁאַר[6] be over, left. שְׁאָר* *m.* rest, remnant. שְׁאֵרִית *f.* remnant.
שָׁבָה[7] carry (away) captive. שְׁבִי *m.* captivity. שְׁבוּת *f.* captivity.

[1] Mn. "Ahaz" (אָחָז) who *possessed* the throne in the time of Isaiah. [2] Mn. "Mahanaim," i.e., two camps: Gen. xxxii. 3. [3] The spear was so called from its elasticity. [4] Name of Abner's father: 1 Sam. xiv. 50. [5] Mn. "Zipporah," wife of Moses; also mimetic. [6] Mn. "Shear-jashub" (שְׁאָר יָשׁוּב) = a remnant shall return: Isa. vii. 3. [7] Mn. "Tishbeh" (תִּשְׁבֶּה), the home of "Elijah the Tishbite." What has the name to do with the idea?

Exercise. — *I* (am) Jehovah the God[a] (*pl.*) of Israel (יִשְׂרָאֵל). Righteous[13] (are) we. A possession of a burying-place.[15] The camp of Israel. With (בְּ) a sword[8] and with a spear. The spear of the king. (Meal) offerings. An offering in righteousness. The candlesticks of silver.[12] And he (w.c.) shall kill[24] the bird.[b] And he (w.c.) has kept[15] the statutes[2] (*m.*). Statutes (*f.*). Asses[11] of. The Altars[18] (חוֹת). The queen[13] of Šᵉbhâ'. Borders[22] of Israel. The mighty men[22] of 'Ĕdôm. Cherubim.[24] (Into) Sheol.[12] Ye shall cast[22] every son (כָּל־הַ·)[c] (into) the river (Nile).[3]

[a] Rem. 1. — A noun in the construct does not take the article, being made definite by its connection with the following word.

[b] Rem. 2. — The definite accusative is generally marked in prose by אֶת־ (or אֵת, § 2). A noun is regarded as definite when it has the article; is a proper name; is in the construct state (with a definite noun); when it has a pronominal suffix (§ 28), and in some other cases.

[c] Rem. 3 — כֹּל is a noun (*cstr.* כָּל־), and when followed by the article carries the idea of totality; without it, it is used distributively. כָּל־עָם every people; כָּל־הָעָם the whole people.

§ 28. THE NOUN WITH PRONOMINAL SUFFIXES.

1. *Suffixes with a Sing. Noun.* *Suffixes with a Pl. and Du. Noun.*

	Sing.	Plur.		Sing.	Plur.
1. c.	ִי my	נוּ, ֵנוּ our	1. c.	ַי my	ֵינוּ our
2. *m.*	ךָ, ְךָ } thy	כֶם, ְכֶם } your	2. *m.*	ֶיךָ } thy	ֵיכֶם } your
2. *f.*	ךְ, ֵךְ } thy	כֶן, ְכֶן } your	2. *f.*	ַיִךְ } thy	ֵיכֶן } your
3. *m.*	הוּ, וֹ ; וֹ, ֹה his	הֶם, ָם } their	3. *m.*	ָיו his	ֵיהֶם } their
3. *f.*	הָ, ָהּ, ֶהָ her	הֶן, הֵן, ָן } their	3. *f.*	ֶיהָ her	ֵיהֶן } their

Rem. 1. — In the suffixes of the 2. *pers.* throughout, כ — by a not uncommon interchange of these letters — has taken the place of ת. Otherwise the fragmentary endings may be readily traced to their origin in the Personal Pronoun (*sing.* 3. *f.* ָהּ = ָה ; *sing.* 3. *m.* ו (ֹה) is a contraction from ָהוּ).

Rem. 2. — With Nouns in the *sing.* are given forms both with and without a preceding vowel, or Šᵉwâ. The former are used with nouns ending in a consonant, the latter with those ending in a vowel. This so-called "connecting" vowel is really an original final vowel of the noun, which here in a form more or less modified reappears before most of the suffixes.

Rem. 3. — In the case of *pl.* and *du.* nouns, the original form of the *cstr.* (*ay*) is taken as the basis for the appended suffixes. This is generally contracted to *ê* (*pl.*); *a* is once lengthened to *â* (*sing.* 3. *m.*), and twice deflected to *ĕ* (*sing.* 2. *m.*, 3. *f.*). In the *sing.* 1. *c.* the pronominal ending is absorbed in the *ay* of the ground-form; and in the *sing.* 2. *f.* a helping vowel (*ĭ*) is used.

Rem. 4. — The suffixes כֶם, כֶן, הֶם, הֶן are called "heavy" suffixes, and strongly attract the tone; the other suffixes are "light."

Rem. 5. — For the endings ־ָיו, ־ֵיהֶם, the poetic forms ־ָיהוּ, ־ֵימוֹ may be found. The effect of a Pausal accent on the suffixes falls under the general rules for Pause (§ **6. 4.** r.).

2. *Singular Noun.* *Plural Noun.*

		Masc.	Fem.	Masc.	Fem.
Sing.	1. *c.* my	סוּסִי	סוּסָתִי	סוּסַי	סוּסוֹתַי
	2. *m.* thy	סוּסְךָ	סוּסָתְךָ	סוּסֶיךָ	סוּסוֹתֶיךָ
	2. *f.* thy	סוּסֵךְ	סוּסָתֵךְ	סוּסַיִךְ	סוּסוֹתַיִךְ
	3. *m.* his	סוּסוֹ	סוּסָתוֹ	סוּסָיו	סוּסוֹתָיו
	3. *f.* her	סוּסָהּ	סוּסָתָהּ	סוּסֶיהָ	סוּסוֹתֶיהָ
Pl.	1. *c.* our	סוּסֵנוּ	סוּסָתֵנוּ	סוּסֵינוּ	סוּסוֹתֵינוּ
	2. *m.* your	סוּסְכֶם	סוּסַתְכֶם	סוּסֵיכֶם	סוּסוֹתֵיכֶם
	2. *f.* your	סוּסְכֶן	סוּסַתְכֶן	סוּסֵיכֶן	סוּסוֹתֵיכֶן
	3. *m.* their	סוּסָם	סוּסָתָם	סוּסֵיהֶם	סוּסוֹתֵיהֶם
	3. *f.* their	סוּסָן	סוּסָתָן	סוּסֵיהֶן	סוּסוֹתֵיהֶן

Rem. 1. — The word here used, it will be noted, has immutable vowels. It is representative of all such nouns. The effects of the pronominal suffixes on the mutable vowels of a word will be shown in the following section.

Rem. 2. — The suffixes of nouns denote the Genitive relation, and the words to which they are attached are in the *cstr.* state in fact, if not in form. Hence the *cstr.* of the *fem.* (־ַת), whose vowel, however, when falling in an open syllable (always except with the heavy suffixes) is lengthened.

Rem. 3. — In the *fem.* of *pl.* nouns there is a double indication of the *pl.*: that of the *masc.* in addition to the *fem.*; but in the 3. *Pers. pl.* the endings ־ָם, ־ָן are oftener found than those given.

Rem. 4. — The omission of Dāghēš from כ in the 2. *m.* and *f.* of the *sing. fem.* noun with *pl.* suffix is due to the loosely closed syllable (§ **3. 4**).

דּוֹד[1] *m.* uncle, beloved (one).
דּוֹר[2] *m.* generation.
סֻכָּה*[3] *f.* booth, tabernacle.
עַד[4] *m.* forever.

עַד (*prep.* and *adv.*) till, as far as. עֵד (*f.* עֵדָה) *m.* witness. עֵדוּת *m.* testimony. עוֹד again, still.
צָוָה[5] command. מִצְוָה *f.* commandment.

רִיב[6] strive. רִיב *m.* strife, cause (legal).
שִׁפְחָה[7] *f.* maid-servant, handmaid. מִשְׁפָּחָה *f.* family.

[1] Mn. "David" (דָּוִד) the beloved. [2] R. דּוּר = revolve. Mn. "door." [3] *Pl.* "Succoth," where Jacob built "booths": Gen. xxxiii. 17. [4] Mn. "add" (the common idea at the basis of this list of words). עַד (r. עָדָה go on) forever; עֵד, עֵדוּת (r. עוּד repeat over) = witness; עוֹד (*adv.*) again, still. [5] R. = be hard, solid, and from it comes צִיּוֹן = "Zion," which may serve as mn. [6] Mn. "Reeve," an old term for officer. Sheriff = Shire-*reeve*. [7] If r. = join, then so called as one *joined* to the family; and the family, as those *joined together*.

Exercise.—My beloved. His uncle. Our witness (vowel immutable). Your witnesses. Their witnesses (*f.*). Her commandment. Your commandment. The tabernacle of David. Strifes of. Thy handmaid. His maidservants. Upon (עַל) the maidservants in those days.[10] This (is) the commandment which Jehovah sent.[22] Great[10] (is) the day of Yehôwāh. Yisr'âēl has not kept[15] my precepts.[15] Jehovah (is) a man[9] of war.[24] The horses of Par'ōh and all his mighty men.[22] It (is) thy voice.[9] Jehovah our God (*pl.*) (is) holy (*sing.*).[0] Our rock[26] (is) not as their rock. בֶּן־הַמֶּלֶךְ הַגָּדוֹל the eldest son of the king.[a]

[a] Rem.—An Adj. modifying a noun in immediate connection with a Genitive (i.e., in the *cstr.* state) is placed after the compound expression; and the noun being (by its connection) definite, the adjective has the article (*cf.* § **10**. 2).

§ 29. FIRST CLASS OF NOUNS.

1. Nouns with mutable vowels may be divided into classes according as they are affected by the *pl.*, *du.*, and *fem.* terminations, pronominal suffixes, and the *cstr.* state. In each of these cases the tone moves forward one or two places, producing the effects described in § **6** (which should now be reviewed).

	Abs.	Cstr.	Light Suff.	Heavy Suff.
Sing.	נָדִיב,	נְדִיב,	נְדִיבִי,	נְדִיבְכֶם.
Pl.	נְדִיבִים,	נְדִיבֵי.	נְדִיבַי,	נְדִיבֵיכֶם.

2. As a first class, those nouns (including adjectives and participles) may be designated which have a mutable vowel in the penult only. Inasmuch as that vowel is volatilized by any moving forward of the tone, the form of the word thus becomes fixed, and to it, as a base. the several terminations and suffixes are added without further change.

Rem. 1. — If a word begin with a guttural, the general rule for gutturals in the same circumstances is to be followed (§ 5. 3. עָוֹן, עֲוֹן, עֲוֹנִי, עֲוֹנוֹת, עֲוֹנוֹתַי). The same is true of a word ending in a guttural. § 5. 2. נָבִיא, נְבִיאֲכֶם, מָשִׁיחַ, מְשִׁיחִי.

Rem. 2. — Feminines of the form גְּדוֹלָה (from m. גָּדוֹל) follow the analogy of סוּסָה in the previous section.

Rem. 3. — Words of the form עָנִי, in addition to the changes spoken of in R. 1, become עֲנִיִּים (עֲנִיֵּי, עֲנִיֵּיכֶם) in the pl.; those of the form עֳנִי become עָנְיִי (my affliction) with a suffix.

חֶסֶד[1] m. mercy. חָסִיד* merciful, godly.

נָבָא[2] prophesy. נָבִיא prophet.

נָבַט look upon, regard.

נָגַד[3] tell, narrate. נֶגֶד over against, before. נָגִיד* m. prince, leader.

נָדִיב* liberal, noble. Mn. "Nadab."

נָשָׂא[4] lift up, bear, forgive. נָשִׂיא m. prince. מַשָּׂא[4] burden, portion.

עָוָה†[5] do iniquity. עָוֹן m. iniquity.

עָנָה[6] oppress. עָנִי poor. עֳנִי* m. affliction, oppression.

[1] חֲסִידָה the Stork, was so named from its *tenderness* to its young. [2] To be associated with the next root; the idea of the r. being to bubble forth, as the prophet's words from his soul, as the eye from the lids. [2] Mn. for the second root "Nebat," father of the notorious Jeroboam. [3] R. = be high, sightly. Note three words for *Noble* beginning with נ (נגיד, נדיב, נשיא). [4] To be disting. from נָסָה (mn. "Massah": Ex. xvii. 7), which also means *to lift up*, but with the idea of *trying, proving*. [5] Mn. *Awa*, an iniquitous strong-drink of the Hawaiian Islands. [6] Mn. "Anna" (an *oppressive* empress of Russia, A.D. 1730-1740). Distinguish עָנָה answer, § 47.

Exercise. — Collect[23] (*pl.*) my godly (ones). Our prophets. The prophets of Jehovah. Thy (*f.*) prophets. He went forth[5] from his place.[19] Ruler (נגיד) of the house[3] of God. The princes (נשיא) of the earth.[9] Our iniquity. Their iniquities. Forgiving (Part.) iniquity and transgression.[25] Thy poor (*pl.*). The poor of the flock.[2] Their affliction. And all her multitude (הָמוֹן). Pray for (ask,[12] *pl.*) the peace[20] of Jerusalem.

§ 30. SECOND CLASS OF NOUNS.

1. עוֹלָם, קָרְבָּן, אֹיֵב, קֹטֵל, הֹוֶה. A second class of nouns are those which have a mutable vowel in the final syllable only: while that of the penult is (by nature or position) immutable.

	Abs.	Cstr.	Light Suff.	Heavy Suff.
Sing.	עוֹלָם,	עוֹלַם,	עוֹלָמִי,	עוֹלַמְכֶם.
Pl.	עוֹלָמִים,	עוֹלְמֵי,	עוֹלָמַי,	עוֹלְמֵיכֶם.

2. The law of inflection for nouns (or participles and adjectives) of the form עוֹלָם is that *ā* remains in an open syllable; is changed to *a* in a loosely shut syllable (*cstr.* and with heavy suff. in the *sing.*); and volatilized when the tone is moved forward two places (*cstr.* and with heavy suff. in the *pl.*).

Rem. 1.—The Ni., Qu., and Ho. Participles of the Strong verb follow in inflection the analogy of עוֹלָם, as the Q. (act.), Qi. and Hithq. Participles follow that of אֹיֵב.

Rem. 2.—Monosyllables with a mutable *ā* belonging to this class of words have some peculiarities, represented by יָד, יַד, יֶדְכֶם, יָדַיִם, יָדָיו, יְדֵי, יְדֵיהֶם; and דָּם, דַּם, דָּמִי, דִּמְכֶם, דָּמִים, דְּמֵי, דְּמֵיהֶם. The special peculiarity consists in thinning *ā* to *i* or *e*, with heavy suff. in the *sing.*, and in the *cstr.* and with heavy suff. in the *pl.*

	Abs.	Cstr.	Vocal Suff.	Conson. Suff.
Sing.	אֹיֵב,	אֹיֵב,	אֹיְבִי,	אֹיִבְךָ.
Pl.	אֹיְבִים,	אֹיְבֵי,	אֹיְבַי,	—.

3. In words of the form אֹיֵב, or the Act. Part. Qal (i.e., words having *ē* in the final syllable and an immutable vowel in the penult), the last vowel is volatilized with suffixes beginning with a vowel, and is shortened to *e* or *i* before those beginning with consonants. The *cstr. sing.* is like the *abs.* except before Maqqēph.

Rem.—Monosyllabic nouns with *ē* naturally follow this law of inflection. שֵׁם, שְׁמִי, שִׁמְךָ, שֶׁם־.

4. חֹזִי, חֹזִים, חֹזְכֶם. In words of the form חֹזֶה, מַטֶּה, the *cstr. sing.* is חֹזֵה (§ **27.** 5). Before suffixes, ה and the vowel are dropped, and the suffixes are added directly to the word as thus apocopated.

אֹיֵב[1] *m.* one hating, enemy.
חָזָה*[2] see, behold (a vision). חֹזֶה† *m.* seer. חָזוֹן* *m.* vision.
נָטָה[3] stretch out, turn aside. מִטָּה* *f.* bed. מַטֶּה *c.* staff, tribe.

עוֹלָם *m.* antiquity, age, eternity.
קָנָה acquire, buy. קָנֶה[4] (*cstr.* קְנֵה) *m.* cane, stalk. מִקְנֶה *m.* property (in cattle), cattle.
רָאָה[5] see. מַרְאֶה sight, appearance.
שָׁפַט[6] judge. מִשְׁפָּט judgment, rule.

[1] An interesting fact about this word is that it is used in this (Part.) form about 280 times in the Bible and only once in another form: Ex. xxiii. 22. [2] Not the r. of "Hosea," the prophet; but חֹזֶה is a syn. of נָבִיא[20] and רֹאֶה (seer). [3] Mn. Lat. *Nata-re* (= *stretch out* hands) to swim. [4] Mn. *cane.* The idea of acquisition in the r. comes through that of setting upright, establishing. [5] Note that all the letters are weak, and the first is a "vibrating" letter. [6] Mn. "Jehosaphat" (יְהוֹשָׁפָט), Jehovah has judged.

Exercise. — By (בְּ) means of (hand of) all the seers. Your blood.[26] Your hand. Their hands. The hand of his enemies. The seer of the king.[13] Upon (עַל) the bed of the man[9] of God. Thy rod. And I (w.c.) will break[14] the staff of bread.[24] Possession (property) of flocks (*sing.*).[2] His cattle. Our cattle. In the name[10] of Jehovah. The name of that place.[19] What[11] is thy name? His judgments are in all the earth.[9] The priests[12] and the judges (Part.). I have taught[18] (Qi.) statutes[2] and judgments. And the appearance of the glory[11] of Jehovah. Their appearance. The names of the tribes (־וֹת) of Israel.

---

§ 31. THIRD CLASS OF NOUNS.

1. דָּבָר, לֵבָב, זָקֵן, שָׂדֶה (see vocab. § **40**). This class includes words with two mutable vowels. The law of vowel changes, when additions are taken, is found § **6.** 4–6.

	Abs.	Cstr.	Light Suff.	Heavy Suff.
Sing.	דָּבָר,	דְּבַר,	דְּבָרִי,	דְּבַרְכֶם.
Pl.	דְּבָרִים,	דִּבְרֵי,	דְּבָרַי,	דִּבְרֵיכֶם.

Rem. 1.—The thinning of the original *a* to *i* (*cstr. pl.*, etc.) takes place, except in cases where one of the first two letters is a guttural (חֲכָמִים, חַכְמֵי, נְהָרִים, נַהֲרֵי), and in a few other words. כָּנָף, כַּנְפֵי.

Rem. 2.—Words of the form זָקֵן become זְקַן in the *cstr. sing.*

Rem. 3.—שָׂדֶה having (unlike חֹזֶה, § **30**) a mutable vowel in both syllables belongs to this class. *Cstr.* שְׂדֵה, שָׂדַי, שָׂדִים (or שָׂדוֹת), *cstr. pl.* שְׂדֵי.

Rem. 4.—Words of this class occasionally take with additions D. forte (*characteristic*, § **4. 2.** R.) in their final radical, in order to keep the pretonic vowel short. גְּמַלִּים for גְּמָלִים.

	Abs.	Cstr.	Light Suff.	Heavy Suff.
Sing.	צְדָקָה,	צִדְקַת,	צִדְקָתִי,	צִדְקַתְכֶם.
Pl.	צְדָקוֹת,	צִדְקוֹת,	צִדְקוֹתַי,	צִדְקוֹתֵיכֶם.

2. In feminines of this class ending in ָה, the original form in *ath* (*ā-th* in open syllable) is assumed, and the law of vocal changes is then applied, as in the masculines.

Rem.—The *dual* has the form (שָׂפָה) שְׂפָתַיִם, *cstr.* שִׂפְתֵי, שְׂפָתַי, שִׂפְתֵיכֶם.

אָדָם *m.* man, Adam. אֲדָמָה[1] *f.* ground, earth.

בָּקָר[2] *c.* (large) cattle, herd. בֹּקֶר *m.* morning.

בִּשֵּׂר †[3] (Qi.) bring good tidings. בָּשָׂר *m.* flesh.

כָּנָף[4] *c.* wing, border.

נָהָר[5] *m.* river. Syn. יְאֹר.

שָׂפָה[6] *f.* lip, border, shore.

שָׁנָה † change. מִשְׁנֶה[7] *m.* second, copy. שָׁנָה *f.* year. שֵׁנִי *m.* (*f.* שֵׁנִית) second. שְׁנַיִם two.

[1] Associate with preceding word. [2] R. = break through: cattle, the clods (in ploughing); morning, the mists and darkness. [3] Idea of r., to smooth the skin, rub out its wrinkles. *Cf.* Germ. glätten, Eng. gladden. [4] R. כן = cover. The three root-letters are in "canopy." [5] Associate with הַר (*river* and *mount*). [6] Idea of r. שׂף, סף, is *to rub*. *Cf.* סֵפֶר = rub pen on the paper. [7] It is easy to see how the idea of year comes from that of change. The two following words are from an allied r. Mn. "Mishna" (מִשְׁנָה), i.e., the text of the Talmud, so called as a *repetition* of the law.

Exercise.—From the elders[17] of Israel. The wisdom[3] of his wise (men).[3] According to (כְּ) the word[6] of Jehovah. He wrote[4] all the words in a book.[12] The words of the lips of Jehovah. His words. Their words. In the heart[23] of the righteous[13] (*pl.*). Which is upon (עַל) the shore of the sea (יָם). In the house[3] and in the field (שָׂדֶה). The waters[3] of the river. Flock[2] and herd. I will give (אֶתֵּן) thy flesh to the birds of (לְעוֹף) heaven.[10] The righteous acts (righteousnesses) of Jehovah. Jehovah our righteousness.

---

§ 32. FOURTH CLASS OF NOUNS.

1. מַלְךְ, סִפְר, בֻּקְר (בָּקְר). Numerous nouns of a peculiar formation (originally monosyllabic) may be reckoned as a fourth class. Their vowels were respectively *a*, *i*, and *u* (or *o*).

2. מֶלֶךְ, סֵפֶר (קֶרֶב), בֹּקֶר. On account of the difficulty of pronouncing these words as monosyllables, a helping vowel was used under the second radical; and as this vowel was ordinarily Seghôl (see, however, the following section) they are generally known as Segholates. They are named Segholates of the *a*, *i*, or *u* (or *o*) class, according to the vowel which originally characterized them.

Rem. 1. — In Segholates of the *a* class this vowel has been ordinarily deflected to *e*. מֶלֶךְ from מַלְךְ.

Rem. 2. — In Segholates of the *i* and *u* (or *o*) class these vowels (now standing in an open syllable with the tone) are changed to *ē* and *ō*.

Rem. 3. — It is not possible to judge from their absolute form to which of the first two classes a Segholate belongs, if the vowel of the first syllable be *e*. Accordingly, those of the *i* class have been indicated in our vocabularies.

Rem. 4. — Certain words of this class have not been given a helping vowel, but remain in their original monosyllabic form. חֵטְא, חֶטְאוֹ, חֲטָאִים.

Sing.	*Abs.*	מֶלֶךְ	סֵפֶר	בֹּקֶר
	Cstr.	מֶלֶךְ	סֵפֶר	בֹּקֶר
	Light suff.	מַלְכִּי	סִפְרִי	בָּקְרִי
	Heavy suff.	מַלְכְּכֶם	סִפְרְכֶם	בָּקְרְכֶם
Pl.	*Abs.*	מְלָכִים	סְפָרִים	בְּקָרִים
	Cstr.	מַלְכֵי	סִפְרֵי	בָּקְרֵי
	Light suff.	מְלָכַי	סְפָרַי	בְּקָרַי
	Heavy suff.	מַלְכֵיכֶם	סִפְרֵיכֶם	בָּקְרֵיכֶם
Du.		רַגְלַיִם	—	—

3. The law for the inflection of Segholates is that in the *sing.* and *du.* of the word, and in the *cstr.* and the forms having heavy suffixes of the *pl.*, the pronominal suffixes are appended to the original monosyllabic form. In the other forms (*pl.* and the *pl.* with light suffixes) a "helping" vowel (ă) is used with the second radical, its own being volatilized, and the suffixes are then added without further change.

Rem. 1. — It will be noted that the *cstr. sing.* is like the *abs.* This law is nearly universal.

Rem. 2. — In Segholates of the *u* (or *o*) class, the characteristic vowel of the inflected forms is generally *o*, but there are examples of the use of *u*, and even *i*. גִּדְלוֹ from גֹּדֶל greatness.

Rem. 3. — On the exceptional *pl.* forms of שֹׁרֶשׁ and קֹדֶשׁ, see § **2.** 3. R. 2.

Rem. 4. — The *cstr. pl.* is really formed from the *abs. pl.* by volatilizing the "helping" vowel ă, and restoring in the first syllable the original *a* (*i* or *o*); but, for practical reasons, it seemed better to state the rule as above.

Rem. 5. — A more characteristic mark of words of this class than ֶ is the tone on the penult.

אָזַן* (Hi.) give ear. אֹזֶן[1] *m.* ear.

בְּכוֹר[2] *m.* firstborn. בְּכֹרָה† *f.* firstling, birthright.

יָלַד beget, give birth. יֶלֶד[3] *m.* boy, son.

נָדַר* vow. נֶדֶר[4] (and נֵדֶר) (i) *m.* a vow.

נֶפֶשׁ *c.* soul, life, self.

רָגַל*[5] go, (go about to) calumniate, spy out, tread. רֶגֶל *f.* foot.

שֶׁמֶן[6] (i) *m.* oil.

שֶׁמֶשׁ[7] *c.* the sun.

שֹׁרֶשׁ*[8] *m.* root.

[1] *Cf.* ὠσίν, *dat. pl.* of οὖς. [2] R. = break through. *Cf.* בָּקַר. [3] A mn. will, perhaps, suggest itself. [4] R. akin to נזר, mn. "Nazirite" (נָזִיר). [5] R. רג carries the idea of (excited) movement. [6] Mn. "Gethsemane" (Aram. גַּת שְׁמָנָה oil press). [7] Mn. "Beth-shemesh" (Josh. xv. 10), house of the sun. [8] Assoc. with קֹדֶשׁ (see § **2.** 3. R. 2).

Exercise. — In their ears. In the ears of the people[9] of the land.[9] All[2] the firstborn. The firstborn according to (בְּ) his birthright. My sons. Their sons. Where (§ **10.** 4) thou hast vowed a vow. His vows. Your vows. Bless[6] (Qi.), my soul, Jehovah. For (לְ) the sole[3] of her foot. From between (מִבֵּין) his feet. At (בְּ) their feet. We (are) your servants.[8] Cause (me) to hear[18] in the morning[31] thy lovingkindness.[29] The root of the righteous[13] (*pl.*). And he (w.c.) wrote[4] these words[6] in the book[12] of the law (תּוֹרָה) of God.

§ 33. FOURTH CLASS OF NOUNS (*Continued*).

Sing. Abs. and Cstr.	נַ֫עַר	נֵ֫צַח	פֹּ֫עַל
Light suff.	נַעֲרִי	נִצְחִי	פָּעֳלִי
Heavy suff.	נַעַרְכֶם	נִצְחֲכֶם	פָּעָלְכֶם
Pl. *Abs.*	נְעָרִים	נְצָחִים	פְּעָלִים
Cstr.	נַעֲרֵי	נִצְחֵי	פָּעֳלֵי
Light suff.	נְעָרַי	נְצָחַי	פְּעָלַי
Heavy suff.	נַעֲרֵיכֶם	נִצְחֵיכֶם	פָּעֳלֵיכֶם

1. Segholates having a guttural for their second or third radical generally take *a* instead of *e* as a helping vowel; and in those having a guttural as their second radical, an original *a* in the first syllable is usually retained, i.e., the word does not assume an actual *Segholate* form in either case.

Rem. 1. — To the second part of this rule there are occasional exceptions. לַחְמָם from לֶ֫חֶם.

Rem. 2. — Segholates of the *u* (or *o*) class sometimes retain the *ō* in the *pl. abs.* and in the *pl.* with light suffixes. אֹהָלָיו, אֹהָלִים from אֹ֫הֶל.

Rem. 3. — Segholates of the *i* class whose first letter is a guttural (ע, ח) usually take *e* with suffixes instead of the original vowel. עֶזְרִי from עֵ֫זֶר.

Sing. Abs.	מַלְכָּה	חֶרְפָּה	חָרְבָּה
Cstr.	מַלְכַּת	חֶרְפַּת	חָרְבַּת
Light suff.	מַלְכָּתִי	חֶרְפָּתִי	חָרְבָּתִי
Heavy suff.	מַלְכַּתְכֶם	חֶרְפַּתְכֶם	חָרְבַּתְכֶם
Pl. *Abs.*	מְלָכוֹת	חֲרָפוֹת	חֳרָבוֹת
Cstr.	מַלְכוֹת	חֶרְפוֹת	חָרְבוֹת
Light suff.	מַלְכוֹתַי	חֶרְפוֹתַי	חָרְבוֹתַי

2. Feminines from *masc.* Segholates (like מֶ֫לֶךְ, חֶ֫רֶף, חֹ֫רֶב) require no new principle in their inflection. The *fem.* ending affects the word as the ordinary suffix affects the *masc.* — throws it into its monosyllabic form. The *fem. pl.* form is also precisely analogous

to the *masc.* All suffixes in both *sing.* and *pl.* are appended to the *cstr.* (as in *fem.* nouns of the third class), the final *a* in the *sing.* becoming *ā* in an open syllable.

REM. — חֶרְפָּה *f.* reproach. See *s.v.* חרף, Ap. 1.

Sing. Abs. and cstr.	מַמְלֶכֶת	קֹטֶלֶת	גְּבֶרֶת	mistress	נְחֹשֶׁת
Light suff.	מַמְלַכְתִּי	קֹטַלְתִּי	גְּבִרְתִּי		נְחָשְׁתִּי
Pl. Abs.	מַמְלָכוֹת	קֹטְלוֹת	—		—
Cstr.	מַמְלְכוֹת	קֹטְלוֹת	—		—

3. Besides the *fem.* form of *masc.* Segholates, there are also proper *fem.* Segholates. They are nouns with the *fem.* ending ת and a helping vowel (ֶ, ַ). They are inflected in the *sing.* like the *masc.* Segholates. In the *pl.* the first form follows the analogy of the *fem.* of *masc.* Segholates; the second (the *fem. act. Part.* Q., Qi., Hithq.) drops the pretonic vowel in the *pl.*; the third and fourth are rarely met with in the *pl.*

REM. — Some *fem.* nouns have an *abs.* form in ָה as well as in ֶת (מִלְחָמָה or מִלְחֶמֶת, קֹטְלָה or קֹטֶלֶת); while there are some whose *abs.* form is in ָה and their *cstr.* always in ֶת. מַמְלָכָה, אִשָּׁה.

אֹהֶל *m.* tent. Mn. "Oholiab": Ex. xxxi. 6.

יַעַר *m.* forest. Mn. (*pl.*) "Jearim": Josh. xv. 10 ("forest-city").

נְחֹשֶׁת[1] *c.* copper, brass (bronze).

נַעַר[2] young man; נַעֲרָה *f.*; נְעוּרִים youth.

נָצַח[3] (Qi.) lead, especially a choir.

נֵצַח (or נֶצַח) glory, eternity.

פֶּסַח* *m.* Passover; Gr. πάσχα.

פָּעַל[4] do, make. פֹּעַל* *m.* deed, work.

פַּעַם[5] *c.* stroke, step, a time (once).

שַׁעַר *c.* gate. R. divide. Mn. "share."

[1] The memory may be aided by combining the p.n. "Necho" (Pharaoh) and "Seth" (שֵׁת), though the latter may have been nearer the *bronze* age: Gen. iv. 22. [2] Mimetic, referring to time of puberty. *Cf.* gnär (= gnarl, snarl, growl). [3] The *Qi. Part.* מְנַצֵּחַ with לְ is found over fifty times in headings of Psalms in the sense of choir-leader. [4] May be associated with the *usual* names of the Voices, as "Niph'al," "Pu'al," etc. (§ 19). It is used in poetry for עָשָׂה. [5] The original monosyllabic form פַּעְם suggests better the idea of stroke, step.

Exercise. — He sent[22] (Qi.) each man[9] (= a man) to (לְ) his tent (*pl.*). As a lion[12] in the forest. Its brass. In silver[12] and in brass. He spoke[5] to his young man. And thou (w.c. Impf. in *a*) hast cleaved[22] to (בְּ) the maidens of Bō'az. "To the chief musician." To cut off[20] (Hi.) from the city (עִיר) of Jehovah all workers of iniquity (אָוֶן). Ask[12] (*pl.*) concerning (עַל) my sons[11] and concerning the work of my hands.[3] And I (w.c.) will reward[20] (Qi. of שָׁלֵם) them (לָהֶם) according to their works. My steps. Twice (*du.*).

§ 34. NOUNS OF PECULIAR FORMATION.

Sing.	*Abs.*	אָח	אָחוֹת	אָמָה	כְּלִי	עִיר
	Cstr.	אֲחִי	אֲחוֹת	—	—	עִיר
	Light suff.	אָחִיו	אֲחוֹתִי	אֲמָתִי	כֶּלְיְךָ	—
	Heavy suff.	אֲחִיכֶם	—	—	—	—
Pl.	*Abs.*	אַחִים	אֲחָיוֹת	אֲמָהוֹת	כֵּלִים	עָרִים
	Cstr.	אֲחֵי	—	אַמְהוֹת	כְּלֵי	עָרֵי
	Light suff.	אַחֶיךָ	אַחְיֹתָיו	אַמְהֹתָיו	כֵּלַי	—
	Heavy suff.	אֲחֵיכֶם	(אַחְוֹתֵיכֶם)	—	כְּלֵיכֶם	—

Rem. — 1. In אַחִים the vowel of the first syllable is possible because there is a D. forte implied. For אַחָיו (*pl.* with light suff.), אֶחָיו is always found by exception. 2. In אָחוֹת the ending is not that of the *fem. pl.*, but is a contraction for -*awath*. 3. The ה in אֲמָהוֹת is used as a consonant, and not as in אָמָה. 4. The *pl.* of כְּלִי is formed as if from כֵּל, and of עִיר as if from עָר, the latter form being still found in proper names. 5. The remaining nouns usually reckoned under this head have already been given in preceding vocabularies, but should now be reviewed: אָב (§ 8); אִשָּׁה, אִישׁ (§ 9); בַּיִת (§ 3); בֵּן, בַּת (§ 11); יוֹם (§ 10); מַיִם, פֶּה, רֹאשׁ (§ 3); שֵׁם, שָׁמַיִם (§ 10).

אָבָה wish, will. אֶבְיוֹן[1] poor.
אָוָה* wish, desire. תַּאֲוָה *f. ibid.*
אוֹ (§ 2) or.
אָח[2] brother. אָחוֹת sister.
אָחוֹר back side, backwards. אַחַר *m.* after. אַחֵר another. אַחֲרוֹן[3] latter, later. אַחֲרִית *f.* latter time, future.
מָחָר, מָחֳרָת* *f.* to-morrow.

אֵם[4] (with suff. אִמִּי, *pl.* אִמּוֹת) *f.* mother. אַמָּה cubit, mother-city, metropolis.
אָמָה[5] *f.* maidservant.
כָּלָה[6] complete, end. כַּלָּה* bride, daughter-in-law. כְּלִי vessel, weapon, thing. כִּלְיָה, (only *pl.*) כְּלָיוֹת reins, inward parts.
עוּר be astir, awake. עִיר *f.* city.

[1] Mn. and deriv. "Ebionite." The idea of "poor" as coming from this r. is obvious. [2] The same word as interjection = Alas! [3] Mn. for this series of words "Acheron" (Ἀχέρων), a fabled river of the *after* world. אַחַר (note vowel and D. forte implied as in אַחַר) = one after, i.e., another. מָחָר apparently = מְאַחַר. i.e., the (day) after. [4] R. אמם (in Assyr.) = be broad, roomy; hence cubit. [5] *Cf.* Germ. *Amme*, nurse; Lat. *mamma*. All seem to be mimetic. [6] Idea of r. is to be rounded out, complete. כֹּל (§ 2) is from an allied r. The bride was so called as the full grown maiden; the reins, from the conception of them, probably, as a sort of vessel (כְּלִי). [7] Note idea of a city. עִיר is equivalent to עָר, as in עָר־מוֹאָב city of Moab: Num. xxi. 28.

Exercise.—He slept[19] with[9] his fathers. The wife[9] (woman) of thy youth.[33] All the men of Israel. The house of the women. A place[19] for (לְ) houses. My sons and my daughters. In the days of your fathers. According to (עַל) the word (mouth) of Jehovah. His brethren (R. 1) were not able.[9] Say[5] (*f.*) thou (art) my sister. His wife (formed from אִשָּׁה) and his maidservants. The vessels (are) holy (holiness).[6] And (w.c.) the elders[17] of that city shall take[19] the man. I have-made-to-cease[16] from the cities of Yᵉhûdhāh the voice[9] of joy.[3]

§ 35. THE CARDINAL NUMBERS.

1.

	ABS.	CSTR.	ABS.	CSTR.
1	אֶחָד	אַחַד	אַחַת	אַחַת
2	שְׁנַיִם	שְׁנֵי	שְׁתַּיִם	שְׁתֵּי
3	שְׁלֹשָׁה	שְׁלֹשֶׁת	שָׁלֹשׁ	שְׁלֹשׁ
4	אַרְבָּעָה	אַרְבַּעַת	אַרְבַּע	אַרְבַּע
5	חֲמִשָּׁה	חֲמֵשֶׁת	חָמֵשׁ	חֲמֵשׁ
6	שִׁשָּׁה	שֵׁשֶׁת	שֵׁשׁ	שֵׁשׁ
7	שִׁבְעָה	שִׁבְעַת	שֶׁבַע	שְׁבַע
8	שְׁמֹנָה	שְׁמֹנַת	שְׁמֹנֶה	wanting
9	תִּשְׁעָה	תִּשְׁעַת	תֵּשַׁע	תְּשַׁע
10	עֲשָׂרָה	עֲשֶׂרֶת	עֶשֶׂר	עֶשֶׂר

REM. — 1. The vowels *e* and *a* in the first syllable of the word for *one* are not in an open syllable; but D. forte is implied in ח. 2. The Dāghēš in שְׁתַּ֫יִם and its *cstr.* is not D. forte, but, by exception (§ 3. 1. R. 2), a D. lene, the word being for אשתים.

2. [1]יוֹם אֶחָד· [2]עָרִים שְׁתַּ֫יִם· [3]שְׁתֵּי נָשִׁים· The numeral for *one* is rarely used except as an *adj.;* hence it is found after its word, and agrees with it in gender and number.[1] The numeral for *two* is an abstract noun; hence it may be found standing in apposition before or after the thing enumerated,[2] or in the construct state before it.[3]

3. שָׁלֹשׁ עָרִים· עָרִים שָׁלֹשׁ· The numerals from 3 to 10 are also abstract nouns; but as a rule they *disagree in gender* with the things they enumerate, a *masc.* being used with a *fem.* and *vice versâ.*[a]

11	אַחַד עָשָׂר	אַחַת עֶשְׂרֵה
	עַשְׁתֵּי עָשָׂר	עַשְׁתֵּי עֶשְׂרֵה
12	שְׁנֵים עָשָׂר	שְׁתֵּים עֶשְׂרֵה
	שְׁנֵי עָשָׂר	שְׁתֵּי עֶשְׂרֵה
13	שְׁלֹשָׁה עָשָׂר	שְׁלֹשׁ עֶשְׂרֵה
	Etc.	Etc.
20	עֶשְׂרִים	30 שְׁלֹשִׁים
100	מֵאָה	200 מָאתַ֫יִם (*du.*)
1000	אֶ֫לֶף	2000 אַלְפַּ֫יִם (*du.*)
10000	רִבּוֹא (רִבּוֹ)	רִבֹּאוֹת (רִבּוֹת) (*pl.*)
	רְבָבָה	רְבָבוֹת (*pl.*)

4. The numerals from *eleven* to *nineteen* are formed by prefixing the units to the numeral for *ten.*

REM. 1. — The form עַשְׁתֵּי represents a root not elsewhere found in Hebrew, but that appears in Assyrian in the word *ištin*, one.

REM. 2. — The forms שְׁתֵּים, שְׁנֵים (contracted from שְׁתַּ֫יִם, שְׁנַ֫יִם) stand for שְׁתֵּי, שְׁנֵי, and come under the head of perpetual *Qᵉrês*, though only used in this connection.

[a] The *fem.* form of the numeral, being the original, is used with the more common *masc.* nouns; while the *masc.* form of the numeral, as shorter, is used with the *fem.* nouns.

5. The numeral for *twenty* is the *pl.* of that for *ten*; while those from *thirty* to *ninety* are the plurals of the respective units.

6. [1] שְׁלשֶׁת בָּנִים · [2] שְׁלשָׁה בָּנִים · [3] בָּנִים שְׁלשָׁה ·
The numerals from *two* to *ten* generally stand in the *cstr.* before their nouns;[1] but may stand before them,[2] or, still less frequently, after them,[3] in the *abs.*

Rem.—The *fem. du.* of the corresponding cardinal is used to express the idea of *-fold.* שִׁבְעָתַיִם sevenfold.

7. רִאשׁוֹן, (*f.*) רִאשׁוֹנָה first. שֵׁנִי, (*f.*) שֵׁנִית second. שְׁלִישִׁי, (*f.*) שְׁלִישִׁית third. The *ordinal numbers* (1 to 10), except that for *first*, are formed from the corresponding cardinals by inserting an ִ י after the 2d and 3d consonants. They are adjectives, and so construed. Above *ten* the cardinals are used for the ordinals, as also often in other cases in counting years and the days of the month.

Rem.—רְבִיעִי *fourth*, drops the weak א of אַרְבַּע on becoming an ordinal.

8. The following idiomatic expressions are worth noting:[a]—

1. זֶה שָׁלוֹשׁ שָׁנִים these three years.
2. בֶּן־שֶׁבַע שָׁנִים seven years old.
3. שְׁנֵי הַמְּלָכִים אֵלֶּה these two kings.
4. עֶשֶׂר בָּאַמָּה הַכְּרוּב the cherub was ten cubits (high).
5. שְׁנֵיכֶם you two (or) two of you.
6. שְׁנֵי הַמְּלָכִים the two kings.
7. שְׁנֵי בָנֶיךָ thy two sons.

---

§ 36. THE STRONG VERB WITH SUFFIXES.

1. The *Inf. cstr.* and *Part.* (Q.): קְטֹל, קֹטֵל. [1] קָטְלֵנִי killing me. [2] קָטְלִי my killing, killing me. קָטְלְךָ etc. Being themselves properly nouns, the *Inf. cstr.* and *Part.* take the pronominal suffixes of nouns; except the suffix of the 1*st Pers. s.*, where ֵ נִי may be used for ִ י. The former always denotes the object of the verb (me),[1] the latter the subject or object (my *or* me).[2]

Rem. 1.—The ending ֵ נִי is found with the *Part.* only in poetry.

Rem. 2.—The *Part.* in this form, it will be remembered, belongs to the second class of nouns (§ **30**); the *Inf.* to the fourth class (§ **32**). The vowel ō, in the latter, is drawn back and used under the first radical, where, falling in a shut syllable without the tone, it becomes *o* (or *u*), and is inflected (with the exception of the 1*st Pers.*) much like בֹּקֶר.

---

[a] *Cf.* Kennedy's *Introd. to Bib. Hebrew* (Lond., 1889), p. 106.

REM. 3.—With the suffixes ךָ, כֶם, כֶן, the *Inf.* generally takes the vowel under the 2d radical. קְטָלְךָ, קְטָלְכֶם.

REM. 4.—The *Inf.* of the form קְטַל (*Intrans.*, etc.) becomes קִטְלִי (קִטְלֵנִי), קִטְלְךָ, etc., when inflected.

3. SING. MASC.	3. SING. FEM.	2. SING. MASC.	2. SING. FEM.	3. PLUR. COM.	2. PLUR. COM.
קָטַל	קָטְלָה	קָטַלְתָּ	קָטַלְתְּ	קָטְלוּ	קְטַלְתֶּם
קְטָלַנִי	קְטָלַתְנִי	קְטַלְתַּנִי	קְטַלְתִּנִי	קְטָלוּנִי	קְטַלְתּוּנִי
קְטָלְךָ	קְטָלַתְךָ	—	—	קְטָלוּךָ	—
קְטָלֵךְ	קְטָלָתֶךְ	—	—	קְטָלוּךְ	—
קְטָלוֹ	קְטָלַתְהוּ	קְטַלְתּוֹ	קְטַלְתִּהוּ	קְטָלֻהוּ	etc.
קְטָלָהּ	קְטָלַתָּה	קְטַלְתָּהּ	קְטַלְתִּהָ	קְטָלוּהָ	as 3. *pl.*
קְטָלָנוּ	קְטָלַתְנוּ	קְטַלְתָּנוּ	קְטַלְתִּנוּ	קְטָלֻנוּ	
wanting	wanting	—	—	קְטָלוּכֶם	—
wanting	wanting	—	—	wanting	—
קְטָלָם	קְטָלָתַם	קְטַלְתָּם	קְטַלְתִּים	קְטָלוּם	
קְטָלָן	קְטָלָתַן	קְטַלְתָּן	קְמַלְתִּין	קְטָלוּן	

2. *The Perf.* The accusative of the *Pers. Pron.* is sometimes expressed with the verb by means of the particle אֵת and a suffix (§ **39**). When this is not the case, the pronominal fragment is attached to the verb itself.

REM.—1. The suffixes of the verb here, too, it will be seen, with the exception above noted, are the same as those of the noun (§ **28**). 2. As in the case of the noun, also, a union vowel (originally found with the word) is generally used before suffixes beginning with a consonant, after forms ending in one. In the verb it is ordinarily *a* in the *Perf.*, as in ַנִי (the only exceptions being ē before the suffix of the 2. *f.* and ְ before ךָ 2. *m.* of קָטַל, קָטְלָה), and ē in the *Impf.* and *Imper.* 3. Before appending the suffixes the verb assumes in some instances (3. *s. f.*, 2. *s. f.*, 2. *pl. c.*) a different (older) form, already indicated, better suited to the additions to be made (ָה becoming ַת); תְּ (from אַתְּי), תִּי or תִּ; תֶּם, תּוּם, and then (eliding ם) תּוּ. 4. The changes produced by the suffix on the preceding vowels are in harmony with previous rules: the vowel in the pretone is dropped; that in the tone preserved, *a* becoming *ā* in an open syllable. 5. The ending ַת (3. *s. f.*), it will be noted, always has the tone, while נִי, נוּ, הוּ, ָה never have it. 6. The remaining parts of the verb in the *Perf.*, as ending in a vowel, present no difficulty, the suffix being added directly (1. *s. c.* קְטַלְתִּיךָ; 1. *pl. c.* קְטַלְנוּךָ, etc.). 7. In place of the form

קְטַלְתַּהוּ (3. s. f.) of the table, the ending ַ֫תּוּ may be found; for קְטַלְתּוֹ (2. s. m.), the ending ָ֫תְהוּ_; and for קְטַלְתִּ֫יהוּ (1. s. c.), the ending ִ֫יו_.

3. Reflexive action (kill one's self) cannot be expressed by means of suffixes appended to the verb, but only by the reflexive voices of the verb itself (Ni., Hithq.).

4. קִטְּלְךָ, קִטֶּלְךָ, קִטְּלַנִי; הִקְטִילְךָ, הִקְטִילֵךְ, הִקְטִילַנִי.
In the *Hi.* Perf. with suffixes no new principle is introduced. Its vowels are unchangeable. The *Qi.* (and *Hithq.*) form has a changeable vowel only in the last syllable, and is treated, with the exceptions already named (1st Pers.), like a noun of the second class.

5. כִּבַּדְכֶם, כִּבֶּדְךָ, כִּבְּדַנִי, כִּבֵּד. Intransitive verbs of this form simply retain *ē* in an open syllable where the transitives have *ā*.

פָּחַד*[1] fear. פַּחַד *m.* fear.

פַּח* *m.* snare.

קָצַר[2] cut off, reap; be short. קָצִיר *m.* harvest.

רָגַז*[3] be moved, angry, afraid.

רָחַב*[4] be broad, enlarged. רֹחַב *m.* breadth. רְחוֹב* *f.* a broad street, place.

רָחַץ[5] wash.

רָכַב[6] ride. רֶכֶב (i) *m.* rider, wagon. מֶרְכָּבָה *f.* chariot.

שָׂכַל[7] have sagacity, act wisely.

שָׁפַךְ[8] pour out, shed.

[1] Idea of r. letters פח is swell up, spring up, as the flesh from fear, as the snare, etc. [2] Idea of קץ is cut, break. *Cf.* קָצַף, § 16. [3] Idea of רג is commotion. *Cf.* רגל, § 32. [4] רח in this word is connected with the r. רוח be airy, then broad. "Rehob," king of Zoba (2 Sam. viii. 3), had a name indicative of breadth. [5] Idea of רח in numerous words is to be soft; here make soft by washing. [6] Mn. "Rechabite" (רֵכָבִי, 2 Sam. iv. 2), so called from their riding on camels. [7] Mn. "Maschil" (מַשְׂכִּיל), a title of certain Psalms (32d, etc.), as *skilfully wrought* perhaps. [8] Used especially of shedding blood (דָּם).

Exercise.—In his reigning.[13] Thou hast honored me (Qi.).[11] And (w.c.) shalt honor him (Qi.). They have honored me (Qi.). And we (w.c.) will honor thee. And (he that) honoreth him (Qi. Part. s.). To honor thee (Qi., in P.). Wherefore[11] hast thou disquieted (moved, Hi.) me? And (w.c.) thy heart[23] (*f.*) shall fear and shall be enlarged. And I (w.c.) will make thee ride. To make thee sagacious. Until[28] he hath destroyed[20] (Hi. Inf.). To till[8] it (*f.*) and to keep[15] it. I have sanctified[6] thee (Hi.). I will teach[18] you (Qi.) the fear[17] of God. They sought[15] him with (בְּ) all the heart.

§ 37. THE STRONG VERB WITH SUFFIXES (Continued).

1. *The Imperfect.*   *The Imperative.*

3. Sing. Masc.	With ‏ נ ‏ Demon.	3. Plur. Masc.	Sing.	With ‏ נ ‏ Demon.	Plur.
יִקְטֹל	—	יִקְטְלוּ	קְטֹל	—	קִטְלוּ
יִקְטְלֵ֫נִי	יִקְטְלַ֫נִּי	יִקְטְלוּ֫נִי	קָטְלֵ֫נִי	קָטְלַ֫נִּי	קִטְלוּ֫נִי
יִקְטָלְךָ	יִקְטְלֶ֫ךָּ	יִקְטְלוּךָ	—	—	—
יִקְטְלֵךְ	—	יִקְטְלוּךְ	—	—	—
יִקְטְלֵ֫הוּ	יִקְטְלֶ֫נּוּ	יִקְטְלוּהוּ	קָטְלֵ֫הוּ	קָטְלֶ֫נּוּ	etc.
יִקְטְלֶ֫הָ ‏ ָה	יִקְטְלֶ֫נָּה	יִקְטְלוּהָ	קָטְלֶ֫הָ ‏ ָה	קָטְלֶ֫נָּה	as
יִקְטְלֵ֫נוּ	—	יִקְטְלוּנוּ	קָטְלֵ֫נוּ	—	Impf.
יִקְטָלְכֶם	—	יִקְטְלוּכֶם	—	—	—
יִקְטָלְכֶן	—	יִקְטְלוּכֶן	—	—	—
יִקְטְלֵם	—	יִקְטְלוּם	קָטְלֵם	—	—
יִקְטְלֵן	—	יִקְטְלוּן	קָטְלֵן	—	—

Rem. — 1. In both the *Impf.* and *Imp.*, forms ending in a vowel take the suffix directly (תִּקְטֹ֫לְנָה, 2. and 3. *f. pl.*, becomes תִּקְטְלוּ before suffixes). 2. The final ō of forms of the *Impf.* is volatilized before the suffix, except with ךָ, כֶם, כֶן, when it becomes o. The final ō of the *Imp.* is drawn back under the first radical, after the analogy of the *Inf.*, and becomes o. 3. The union vowel which by the rule is here ē (§ 36. 2. R. 2) appears in the *Impf.* as ֵ before the suffixes ךָ, כֶם, כֶן, and è before ה (sometimes contracted to הָ ֶ) in the *Impf.* and *Imp.* 4. The alternative (strengthened) forms before the suffixes נִי, ךָ, הוּ, הָ, are due to the presence of the syllable *an*, now mostly reduced to נ. This נ is assimilated to a following ךָ and ה; while a ה following is assimilated to it, as indicated by the D. forte in both cases. This נ is called נ demonstrative, and is found mostly with pausal and emphatic (cohortative) forms. It will be noted that every syllable where it is found has the vowel *e* with the tone.

2. יִכְבַּד, יִכְבְּדֵ֫נִי, יִכְבָּדְךָ. Verbs having *a* in the last syllable of the *Impf.* and *Imp.* (Intrans., etc.) retain it, and, in an open syllable, heighten it to *ā*.

3. יַקְטִיל יַקְטִילֵ֫נִי יַקְטִילְךָ; יִקְטַל יִקְטְלֵ֫נִי יִקְטָלְךָ. The Hi. *Impf.*, having unchangeable vowels, presents no difficulties; while the Qi. *Impf.* follows the analogy of the *Perf.*, with the difference of the union vowel.

בָּדַל[1] separate.
בִּקֵּשׁ[2] (Qi., Qu.) seek.
דְּבַשׁ[3] *m.* honey, syrup.
יַיִן[4] *m.* wine.
יָם[5] (*pl.* יַמִּים) *m.* sea.
יָמִין[6] *m.* right hand.

סָלַח*[7] (akin to שָׁלַךְ, § 22) forgive.
צָרַף[8] try, prove.
קָטַר[9] burn incense, sacrifice. קְטֹרֶת *f.* incense.
שֶׁקֶל (r. = weigh) *m.* Shekel. מִשְׁקָל* *m.* weight.

[1] R. בדר = separate. *Cf.* בַּד, § 38). [2] "Backshish" = a gratuity in the East. [3] Mn. *dibs*, a syrup much used in the East. [4] Substituting ו for י, we have וַיִן, a word approaching "wine" in sound. [5] The "Yam" is mostly from over the seas. [6] Mn. "Benjamin" (בִּנְיָמִין). [7] Idea of send, fling away, and forgive are closely allied. [8] *Cf.* שָׂרַף, though the r. idea is different. [9] Mn. "Keturah" (קְטוּרָה), name of Abraham's second wife (= sweet odor).

Exercise.—And I (w.c.) will keep[15] thee. He who keepeth thee (Q. Part.). To keep him. And from his keeping (*Inf. cstr.*). Keep (*sing.*) them. I *will* keep (Cohort.). He will keep me. And he (w.c.) has kept us. He will keep him. He will keep him (נ denom.). The lips[31] of the wise (*pl.*)[3] will keep them. For[2] thou didst separate them. And I (w.c.) washed[36] thee in (the) water.[3] Jehovah will surely separate (separating will separate, Hi.) me. Seek ye me (*pl.* Qi.). Thou hast tried us as the trying of (כְּ with *Inf. cstr.*) silver.[12] We ceased[15] to burn incense (Qi.). And they (w.c.) shall pursue[21] thee. He was pursuing (*Inf. cstr.*) with (ב) a sword[8] his brother.[34] Seek (Qi.) peace[20] and pursue it (*m.*). And he (w.c.) pursued them. And they (w.c.) shall burn[24] it (*f.*). For thou wilt visit[15] him (נ demon.). Ye shall seek[15] me with (ב) all your heart.[23]

---

§ 38. PARTICLES WITH SUFFIXES.—ADVERBS.

1.

אַי (אַיֵּה)	אַיִן	הֵן (הִנֵּה)	יֵשׁ	עוֹד
אַיֶּכָּה ךָ	אֵינְךָ	הִנְנִי (הִנֵּנִי)	יֶשְׁךָ	עוֹדֶנִּי
אַיּוֹ	אֵינֶנּוּ	הִנְּךָ	יֶשְׁכֶם	עוֹדְךָ
אַיָּם	אֵינֶנָּה	הִנְנוּ (הִנֶּנּוּ)	—	עוֹדֶנּוּ
—	אֵינֶנּוּ	הִנָּם	—	עוֹדֶנָּה

REM. — 1. In some cases typical forms only are given in the table; in others, all that are in use. 2. While these particles have, in general, the suffixes of the noun, all in this table may also have נ demonstrative (יֶשְׁנוֹ: Deut. xxix. 14), and the union vowel frequently differs from that of the noun. 3. These particles all involve a verbal idea, and may include the copula (Where art thou? Thou art not. Behold I am here, etc.). 4. Excepting עוֹד, each of these words has a *cstr.* form (אֵי, אֵין, הֶן־, יֶשׁ־).

2. לְבַדְּהֶן, לְבַדְּךָ, לְבַדִּי. (יַחְדָּיו) יַחְדָּו. בִּלְתֶּךָ, בִּלְתִּי. סְבִיבָיו, סָבִיב. There are a few other adverbs which take some of the suffixes of the noun.

אָז[1] then.
אַי where (see § 11).
אַיִן[2] (to be) naught, not.
בִּלְתִּי[3] not, except.
הִנֵּה[4], הֵן behold!
יַחְדָּו[5] together.

יֵשׁ (to be) something, there is.
לְבַד[6] alone (לְ is a prefix).
סָבַב[7] turn about. סָבִיב *m.* and *adv.* circuit, roundabout.
עוּד* repeat. עוֹד (עֹד) again, still. See vocab. § 28.

[1] Composed of the demon. ז and א prosthetic. [2] Not צַיִן. May be remembered as the opposite of יֵשׁ. [3] From a verb בלה, meaning to waste away (to *nothing*). It comes from a form בֶּלֶת, with ִי paragogic. It is used principally with the *Inf.* [4] Disting. הִנֵּה from *pron.* הֵנָּה. [5] R. akin to numeral אחד = in its unity, as one, i.e., together. [6] R. בד = separate. *Cf.* בדל. [7] Assoc. the meaning with the form of its letters, especially ס.

Exercise.—And the Canaanite (כְּנַעֲנִי) was then in the land.[9] Where art thou? And man[31] there-was-not to till[8] the ground.[31] And he was not (he, he-was-not). Not-to (To not) hear.[18] Behold-I (am here). Behold-we (are) servants[8] to (לְ) my lord.[2] That[2] there-is a God[2] in (לְ) Israel. Thou-art. Ye-are. Is my father yet alive[11] (Is[11] yet, etc.)? I-alone. They-alone. His blood[26] upon (עַל) the altar[18] round about. What is man[31] that thou rememberest[18] him (Impf.), and the son[11] of man that thou visitest[15] him (נ demon.). Righteous[13] (art) thou, Jehovah, in (בְּ) thy judging[30] (*Inf.*). And they (w.c.) will gather themselves[23] together (Ni.).

§ 39. PARTICLES WITH SUFFIXES. — PREPOSITIONS.

1.

לְ	אֵת	אֵת	כְּמוֹ ,כְּ	מִן
לִי	אִתִּי	אֹתִי	כָּמוֹנִי	מִמֶּנִּי
לְךָ	אִתְּךָ	אֹתְךָ	כָּמוֹךָ	מִמְּךָ
לָךְ	אִתָּךְ	אֹתָךְ	כָּמוֹךְ	מִמֵּךְ
לוֹ	אִתּוֹ	אֹתוֹ	כָּמֹהוּ	מִמֶּנּוּ
לָהּ	אִתָּהּ	אֹתָהּ	כָּמֹהָ	מִמֶּנָּה
לָנוּ	אִתָּנוּ	אֹתָנוּ	כָּמֹנוּ	מִמֶּנּוּ
לָכֶם	אִתְּכֶם	אֶתְכֶם	כָּכֶם	מִכֶּם
לָכֶן	אִתְּכֶן	אֶתְכֶן	כָּכֶן	מִכֶּן
לָהֶם	אִתָּם	אֹתָם	כָּהֶם	מֵהֶם
לָהֶן	אִתָּן	אֹתָן	כָּהֵן	מֵהֶן

Rem. — 1. The forms of מִן, in part, come from doubling (מִמֶּן = מִנְמִן). It is one result of a general effort to give more body to these particles, as in כְּמוֹ (= כְּ and מָה). The latter is mostly used with suffixes; only in poetry before substantives (§ 12. R. 2). 2. The difference between אֵת *with*, with suffixes, and אֵת, the sign of the definite accus., will be noticed. They are somewhat mixed in the books of Kings, Jer., and Ezek. Like the former, עִם is treated, excepting a few forms (עִמִּי or עִמָּדִי, עִמָּכֶם, עִמָּכֶן); and like לִי, for the most part, בִּי. 3. The idiomatic phrase מַה־לִּי וְלָכֶם = What have I to do with thee? 4. The prep. לְ with a pronominal suffix is often used (especially after verbs of motion) somewhat pleonastically. As denoting an intimate participation of the subject in the act, it is named by some grammarians the *ethic dative*. הִשָּׁמֶר לְךָ take heed (to yourself).

2. אֵלַי, אֲלֵיכֶם. עָדַי, עָדֶיךָ. עָלַי, עֲלֵיכֶם. The three prepositions אֶל, עַד, and עַל, having ended originally in ־ַי, assume this form with pronominal suffixes. By some grammarians they are called plurals. In poetry their *cstr.* is used independently of suffixes.

3. אַחַר[34], אַחֲרֵי. תַּחַת, תַּחְתַּי. בֵּין, בֵּינֵינוּ. There are certain other prepositions which actually take the plural form with

suffixes, the last of the three named, however, only with plural suffixes.

אֵשׁ[1] *c.* fire. אִשֶּׁה* "firings" (sacrifices by fire).
בַּרְזֶל[2] *m.* iron.
הֶבֶל[3] *c.* breath, Abel.
הָרַס*[4] break, throw down.
חֶבֶל[5] *c.* cord, region (measured).

חוֹמָה[6] *f.* wall.
עָלָה go up. עַל upon, by, etc. עֹלָה *f.* burnt-offering. עֶלְיוֹן Most High.
מַעַל[7] above, (מַעְלָה) upwards.
מַעֲלָה* *f.* steps.
תַּחַת beneath.

[1] Discrim. from אִשָּׁה, אִישׁ. [2] Mn. "Barzillai" (בַּרְזִלַּי), iron (man): 2 Sam. xvii. 27. [3] Mn. "Abel" (הָבֶל in Pause). [4] Eng. *harass* approaches it in sound and idea. [5] Discrim. from הֶבֶל. [6] Gr. χῶμα, equiv. in sound and sense. [7] Idea of r. may be associated with עַל, already used several times. The burnt-offering was so called from being wholly consumed (*going up* in fire and smoke).

Exercise. — And I (w.c.) burnt[24] it (*m.* with אֵת) with (בְּ) fire. To her. With thee (*f.*). From us. From her. Thy heavens[10] which are over thy head[3] (shall be) copper,[33] and the earth[9] which is under thee (shall be) iron. Where (§ **11.4**) is Abel thy brother?[34] Two (שְׁנֵי) lines. The king[13] of Israel (was) passing (Q. Part.)[23] on the wall, and a woman cried[24] unto him (אֵל). And they (w.c.) shall break down thy (*f.*) walls. An offering (made by fire) unto (לְ) Jehovah. Sacrifices[18] and burnt-offerings. Sheol[12] from beneath is moved[36] (Perf. *f.*) for thee. With (עִם) me. With you. Like us. After him.

---

§ 40. DEGREES OF COMPARISON.

1. [1]חָכָם אַתָּה מִדָּנִאֵל thou art wiser than Daniel. [2]בְּנָהּ הַגָּדוֹל the elder of her sons. [3]כָּבֵד מִמֶּנִּי too heavy for me. The Hebrew has no special forms for indicating degrees in the comparison of Adjectives. The comparative degree is expressed by prefixing מִן to the word with which the comparison is made;[1] or, if the objects compared do not immediately succeed one another, by the use of the article.[2] מִן is also used to express the idea that a thing is *too* great or *too* little, or the like, for a specified purpose.[3]

2. [1]הַקָּטֹן the youngest son; בְּנוֹ הַקָּטָן (or קְטֹן בָּנָיו) the youngest of his sons. [2]טוֹבָם the best of them; עֶבֶד עֲבָדִים servant of servants. [3]לְדֹר דֹּר to generations of generations; גָּדוֹל מְאֹד מְאֹד exceedingly great. The Hebrew has a variety of ways to express the idea of superlativeness: as by the use of the article with the adjective[1]; or by a Genitive following the object compared (it may be a pronominal suffix)[2]; or, a less definite superlativeness, by a repetition of a word, or the use of an adverb.[3]

יָבֵשׁ[1] dry up. יַבָּשָׁה† *f.* dry ground.
יָרָה cast, found. תּוֹרָה *f.* law, Torah.
לָשׁוֹן[2] *c.* tongue.
מָדַד*[3] measure. מִדָּה *f.* measure.
תָּמִיד continually.
צָפָה[4] look about, watch, overlay.
קֵץ *m.*, קָצָה*[5] *f.*, קָצֶה *m.* end.

קָשָׁה*[6] hard, rough. קֶשֶׁת *c.* bow.
רָשַׁע*[7] be wicked. רָשָׁע wicked.
רֶשַׁע* (i) *m.* wickedness.
שָׂדֶה *m.* field.
שָׁלָל[8] *m.* spoil.
תָּוֶךְ[9] (*cstr.* תּוֹךְ) *m.* middle, midst.
תּוֹעֵבָה[10] *f.* abomination.

[1] Mn. "Jabesh" Gilead = dry Gilead. [2] R. לָשָׁה = lick. Note also shape of first letter. [3] Sansc. Mâd, Eng. mete. [4] Mn. "Mizpeh" (מִצְפָּה), watch-tower. Idea of r. is *cover, conceal* (*cf.* צפן). One conceals himself to watch, spy out. [5] Letters קץ = cut off. *Cf.* קצר, קצף. [6] Easy to see how the word for bow, on account of its stiffness, rigidity, comes from this r. קַשׁ = stubble. [7] Mn. "rash," which in its original meaning, *be in commotion*, corresponds pretty well with רשׁע be loose, without firmness. *Cf.* Isa. lvii. 20, "troubled sea." [8] R. = draw out, away, akin to שׁאל (draw out by) question. [9] To be associated with קֶרֶב, both much used for *midst.* [10] Used more than 100 times in the Bible, often in the expression תּוֹעֲבַת יְהוָֹה.

Exercise.—His eldest[10] son.[11] More righteous[13] than (from) he. Is this your youngest[17] brother?[34] Is it too little (מְעַט) for (from) you? A day[10] in thy courts (חָצֵר) is better[10] than a thousand.[3] The most glorious song[26] (song of songs). The earth[9] became dry. The law of mercy[29] (is) on[39] her tongue. (He) passes[23] (Part.) by us (עַל) continually. At (לְ) the end of the days. He maketh wars[24] cease[16] unto[28] the end (קָצֶה) of the earth; (the) bow he breaketh in pieces[14] (Qi.). An abomination unto (of) Jehovah (is) the way[12] of the wicked (*sing.*). Divide ye (חָלַק) the spoil of your enemies[30] with (עִם) your brethren. In (בְּ) the mount[9] from the midst of the fire.[39]

§ 41. WEAK VERBS.—VERBS פ״א.

1. The distinction between the Strong and Weak verbs, and the nomenclature of the latter, have already been noted (§ **14**. 1. 2). Verbs having א as their first radical are properly gutturals. In certain of them, however, א is not so treated throughout, but as a quiescent letter, losing its power as a consonant, and becoming blended with the preceding vowel (§ **5**).

Impf. s. 3. *m.*	יֹאכַל	....	*pl.* 3. *m.*	יֹאכְלוּ
3. *f.*	תֹּאכַל	....	3. *f.*	תֹּאכַלְנָה
2. *m.*	תֹּאכַל	....	2. *m.*	תֹּאכְלוּ
2. *f.*	תֹּאכְלִי	....	2. *f.*	תֹּאכַלְנָה
1. *c.*	אֹכַל	....	1. *c.*	נֹאכַל

2. In the *Impf.* Q. of six verbs beginning with א this letter quiesces in ô, which is an obscured â (*ya'ăkhal* = *yâkhal* = *yôkhal*). In the 1. *pers. s.* (rarely elsewhere) the radical letter א itself disappears.

Rem. 1.—These verbs may be easily remembered by arranging them as follows: He said (אָמַר), he wished (אָבָה), to eat (אָכַל); he baked (אָפָה), he seized (אָחַז), he perished (אָבַד). א in אחז does not always so quiesce.

Rem. 2.—There are two other verbs beginning with א which occasionally follow this analogy: אָסַף, three times, twice with a dropping of the א (תֹּסֵף, וַיֹּסֶף), which might lead to a confounding of the word with some forms of יָסַף; and אָהַב *love*, in the 1. *s.* Impf. (אֹהַב).

אוֹצָר[1] *m.* granary, treasury.

אַיִל[2] *m.* ram; *pl.* אֵלִים the mighty, the foremost.

אָכַל[3] eat. אֹכֶל (*f.* אָכְלָה) food.

מַאֲכָל food.

אָפָה*[3] bake (אֹפֶה baker).

אֹרַח[4] *m.* way, course.

אָרַךְ* be long, tarry. אֹרֶךְ *m.* length.

בּוֹר[5] *m.* cistern, pit.

בָּחַר[6] choose. בָּחוּר* *m.* chosen one (youth, etc.).

בָּכָה[7] weep. בְּכִי* *m.* weeping.

בָּמָה[8] *f.* height, high place.

יָסַף[9] add, (with other verbs) again.

[1] Mn. "*Oats are*" (there). [2] Mn. "Aijalon" (place of deer). [3] It will be remembered best as a פ״א verb in connection with the sentence above. [4] To be associated with, and discriminated from, the next word (ח marks the word meaning *way*, ךְ that meaning *be long*). [5] Mn. "Bore," to which its r. is nearly equivalent. *Cf.* בְּאֵר. [6] Associate the three words of similar sound thus: בָּחַר בִּבְכֹרוֹת בְּקָרִים he chose the firstborn of the cattle. Note the order of

the consonants (ח, כ, ק). [7] Mn. "Baca" (בָּכָא a dropping (weeping) balsam): Ps. lxxxiv. 7. [8] Mn. "Bema" (βῆμα) raised place. [9] Mn. and deriv. "Joseph" (יוֹסֵף): Gen. xxx. 24, "the Lord *add*," etc.

Exercise.—The treasury of the house[3] of Jehovah. And behold![38] a ram caught[27] (Ni. Part.) by (בְּ) his horns (קֶרֶן). Thou mayest surely eat (eating thou mayest eat). Teach[18] me (Qi.) thy ways (*pl.* in וֹת). Lengthen (Hi.) thy cords.[39] As to (לְ) its (*f.*) length. We will cast[22] him (Hi.) into (בְּ) one[35] of the pits (*pl.* in וֹת). Choose ye (for you[39]) to-day[10] whom (אֶת־מִי) ye will serve.[8] The people[9] (were) sacrificing[18] and burning incense[37] (both Qi. Parts.) in the high places. And (w.c.) said to them.[39] And they (w.c.) took[27] him (אוֹתוֹ) and slew him.[24] And they (w.c.) said, let us not[15] perish[8] (Cohort.) for (בְּ) this man's[9] life[32] (soul).

§ 42. VERBS פ״נ.

	Q.	*Ni.*	*Hi.*	*Ho.*
Perf. s. 3. *m.*	נָגַשׁ	נִגַּשׁ	הִגִּישׁ	הֻגַּשׁ
3. *f.*	נָֽגְשָׁה	נִגְּשָׁה	הִגִּ֫ישָׁה	הֻגְּשָׁה
2. *m.*	נָגַ֫שְׁתָּ	נִגַּ֫שְׁתָּ	הִגַּ֫שְׁתָּ	הֻגַּ֫שְׁתָּ
pl. 2. *m.*	נְגַשְׁתֶּם	נִגַּשְׁתֶּם	הִגַּשְׁתֶּם	הֻגַּשְׁתֶּם
Inf. cstr.	גֶּ֫שֶׁת	הִנָּגֵשׁ	הַגִּישׁ	הֻגַּשׁ
Inf. abs.	נָגוֹשׁ	הִנָּגֹשׁ	הַגֵּשׁ	הֻגֵּשׁ
Imp. s. m.	גַּשׁ	הִנָּגֵשׁ	הַגֵּשׁ	wanting
f.	גְּשִׁי	הִנָּגְשִׁי	הַגִּ֫ישִׁי	
pl. f.	גַּ֫שְׁנָה	הִנָּגַ֫שְׁנָה	הַגֵּ֫שְׁנָה	
Impf. s. 3. *m.*	יִגַּשׁ	יִנָּגֵשׁ	יַגִּישׁ	יֻגַּשׁ
2. *f.*	תִּגְּשִׁי	regular	תַּגִּ֫ישִׁי	תֻּגְּשִׁי
1. *c.*	אֶגַּשׁ		אַגִּישׁ	אֻגַּשׁ
pl. 3. *f.*	תִּגַּ֫שְׁנָה		תַּגֵּ֫שְׁנָה	תֻּגַּ֫שְׁנָה
Part. act.	נֹגֵשׁ	נִגָּשׁ	מַגִּישׁ	
Part. pass.	נָגוּשׁ			מֻגָּשׁ

1. Verbs פ״נ show but a few variations from the Strong verb; none at all in the Qi. and Qu. Voices. When, in process of inflection, the נ would come at the end of a syllable and be pointed with a silent Šᵉwâ, it is assimilated to the following radical, the assimilation being indicated by a D. forte (Q. Impf., Ni. Perf. and Part., and in the Hi. and Ho. throughout).

Rem. 1. — Assimilation does not take place, however, in verbs medial guttural, and in a few other cases, especially in Pause.

Rem. 2. — A certain number of these verbs (like נגשׁ), in addition to those medial guttural, have *a* in the Q. Impf., and some others have either *a* or *ō*.

Rem. 3. — In the Ho. the original *u* appears (instead of *o*) in the sharpened syllable.

2. גַּשׁ, גִּשְׁתְּ, גֶּשֶׁת, גִּשְׁתִּי (*i* thinned from *a*), etc. In the Q. of some פ״נ verbs, this letter at the beginning of a syllable, when not supported by a full vowel, is dropped (Inf. cstr., Imp.). In the Inf. cstr. this shortened root is again made triliteral by the addition of ת, marking the feminine, so becoming a Segholate (of the *i* class), and inflected accordingly.

3. קַחַת, קַח, יִקַּח. The verb לָקַח (except in Ni.) follows the analogy of the פ״נ verbs.

4. נָתַתָּ, נָתַתְּ, נְתַתֶּם, נָתַנּוּ. תֵּת (= תְּנֶת with the vowel heightened and the weak consonant assimilated), תִּתִּי etc. תֵּן (תְּנָה), תְּנִי. יִתֵּן. תִּתֵּן. The verb נָתַן assimilates also its final נ before ת (Q. Perf., Inf. cstr.), and naturally before another נ (Q. Perf., 1. Pers. pl.). In the Imp. the final vowel is *ē*, as also in the Impf. in harmony with the Inf. cstr. as ground-form. The Inf. cstr. is inflected like a Segholate noun.

נְאֻם[1] say, utter oracularly.

נֶגֶב[2] *m.* Negeb, the south.

נָגַע[3] touch, smite, plague. נֶגַע *m.* stroke, plague.

נָגַף smite. מַגֵּפָה* *f.* a smiting.

נָחַל[4] inherit. נַחֲלָה *f.* inheritance.

נַחַל *m.* wady, (and its) brook.

נָחַם Ni. repent, Qi. comfort. Mn. "Nahum" (נַחוּם), consoler.

נָטַע[5] plant, drive (tent-pin).

נָסָה*[6] try, prove.

נָסַךְ[7] pour out (a drink-offering). נֶסֶךְ (i) *m.* a drink-offering.

נָסַע[5] pull out (tent-pin), journey.

נָצַב[8] (and יָצַב Hithq.) be set, fixed, stand. מַצֵּבָה *f.* pillar.

נָצַל[9] deliver.

נָצַר preserve.

נָתַן[10] give, set, appoint, etc.

[1] Like אָיַב, used but once except as Part. (נְאֻם). [2] One of the divisions of Southern Palestine. [3] R. נג, in many words, has the idea of *touching* more or

less forcibly. *Cf.* נגשׁ and the following word here. [4] Following word is from a different r. Both may be better remembered by thinking of the wady as a possible boundary of an inheritance. [5] *Cf.* נָטָה. Both words, with נסע, have to do with the tent (נטה to spread it; נטע drive its pins; נסע pull them up). [6] Mn. and deriv. "Massah" (מַסָּה), proving: Ex. xvii. 7. Discriminate from נסע. [7] Associate with "sack" (a dry Spanish wine). [8] Akin to צִיָּה with its mn. צִיּוֹן Zion. [9] This word and the next (note radicals) include in idea much of what God now does for us. [10] Mn. "Nathan," he (God) has given (= Nathanael).

Exercise. — Utterance of Jehovah. And thou, take[10] unto (לְ) thee from all food.[41] And ye shall not touch it (בּוֹ). And (w.c.) Jehovah smote Pharaoh (אֶת־פַּרְעֹה) (with) great smitings. Bring near[14] (Hi.) the burnt-offering.[39] And ye (w.c.) shall be smitten (Ni.) before (לִפְנֵי) your enemies.[30] For[2] thou shalt make this people[9] inherit the land[9] which I swore[25] (Ni.) to their fathers[8] to give to (לְ) them. Comfort ye (Qi. *pl.*), comfort ye my people, saith[5] (Impf.) your God. Where (§ 10. 4) he spread[30] his tent.[33] He shall plant the tents. And (w.c.) Abram journeyed. And they (w.c.) will pour out (Hi.) drink-offerings to (לְ) other[34] gods. Behold[38] I stand (Ni. Part.) by (עַל) the fountain[3] of water.[3] And *I* delivered thee (Hi.) from the hand[3] of Saul (שָׁאוּל). To the keepers (Q. Part.)[15] of his covenant.[20] Give (*pl.*) to me the possession[27] of a burying-place[15] with (עִם) you. My giving (Inf. cstr.) the inheritance of my fathers[8] to thee.

---

§ 43. VERBS פ"י.

	Q.	*Ni.*	*Hi.*	*Ho.*
Perf. s. 3. *m.*	יָשַׁב	נוֹשַׁב	הוֹשִׁיב	הוּשַׁב
3. *f.*	regular	נֽוֹשְׁבָה	הוֹשִׁיבָה	הֽוּשְׁבָה
2. *m.*		נוֹשַׁבְתָּ	הוֹשַׁבְתָּ	הוּשַׁבְתָּ
pl. 2. *m.*		נֽוֹשַׁבְתֶּם	הֽוֹשַׁבְתֶּם	הֽוּשַׁבְתֶּם
Inf. cstr.	שֶׁבֶת	הִוָּשֵׁב	הוֹשִׁיב	הוּשַׁב
Inf. abs.	יָשׁוֹב	wanting	הוֹשֵׁב	wanting

	Q.	Q.	Ni.	Hi.	Ho.
Imp. s. m.	שֵׁב (שְׁבָה)	יְרַשׁ	הִוָּשֵׁב	הוֹשֵׁב	wanting
f.	שְׁבִי	יְרְשִׁי	הִוָּשְׁבִי	הוֹשִׁיבִי	
pl. f.	שֵׁבְנָה	יְרַשְׁנָה	הִוָּשַׁבְנָה	הוֹשֵׁבְנָה	
Impf. s. 3. m. ..	יֵשֵׁב	יִירַשׁ	יִוָּשֵׁב	יוֹשִׁיב	יוּשַׁב
2. *f.* ...	תֵּשְׁבִי	תִּירְשִׁי	תִּוָּשְׁבִי	תּוֹשִׁיבִי	תּוּשְׁבִי
1. *c.* ...	אֵשֵׁב	אִירַשׁ	אִוָּשֵׁב	אוֹשִׁיב	אוּשַׁב
pl. 3. f. ...	תֵּשַׁבְנָה	תִּירַשְׁנָה	תִּוָּשַׁבְנָה	תּוֹשֵׁבְנָה	תּוּשַׁבְנָה
Part. act.	יֹשֵׁב		נוֹשָׁב	מוֹשִׁיב	
Part. pass.	יָשׁוּב				מוּשָׁב

1. Verbs פ״י are of three classes. The first two include those whose first radical was originally ו; the last are the proper פ״י.

2. In the first class of פ״י (or ו) verbs, the original ו appears as י when initial (Q. Perf., Qi., Qu., and, partly, Hithq.), except in the Q. Impf. and related parts. In the latter case, (a) the first radical may be dropped, the stem vowel, originally *i*, becoming under the tone *ē* (*a* with a guttural); while that of the preformative (? from a union of י with *a*) becomes an unchangeable *ê*. The Inf. cstr. (like verbs פ״נ) taking the *fem.* ending ת assumes the form of a Segholate noun, which *when inflected* takes *i* under its first radical. Or (b) if the first radical be retained in the Impf., the stem vowel is *a*, and ו (become י), uniting with the *i* of the preformative forms *ī*.

Rem. 1.—There are but eight פ״י verbs which regularly drop their first radical in the Q. Impf. and related parts (ידע, יחד, ילד, ילך (הלך), יקע be dislocated, ירד, יצא, ישב).

Rem. 2.—There are but three of this class of verbs which retain י invariably in the Imp. (ידה, ירא, ירה). There are others which appear in both forms (ירש, etc.).

3. When in verbs originally פ״ו the ו is *not* initial, it is treated as a consonant at the beginning of a syllable (Ni. Inf. cstr., Imp., Impf., and sometimes Hithq.); and as a vowel at the end of a syllable. As a vowel it either coalesces with a homogeneous vowel (Ho.) or is contracted with an (original) *a* to *ô* (Ni. Perf. and Part., Hi.).

Rem. 1.—In the Qi. and Qu. Voices ו appears always as י, and these Voices are inflected regularly. The same is partly true of the Hithq. (*cf.* 2).

Rem. 2. — The lengthened form of the Imp. is frequent in these verbs. שֵׁב or שְׁבָה from יָשַׁב.

Rem. 3. — The verb יָלַךְ has forms of its own in the Q. Impf. and related parts (וַיֵּלֶךְ ,יֵלֵךְ; לֵךְ (לְכָה), לְכִי; לֶכֶת, לֶכְתִּי my going); but elsewhere הָלַךְ is used.

Rem. 4. — The verb יָכֹל forms its Q. Impf. irregularly (יוּכַל, etc. for יוֹכַל from יוֹכַל; others suppose the form to belong to the Ho. Voice); also its Inf. cstr. יְכֹלֶת.

4. יָצַק. Inf. cstr. צֶקֶת. Imp. יְצֹק and צַק. Impf. יִצֹּק. The second class of verbs originally פ״ו follow the analogy of פ״נ verbs. The first stem letter, when coming at the end of a syllable with silent Š^ewâ, is assimilated to the next; and when standing at the beginning of a syllable unsupported by a full vowel, is dropped. There is considerable variation, however, in their inflection. Their forms may be generally distinguished from those of verbs פ״נ by the fact that פ״י verbs of this class have almost exclusively צ as a middle radical.

5. יָטַב. Q. Inf. cstr. regular; Imp. wanting; Impf. יִיטַב; Part. regular. Hi. הֵיטִיב (הֵיטַבְתָּ, הֵיטִיבָה) הֵיטִיב; Infs. הֵיטִיב, הֵיטֵב; Imp. הֵיטֵב (הֵיטִיבִי); Impf. יֵיטִיב; Part. מֵיטִיב. The third class of verbs פ״י, i.e., verbs whose first radical was originally י, have the following characteristics. In the Q. Impf. this י, which is never dropped, unites with the vowel of the preformative (*i*) and forms î. In the Hi. this radical unites with the original vowel of the preformative (*a*) and forms ê, which being unchangeable appears in all the other forms of this Voice. There are no forms of the Ni. and Ho. Voices. There are but eight verbs in the class altogether, and all are more or less defective.

יָדַע[1] know. דַּעַת *f.* knowledge.

יָלַךְ[2] (and הָלַךְ) go, walk.

יָסַר[3] instruct, chastise. מוּסָר *m.* correction.

יָעַד* appoint, meet. עֵדָה *f.* congregation (of Israel). מוֹעֵד[4] *m.* season, festival, assembly.

יָעַץ counsel. עֵצָה[5] *f.* counsel.

יָצַק[6] pour.

יָצַר[7] form, make.

יָרַד[8] go down.

יָרַשׁ[9] possess, Hi. (sometimes) dispossess. תִּירוֹשׁ *m.* new wine.

[1] *Cf.* εἴδω, οἶδα. [2] *Imp.* לֵךְ, לֶךְ־, לְכָה is very common. לֶךְ לְךָ Get thee! [3] Connect the three פ״י verbs, יָסַר, יָעַץ, יָעַד. Read from the right. [4] One of the names of the Tabernacle was אֹהֶל מוֹעֵד. For two others see §§ 6, 21. [5] Discriminate from *fem.* of עֵץ wood. [6] Assoc. with נָסַךְ (mn. "Sack").

[7] Allied r. צרר, צר (mn. "Tsar"), meaning *press, oppress*. This means, too, *press, impress, form*. [8] Mn. "Jordan" (הַיַּרְדֵּן the descender). [9] Assoc. with other words in רַשׁ, thus: דָּרַשׁ (he sought), גָּרַשׁ (he drove out), יָרַשׁ (he possessed), and note progress of thought.

Exercise.—Know (*pl.*). To know good [10] and evil (וָרָע). And to walk with (עִם) wicked men [9] (men of wickedness [40]). Be instructed (Ni. Imp.), ye judges [30] of the earth.[9] There (שָׁם) hath he appointed it (*f.*). Speak [6] (Qi. *pl.*) to (אֶל־) all [2] the congregation of Israel. He counselled in those days.[10] Pour out for the people [9] that (w.c.) they may eat [41] (Impf.). The man [31] whom he had formed. He that formeth (Part.) the mountains.[9] When (בְּ) he came down (Inf. cstr.) from the mount. And they (w.c.) possessed his land.[9]

§ 44. VERBS ע״ו.

	Q.		*Ni.*	*Hi.*	*Ho.*
Perf. s. 3. *m.*	קָם	מֵת	נָקוֹם	הֵקִים	הוּקַם
3. *f.*	קָמָה	מֵתָה	נָקוֹמָה	הֵקִימָה	הוּקְמָה
2. *m.*	קַמְתָּ	מַתָּה	נְקוּמוֹתָ	הֲקִימוֹתָ	הוּקַמְתָּ
pl. 2. *m.*	קַמְתֶּם	מַתֶּם	נְקוּמוֹתֶם	הֲקִימוֹתֶם	הוּקַמְתֶּם
Inf. cstr.	קוּם		הִקּוֹם	הָקִים	הוּקַם
Inf. abs.	קוֹם		הִקּוֹם	הָקֵם	wanting
Imp. s. m.	קוּם		הִקּוֹם	הָקֵם	wanting
f.	קוּמִי		הִקּוֹמִי	הָקִימִי	
pl. f.	קֹמְנָה		הִקֹּמְנָה	הָקֵמְנָה	
Impf. s. 3. *m.*	יָקוּם		יִקּוֹם	יָקִים	יוּקַם
2. *f.*	תָּקוּמִי		תִּקּוֹמִי	תָּקִימִי	תּוּקְמִי
pl. 3. *f.*	תְּקוּמֶינָה		תִּקֹּמְנָה	תָּקֵמְנָה	תּוּקַמְנָה
Part. act.	קָם, מֵת		נָקוֹם	מֵקִים	
Part. pass.	קוּם				מוּקָם

1. The irregularities in the inflection of verbs ע״ו consist mainly in the elision of the weak middle radical together with one of the vowels, usually the preceding.

Rem. — 1. Q. Perf. was orig. *qawam*, *aw* being elided, and final *a* under the tone becoming *ā*; Inf. cstr. and Imp., orig. *qwum*, wu = û; Impf., orig. *yaqwum*, *a* in an open syllable = *ā*; Part. act., orig. *qâwim*, *w* being rejected and *i* absorbed; Part. pass., orig. *qawûm*, *a* being rejected. 2. Perf. and Part. of intrans. verb were orig. *mawith*, the present form eliding *w* and retaining and heightening vowel. 3. Ni. Perf. and Part., orig. *naqwam*, which is contracted to *nā-qôm*, the final syllable appearing in all subsequent forms of this Voice. 4. Hi. Perf. and Part. were orig. *haqwam* (thinned *a* in first, and, after *Inf. cstr.*, *ī* in second, syllable), *miqwîm* (*i* in an open syllable = *ē*). 5. The forms of the Imp. קֹמְנָה, הֲקֵמְנָה are due to the vocal law that *û* and *ī* cannot stand in a shut penultimate syllable even with the tone (§ 3. 4. R.). 6. Before the affixes beginning with the consonantal afformatives ת and נ (Perf. and Impf.), except in the Ho. and the Q. Perf., an additional syllable is generally found (probably an original vowel of the stem is used for the purpose), which serves to open the stem syllable and protect its vowel. 7. The change of tone works a change in the vowel *ô* of the Ni. Perf. in some parts to *û*. 8. The verb נוּחַ has an alternative form in the Hi. Impf. and Imp. (יַנִּיחַ).

2. The endings ָה, וּ, ִי, it will be noted, do not generally take the tone in this verb, the contracted stem drawing it to itself.

3. בּוֹשׁ, בֹּשְׁתִּי; יֵבוֹשׁ. Intransitive verbs of this class whose middle vowel is *o* retain it throughout the Q.

4. בָּא; Inf. בּוֹא, Impf. יָבוֹא. In the Inf. and related forms, besides the ordinary form with *u* (changed to *û*) in the last syllable, there are some with *a* heightened to *ā*, and then obscured to *ô*.

5. יָקֹם, וַיָּקָם; יָקֵם, וַיָּקֶם. The Jussive and Wāw consecutive forms of the Q. and Hi. should be especially noted. In one case we have *ō* becoming *o* with the tone retracted; in the other, *ē* becoming *e*.

בּוֹא[1] come in. מָבוֹא* *c.* entrance. תְּבוּאָה* *f.* income, increase.
לוּן (לִין) stay over night. לַיְלָה, לַיִל *m.* night.
מוּת[3] die. מָוֶת (*cstr.* מוֹת) *m.* death. מְתִים* men (adults).
נוּחַ rest. נִיחֹחַ* *m.* rest, pleasantness. Mn. "Noah" (נֹחַ).
נוּס flee (? the *noose*).
נוּעַ shake, wander. *Cf.* *nuo*, *nuto*.
נוּף wave. תְּנוּפָה*[4] *f.* wave offering.

[1] Antithetic to יָצָא go out. [2] Note interchange of the liquids נ and ל in verb and noun. [3] To be associated with the following word, which is from an obsolete *sing.* מַת. The roots מתה, מדד, מוּת, etc. = what is *stretched out*, מְתִים as *full grown* men, מֵת as a *dead* man. [4] Assoc. words for offerings (burnt-offerings,[30] peace-offerings,[21] heave-offerings,[17] etc.).

Exercise. — Jehovah shall keep[15] thy going forth (צֵאתְךָ) and thy coming in (Inf. c.). The spirit (רוּחַ) of Jehovah shall cause him to rest. Stay over night (*f.*) to-night (§ **9.** R. 1). For[2] in the day[10] of thy eating[41] (Inf. c.) from it (*m.*) dying (§ **15.** 2) thou shalt die. And he (w.c.) shall die. The men and the women[9] and the children (טַף *sing.*). They flee (Part. *pl.*). And (w.c.) Judah (יְהוּדָה) was smitten[42] (Ni.) before (לִפְנֵי) Israel, and they fled every-man (אִישׁ) to his tent.[33] The daughter[11] of Jerusalem hath shaken (Hi.) her head.[3] I will wave (Hi. Part.) my hand[5] over them.[39] Let him arise[19] (Jussive). And he (w.c.) arose. Let him establish (Hi.). And he (w.c.) hath established his word[6] which he spoke[6] (Qi.) over us.[39] Let them be ashamed.[17]

---

§ 45. VERBS ע״י AND THE INTENSIVE VOICES.

Perf. s. 3. m.	בָּן	*Inf. cstr.*	בִּין	*Imp. s. m.*	בִּין	*Impf. s. 3. m.*	יָבִין
	בָּנָה	*abs.*	בּוֹן	*f.*	בִּינִי	*2. f.*	תָּבִינִי
	בַּנְתָּ			*pl. m.*	בִּינוּ	*Part. act.*	בָּן
						Part. pass.	בּוֹן

1. As in verbs פ״י, we find also in the present class ו not infrequently changed to י. The vocalization being thus changed, there appears in the Q. *some forms* resembling those of the Hi. (Impf.); or of the Hi. apocopated (Inf. cstr., Imp.). In fact, they are regarded as such by some grammarians. These (Q.) forms are inflected like קוּם, except that ִי takes the place of וּ. In the other Voices the inflection of these words conforms in all respects to that of the proper ע״ו verbs.

Rem. 1. — The words of this sort most used are בּוּן (בִּין), גּוּל (גִּיל), חוּל (חִיל), שׂוּם (שִׂים), שׁוּת (שִׁית).

Rem. 2. — It is often not possible to distinguish the Q. Impf. of these verbs from the Hi. Impf. except by the sense.

Rem. 3. — It is probable that in some of the verbs just cited, and certainly in some others, the *original* middle radical was actually י.

2. בִּינוֹתָ, בִּינָה, בִּין, etc. Sometimes י is found as a middle radical in the Q. Perf. It is then inflected like an apocopated Hi. (i.e., a Hi. with its first syllable wanting).

3. [1] קִיֵּם. [2] Perf. קוֹמֵם (קוֹמַם); Inf. c. קוֹמֵם; Impf. יְקוֹמֵם (יְקוֹמַם); Part. מְקוֹמֵם (מְקוֹמַם). [3] קִמְקֵם, קְמִקְם. The intensive Voices (Qi., Qu., Hithq.) are not ordinarily used with verbs ע״ו (ע״י). There are a few examples in ע״י verbs;[1] but only one of an ע״ו. The same effect has been secured by doubling the last radical and then inflecting as a strong verb with unchangeable vowels.[2] These Voices are accordingly to be named in harmony with their vocalization, Qôlēl, Qôlal, Hithqôlēl (or on the basis of פעל, Pô'lēl, Pô'lal, Hithpô'lēl), respectively. More rarely both the first and last radical are repeated, forming so-called Qilqēl, Qulqal (Pilpēl, Pulpal) Voices.[3]

בָּרָא[1] create.
בְּתוּלָה[2] *f.* virgin (= the separated).
גּוּר sojourn. גֵּר *m.* sojourner, stranger.
גִּיל[3] (גּוּל) circle about (in joy), rejoice.
חִיל[4] (חוּל) circle about (in joy or *pain*), be in pain, wait. חוֹל† (round by rolling), *m.* sand. חַיִל, *cstr.* חֵיל (strong by twisting) *m.* might, force (army).
שִׂים[5] (שׂוּם) set, place.
שִׁית set, place. Mn. "Seth" (שֵׁת): Gen. iv. 25.

[1] Gen. i. 1: בְּרֵאשִׁית בָּרָא אֱלֹהִים. [2] *Cf.* בָּדַל, and assoc. with it. [3] Mn. "Abigail" (אֲבִיגַיִל), father's joy. [4] To be assoc. with the preceding. [5] Combine with following as having the same general meaning.

Exercise.—Sojourn (*m. s.*) in this land.[9] And for (לְ) the stranger who sojourneth (Part. with Art.) in the land. My soul[32] shall rejoice in Jehovah. We have been in pain. The virgin of Israel hath fallen.[22] And he (w c.) set (שִׂים) his life[32] in his hand (כַּפּוֹ). All[2] (things) thou hast put (שִׁית) under[30] his feet.[32] My people[9] as (לְ) an enemy[30] riseth up[10] (Qôlēl Impf.). And I, behold I[38] establish (Hi. Part. of קוּם) my covenant[20] with (אֵת) you. The tabernacle[21] was reared up (Ho.).[19] And he shall exalt himself (Hithqô.)[10] and make himself great (Hithq.).[10]

§ 46. VERBS ע"ע.

	Q.	Ni.	Hi.	Ho.
Perf. s. 3. *m.*	קַל סַב סָבֲבָה	נָסַב	הֵסֵב	הוּסַב
3. *f.*	קַלָּה סַבָּה	נָסַבָּה	הֵסֵבָּה	הוּסַבָּה
2. *m.*	קַלּוֹתָ סַבּוֹתָ	נְסַבּוֹתָ	הֲסִבּוֹתָ	הוּסַבּוֹתָ
Inf. cstr.	סֹב	הִסֵּב	הָסֵב	wanting
Inf. abs.	סָבוֹב	הִסּוֹב	הָסֵב	wanting
Imp. s. m.	סֹב	הִסַּב	הָסֵב	wanting
f.	סֹבִּי	הִסַּבִּי	הָסֵבִּי	
pl. f.	סֻבֶּינָה	הִסַּבֶּינָה	הֲסִבֶּינָה	
Impf. s. 3. *m.*	יֵקַל יִסֹּב יָסֹב	יִסַּב	יַסֵּב יָסֵב	יוּסַב
2. *f.*	תִּסְּבִי תָּסֹבִּי	תִּסַּבִּי	תָּסֵבִּי	תּוּסַבִּי
pl. 3. *f.*	תִּסֹּבְנָה תְּסֻבֶּינָה	תִּסַּבֶּינָה	תְּסִבֶּינָה	תּוּסַבֶּינָה
Part. act.	סֹבֵב	נָסָב	מֵסֵב	
Part. pass.	סָבוּב			מוּסָב

1. The chief irregularity in the inflection of verbs ע"ע consists in doubling (by D. forte, where possible) the second radical as representative of both the second and third, which in this class of verbs are identical. On the other hand, the Perf. Q. of nearly all transitive verbs of this class, as well as those parts of other verbs in which the last two consonants are separated by an unchangeable vowel (Q. Inf. abs., Parts., and Qi., Qu., if used) are inflected regularly.

2. The two consonants of the root, which are alike, being doubled, the vowel of the second (as in verbs ע"ו) appears under the first (except in Hi., and Ni. Impf.); and the contracted stem takes the tone from the endings ־ָה, וּ, ־ִי (except when it is thrown forward after a Wāw consecutive of the Perf.).

Rem. 1. — The vowel of the stem in the Perf. Hi. is ē, because ī could not stand before the doubled consonant.

Rem. 2. — The vowels of the preformatives when falling in open syllables are, of course, lengthened (Q. Impf., Ni. Perf., Part., Hi. and Ho. throughout), and an original *a* has in some cases been restored (Q. Impf., Ni. Perf.).

3. To make clear in pronunciation the doubling of the second radical, a helping vowel (Perf. *ō*, Impf. *é*) is used before the consonantal afformatives ת, נ, in four of the Voices. The difference from verbs ע״ו, which uses it only in the Q. Impf. and the Ni. and Hi. Perf., will be noted.

Rem. — This rule with respect to the Ho. rests on an inference from the one example found in the Part. *pl. f.* (מוּסַבּוֹת).

4. To show that a stem is ע״ע in forms where there is no afformative, and consequently no D. forte in the second radical, a D. forte is sometimes put in the first radical, by way of compensation (*cf.* alternative forms in Q. and Hi. Impfs.).

5. יָסֹב, וַיָּ֫סָב· יָסֵב, וַיָּ֫סֶב. The unchanged Jussive forms, and those with Wāw consecutive (Q. and Hi.), as in verbs ע״ו, should here also be especially noted.

6. Qi., Qu. Perf. סוֹבֵב, סוֹבַב; Infs. סוֹבֵב, סוֹבַב; Imp. סוֹבֵב; Impf. יְסוֹבֵב, יְסוֹבַב; Parts. מְסוֹבֵב, מְסוֹבָב. In the intensive stems, the inflection is either regular (D. forte in the middle radical, making contraction impossible), or an unchangeable *ô* is inserted after the first radical, and the inflection then proceeds regularly. In the latter case, the Voices would receive, on the basis of the verb קָטַל, the names Qôṭēṭ, Qôṭaṭ, and Hithqôṭeṭ (from פָּעַל, Pô'ēl, Pô'al, Hithpô'ēl).

7. Nouns from verbs ע״ו and ע״י are represented by מָ֫וֶת (cstr. מוֹת), בַּ֫יִת (cstr. בֵּית); and those from verbs ע״ע by אֵם (אִמִּי), יָם (*pl.* יַמִּים), etc.

אַף[1] also, yea, truly.
אַף[2] *m.* nostril (*du.* אַפַּ֫יִם face), breathing, anger.
גּוֹרָל[3] *m.* (pebble) lot.
חָתַת[4] be in dismay, *trans.* break.
סוּר[5] turn aside, remove.
רָבָה[6] be great, multiply. רַב[6] great, (*f.* רַבָּה) many. רֹב *m.* multitude (last two from allied r. רבב).
רָעַע[7] be evil. רַע (*f.* רָעָה) evil, wicked.
שׁוּב[5] return.

[1] Discrim. from following. [2] Full form and r. אנף (hence D. forte in *du.*). Anger associated with (violent) breathing. [3] Mn. "Coral," which we may imagine to be the "pebble" or lot. [4] Mn. and deriv. "Hittite" (חִתִּי). They seem to have been redoubtable warriors. [5] Assoc. as follows: He turned aside (סוּר), about (סבב[38]), returned (שׁוּב). [6] Mn. and deriv. "Rabbi" (רַבִּי, 'Ραββί).

Cf. רִבּוֹ, etc., § 35. [7] R. means be in commotion (*cf.* רשׁע), without fixed principles or goal.

Exercise.—Also I in my dream.[3] In his nostrils. For[2] in their anger they slew (הרג) a man. And ye (w.c.) shall divide (Hithq. of נחל[42]) the land[9] by (בְּ) lot. They were dismayed. Be not dismayed (Ni. Impf.). They have turned aside from the way.[12] And my mercy[20] I will not remove (Hi.) from (from with עִם) him. For great (*f.*)[10] (was) the evil (*f.*) of the man.[31] Return (*pl.*) unto me (אֶל), and I will return (Cohort.) unto you.

---

§ 47. VERBS ל״ה.

	Q	*Ni.*	*Qi.*	*Qu.*	*Hi.*	*Ho.*
Perf. s. 3. *m.*	גָּלָה	נִגְלָה	גִּלָּה	גֻּלָּה	הִגְלָה	הָגְלָה
3. *f.*	גָּלְתָה	נִגְלְתָה	גִּלְּתָה	גֻּלְּתָה	הִגְלְתָה	הָגְלְתָה
2. *m.*	גָּלִיתָ	נִגְלֵיתָ	גִּלִּיתָ	גֻּלֵּיתָ	הִגְלִיתָ	הָגְלֵיתָ
pl. 2. *m.*	גְּלִיתֶם	נִגְלֵיתֶם	גִּלִּיתֶם	גֻּלֵּיתֶם	הִגְלִיתֶם	הָגְלֵיתֶם
Inf. cstr.	גְּלוֹת	הִגָּלוֹת	גַּלּוֹת	גֻּלּוֹת	הַגְלוֹת	הָגְלוֹת
Inf. abs.	גָּלֹה	נִגְלֹה	גַּלֵּה	wanting	הַגְלֵה	הָגְלֵה
Imp. s. 2. *m.*	גְּלֵה	הִגָּלֵה	גַּלֵּה	wanting	הַגְלֵה	wanting
2. *f.*	גְּלִי	הִגָּלִי	גַּלִּי		הַגְלִי	
pl. 2. *f.*	גְּלֶינָה	הִגָּלֶינָה	גַּלֶּינָה		הַגְלֶינָה	
Impf. s. 3. *m.*	יִגְלֶה	יִגָּלֶה	יְגַלֶּה	יְגֻלֶּה	יַגְלֶה	יָגְלֶה
2. *f.*	תִּגְלִי	תִּגָּלִי	תְּגַלִּי	תְּגֻלִּי	תַּגְלִי	תָּגְלִי
1. *c.*	אֶגְלֶה	אֶגָּלֶה	אֲגַלֶּה	אֲגֻלֶּה	אַגְלֶה	אָגְלֶה
pl. 3. *f.*	תִּגְלֶינָה	תִּגָּלֶינָה	תְּגַלֶּינָה	תְּגֻלֶּינָה	תַּגְלֶינָה	תָּגְלֶינָה
Part. act.	גֹּלֶה	נִגְלֶה	מְגַלֶּה		מַגְלֶה	
Part. pass.	גָּלוּי			מְגֻלֶּה		מָגְלֶה

1. גָּלָה[1] = גָּלַי or גָּלַו; Part. pass. גָּלוּי[2]. Verbs ל״ה are properly ל״י (or ל״ו), the final ה being simply the sign and accompaniment of the preceding long vowel[1] (§ 1. 4). The third radical (י), which is usually dropped when it does not coalesce with the preceding vowel, appears in the Part. pass.,[2] before נָה of the Imp. and Impf., and occasionally elsewhere before afformatives beginning with vowels. Most of the verbs of this class were originally ל״י; but ו is found in place of י in a few forms.

2. By attention to the following comparatively uniform principles the forms of this verb may be easily fixed in the memory. (1) The ending of the Perf. 3. s. in all Voices is ָה; while the old ending *ath* (*ayath* becoming *ᵉthāh*; in p., *āthāh*) has been restored before it in the feminine. (2) The original י reappears in 1. and 2. Pers. of the Perf., always coalescing, however, with the preceding vowel, becoming uniformly *ī* (*ê* is also found) in the active Voices, and *ê* in the passive. (3) Before the afformatives וּ, ִי, ָה, as well י as its representative ה, with their vowels, generally (always with pronominal suffixes) disappear. (4) The Inf. cstrs. end in וֹת; the abs. in ֹה (or וֹ) excepting the Hi., Ho., and generally Qi., which end in ֵה. (5) The ground-form of the Imp. ends in ֵה; of the Impf. and Parts. (excepting Q. Part. pass.) in ֶה. (6) Before the fem. ending נָה (Imp., Impf.) the radical י orthographically reappears (*cf.* § 2. R. 1).

Rem. 1. — The Hithq. Voice follows, as usual, the analogy of the Qi.

Rem. 2. — The *ordinary form* of the Impf. is used for the Cohortative, except in three instances, where the ending ָה is used for ֶה: Ps. lxxvii. 4; cxix. 117; Isa. xli. 23.

הָפַךְ[1] turn, overturn.

זָהָב *m.* gold. R. = shine. *Cf.* "Zif" (זִו), the (blooming) Hebrew month (May–June).

עָנָה[2] respond, answer, sing. עָנָן *m.* cloud (as responding from the skies).

יַעַן because of (in response to). מַעַן (always with לְ) in order that, because of. עֵת (= עֶנֶת) *c.* time (as appointed, fitting). עַתָּה now.

רָעָה[3] (have an eye upon) pasture (flock), seek. רֵעַ (רֵעֶה) friend.

[1] Mn. "Mᵉhuppākh" (Qu. Part.), one of the accents (§ 7) whose form is an *overturned* trumpet (ˆ). [2] Disting. from ענה afflict. [3] *Cf.* ראה and disting. from רעע.

Exercise. — For[2] (there) shall be turned (Ni.) to thee (עָלַי with *f.*) the abundance[9] of the sea.[37] Instead[39] of copper[33] (Art.) I will bring (in)[41] gold, and instead of iron[39] (Art.) I will bring (in) silver.[12] And (w.c.) my righteousness[13] shall answer for (בְּ) me. His brethren[34] were not able[9] to answer him (אֹתוֹ). Incline[30] (Hi.), O Lord, thine ear,[32] answer me. And (w.c.) the woman answered and said.[5] Should (הֲ) a multitude[46] of words not be answered (Ni.)? Jehovah is my shepherd (Part.). And Dāwidh went[43] (Part.) to feed the flock[2] of his father.[8] And the appearance[30] of the glory[11] of Jehovah (was) like a devouring[41] (Part. *f.* Segholate form) fire.[39]

---

§ 48. VERBS ל״ה (*Continued*).

Qi. Imp. …	גַּלֵּה,	apoc. גַּל	*Qi. Impf.* …	יְגַלֶּה,	apoc. יְגַל
Hi. Imp. …	הַגְלֵה,	" הַגְלְ or הֶגֶל	*Hi. Impf.* …	יַגְלֶה,	" יַגְלְ or יֶגֶל
Q. Impf. …	יִגְלֶה,	" יִגְלְ " יִגֶל	*Q. and Hi. Impf.*	יַעֲשֶׂה,	" יַעַשׂ
Q. Impf. …	יִגְלֶה,	" יֵגֶל " יָגֶל	*Q. Impf.* …	יִרְאֶה,	" יֵרֶא וַיַּרְא
Ni. Impf. …	יִגָּלֶה,	" יִגָּל			

1. It is a peculiarity of ל״ה verbs that in their Jussive and Wāw consecutive forms they generally reject the final ֶה. In some of the Voices the Imp. also is shortened by the dropping of ֵה. When this apocopation occurs, changes take place, in some cases, in the remaining vowels, as shown in the table.

Rem. 1. — In the Qi. Imp., the apocopation takes place without further change, except the necessary disappearance of D. forte. In the Hi. Imp., the word remains in its monosyllabic form or takes a helping Seghôl with the middle radical, under whose influence the *a* of the preformative frequently becomes *ĕ* (*cf.* treatment of Segholate nouns).

Rem. 2. — In the Q. Impf., after the apocopation the word may remain in its monosyllabic form either with or without the heightening of its vowel, or it may take a helping Seghôl. In the Ni. and Qi. Impf., the apocopation takes place without further change, except the omission of D. forte in the latter. In the Hi. Impf., a helping vowel may be taken, which works the same change as in the Hi. Imp.

Rem. 3. — If the first radical be a guttural, the apocopated form of the Q. and

Hi. are the same. The verb ראה heightens the vowel of its preformative under the tone when apocopated in the Impf., and with Wāw consecutive in the 3. *s. m.* takes *á*.

2. יִהְיֶה, apoc. יְהִי = יְהִ֫י; with Wāw וִיהִי; with Wāw consecutive וַיְהִי. The verb הָיָה, when apocopated in the Impf., assumes the forms given, and חָיָה follows the same general analogy here and throughout.

Rem. — The Inf. cstr. of היה is הֱיוֹת; the Imp. הֱיֵה. With prefixed letters, the first radical has Šᵉwâ, and the prefixed letter *i* (יִהְיֶה), excepting ו with the Imp. (וֶהְיֵה) and א with the Impf. (אֶהְיֶה). The vowel of the prefixed letter with unapocopated forms takes Methegh (§ **3.** 6).

3. יִשְׁתַּחֲוֶה, apoc. יִשְׁתַּחוּ; יִשְׁתַּחֲווּ contracted, יִשְׁתַּחוּ. The much used verb שחה presents some peculiarities. The final root letter is ו (instead of י), and this radical appears in the unapocopated form because this verb in the reflexive intensive Voice doubles, exceptionally, its *last* radical. When apocopated in the 3. *s. m.*, the ו left over becomes וּ, after the analogy of Segholate nouns of this form; while in the 3. *pl. m.* וּו contracted becomes וּ, thus making it identical with the apocopated 3. *s. m.*

נָכָה[1] strike, smite. מַכָּה* *f.* stroke, wound.

עֵמֶק[2] *m.* valley.

עָשָׂה[3] do, make. מַעֲשֶׂה *m.* work.

פָּדָה[4] redeem (by payment), set free.

פָּנָה[5] turn (face), prepare. פֶּן lest. פָּנִים (*s.* פָּנֶה unused) face; (with ל) לִפְנֵי before, לְפָנַי before me, etc. פִּנָּה* *f.* corner. פְּנִימִי* inner.

שָׁחָה[6] Hithq. worship, bow one's self.

[1] Suggests "knock." This verb as doubly weak, liable to apocopation, and much used, requires special attention. Perf. Hi. הִכָּה, Impf. יַכֶּה; apoc. forms וַיַּךְ, יַךְ, הַךְ, etc. Similarly נָטָה. [2] Syn. of בִּקְעָה. [3] Syn. of פָּעַל, יָצַר, בָּרָא. [4] Syn. of גָּאַל. [5] Idea of r. is *turn*, hence the various meanings (corner = a turn; face, what is turned; the inner place, where the face, presence is). Mn. "Peniel" (פְּנִיאֵל): Gen. xxxii. 31. [6] *Cf.* שַׁחַת; R. שח = be low.

Exercise. — And he (w.c.) saw.[30] And (w.c.) God said,[5] let (there) be light.[5] They bowed themselves to (ל) me. And he (w.c.) bowed himself to the earth (ה ָ locative). And they (w.c.) bowed themselves to (ל) him. Multitudes, multitudes[9] (*pl.*) in the valley. Smite (Hi.) now[3] this people (גּוֹי *m.*). And he (w.c.) smote (Hi.) all[2] the city.[34] And he (w.c.) did evil[46] (Art.) in the eyes[3] of Jehovah.

And he (w.c.) turned and went.[43] Before me. Before them. Before us. Incline[30] (Hi.) thine ear[32] and hear[18] the words[6] of the wise.[3]

Rem. — Apocopated forms of the Imp. and Impf. are to be used where possible in this Exercise.

---

§ 49. VERBS ל״א.

	Q.		Ni.	Qi.	Qu.	Hi.	Ho.
Perf. s. 3. *m.*	מָצָא	מָלֵא	נִמְצָא	מִצֵּא	מֻצָּא	הִמְצִיא	הֻמְצָא
3. *f.*	מָצְאָה	מָלְאָה	נִמְצְאָה	מִצְּאָה	מֻצְּאָה	הִמְצִיאָה	הֻמְצְאָה
2. *m.*	מָצָאתָ	מָלֵאתָ	נִמְצֵאתָ	מִצֵּאתָ	מֻצֵּאתָ	הִמְצֵאתָ	הֻמְצֵאתָ
pl. 2. *m.*	מְצָאתֶם	מְלֵאתֶם	נִמְצֵאתֶם	מִצֵּאתֶם	מֻצֵּאתֶם	הִמְצֵאתֶם	הֻמְצֵאתֶם
Inf. cstr.	מְצֹא		הִמָּצֵא	מַצֵּא	wanting	הַמְצִיא	הֻמְצָא
Inf. abs.	מָצוֹא		נִמְצֹא	מַצֹּא	wanting	הַמְצֵא	wanting
Imp. s. m.	מְצָא		הִמָּצֵא	מַצֵּא	wanting	הַמְצֵא	wanting
f.	מִצְאִי		הִמָּצְאִי	מַצְּאִי		הַמְצִיאִי	
pl. f.	מְצֶאנָה		הִמָּצֶאנָה	מַצֶּאנָה		הַמְצֶאנָה	
Impf. s. 3. *m.*	יִמְצָא		יִמָּצֵא	יְמַצֵּא	יְמֻצָּא	יַמְצִיא יַמְצֵא	יֻמְצָא
2. *f.*	תִּמְצְאִי		תִּמָּצְאִי	תְּמַצְּאִי	תְּמֻצְּאִי	תַּמְצִיאִי	תֻּמְצְאִי
1. c.	אֶמְצָא		אֶמָּצֵא	אֲמַצֵּא	אֲמֻצָּא	אַמְצִיא	אֻמְצָא
pl. 3. *f.*	תִּמְצֶאנָה		תִּמָּצֶאנָה	תְּמַצֶּאנָה	תְּמֻצֶּאנָה	תַּמְצֶאנָה	תֻּמְצֶאנָה
Part. act.	מֹצֵא		נִמְצָא	מְמַצֵּא		מַמְצִיא	
Part. pass.	מָצוּא				מְמֻצָּא		מֻמְצָא

1. The peculiarities in the inflection of verbs ל״א arise from two principal causes: (1) the fact that the letter א is treated either as a guttural (consonant), or a quiescent (vowel) letter, according to its position in the syllable (§ 5. 4); and (2) that it follows in some of its forms the analogy of verbs ל״ה.

2. In all forms ending in א, the vowels remain the same as in the Strong verbs, except that when short (*a* everywhere) they are lengthened immediately before it.

Rem. — The Q. Imp. and Impf. take ā (a lengthened *a*) in the final syllable, after the analogy of verbs whose third stem letter is a guttural (§ 25).

3. In like manner, in all other forms where א ends a syllable before afformatives beginning with consonants, it quiesces with the preceding vowel: in the Q. Perf. with Pathaḥ (becoming ā); in all the other Perfects with Çērê, and in all the Imperfects with Seghôl, following in the last two particulars verbs ל״ה. Before afformatives beginning with a vowel, א is detached, and stands as a consonant (guttural) before them.

Rem. 1. — Intransitive verbs, it will be noted, have no peculiarities here not shared by the transitive.

Rem. 2. — The Hithq. Voice follows the analogy of the Qi., as in the Strong verb.

Rem. 3. — Verbs ל״א are not infrequently inflected in other forms than those named, like verbs ל״ה, and *vice versâ*, even to the extent of their exchanging final letters.

הָלַל[1] praise, boast. תְּהִלָּה *f.* praise.
חָלַל[2] bore, wound, profane, begin.
חָלָל wounded (to death). תְּחִלָּה† beginning.
צָבָא (*pl.* צְבָאוֹת) host, warfare. Mn. "Sabaoth" ("Lord of Sabaoth").
צָמֵא[3]† thirst. צָמָא† *m.* thirst.
שׁוֹפָר[4] *m.* trumpet.
שׁוֹר[5] (*pl.* שְׁוָרִים) *m.* (single) ox.
תָּמַם[6] be complete, finished, perfect.
תֹּם* *m.* perfectness. תָּמִים (and תָּם) perfect, upright.

[1] Mn. and deriv. "Hallelujah" (הַלְלוּיָהּ). [2] Discrim. from preceding, and *cf.* חדל cease. [3] Associate with מצא, having the same root letters, and יצא (thirst, go forth, find). [4] R. = shine; metaphor. shine in tone, so be clear. *Cf.* Eng. *clarionet*. [5] An individual of the ox (בָּקָר) species, as שֶׂה* is one of the sheep or goat (צֹאן) species. [6] Mn. "Thummim" (תֻּמִּים), which is associated with the "Urim" (from אוֹר) = Light and Perfection.

Exercise.—Give me to drink[26] (= cause me to drink), I pray,[3] a little (מְעַט) water[3]; for[2] I am thirsty. And they (w.c.) said[5] to (לְ) him: We have found[14] water. The man[31] is not able (Impf.; *cf.* § **43**. 3. R. 4) to find out the work[48] which is done[48] (Ni.) beneath[30] the sun.[32] For all[2] the priests[12] who were found (Ni. Part. *pl.* with Art.) sanctified themselves[6] (Hithq.). And he (w.c.) blew[25] a (בְּ) trumpet. Whose ox (the ox of whom[11]) have I taken.[19] The words[6] of Job (אִיּוֹב) are finished (Q. Perf.). (As for) God (הָאֵל) his way[12] is perfect. They went forth[5] from the ark (הַתֵּבָה). When (ב) I went forth (Inf. צֵאת for צֵאֵת). And (w.c.) Cain (קַיִן) went forth (יֵצֵא) from before[48] Jehovah. Jehovah brought forth (Hi.) Israel. Bring out (*pl.*) the children[11] of Israel.

PARADIGMS, EXERCISES IN TRANSLATION,

AND LIST OF WORDS.

THE STRONG

	Qal.			*Niqṭal.*	*Qiṭṭēl.*
Perf. s. 3. *m.*	קָטַל	כָּבֵד	קָטֹן	נִקְטַל	קִטֵּל, קִטַּל
3. *f.*	קָֽטְלָה	כָּֽבְדָה	קָֽטְנָה	נִקְטְלָה	קִטְּלָה
2. *m.*	קָטַלְתָּ	כָּבַדְתָּ	קָטֹנְתָּ	נִקְטַלְתָּ	קִטַּלְתָּ
2. *f.*	קָטַלְתְּ	כָּבַדְתְּ	קָטֹנְתְּ	נִקְטַלְתְּ	קִטַּלְתְּ
1. *c.*	קָטַלְתִּי	כָּבַדְתִּי	קָטֹנְתִּי	נִקְטַלְתִּי	קִטַּלְתִּי
pl. 3. *c.*	קָֽטְלוּ	כָּֽבְדוּ	קָֽטְנוּ	נִקְטְלוּ	קִטְּלוּ
2. *m.*	קְטַלְתֶּם	כְּבַדְתֶּם	קְטָנְתֶּם	נִקְטַלְתֶּם	קִטַּלְתֶּם
2. *f.*	קְטַלְתֶּן	כְּבַדְתֶּן	קְטָנְתֶּן	נִקְטַלְתֶּן	קִטַּלְתֶּן
1. *c.*	קָטַלְנוּ	כָּבַדְנוּ	קָטֹנּוּ	נִקְטַלְנוּ	קִטַּלְנוּ
Inf. cstr.	קְטֹל	כְּבַד		הִקָּטֵל	קַטֵּל
Inf. abs.	קָטוֹל	כָּבוֹד		נִקְטֹל, הִקָּטֹל	קַטֹּל, קַטֵּל
Imp. s. 2. *m.*	קְטֹל	כְּבַד		הִקָּטֵל	קַטֵּל
2. *f.*	קִטְלִי	כִּבְדִי		הִקָּֽטְלִי	קַטְּלִי
pl. 2. *m.*	קִטְלוּ	כִּבְדוּ		הִקָּֽטְלוּ	קַטְּלוּ
2. *f.*	קְטֹלְנָה	כְּבַדְנָה		הִקָּטַלְנָה	קַטֵּלְנָה
Impf. s. 3. *m.*	יִקְטֹל	יִכְבַּד,	יִקְטַן	יִקָּטֵל	יְקַטֵּל
3. *f.*	תִּקְטֹל	תִּכְבַּד		תִּקָּטֵל	תְּקַטֵּל
2. *m.*	תִּקְטֹל	תִּכְבַּד		תִּקָּטֵל	תְּקַטֵּל
2. *f.*	תִּקְטְלִי	תִּכְבְּדִי		תִּקָּֽטְלִי	תְּקַטְּלִי
1. *c.*	אֶקְטֹל	אֶכְבַּד		אֶקָּטֵל	אֲקַטֵּל
pl. 3. *m.*	יִקְטְלוּ	יִכְבְּדוּ		יִקָּֽטְלוּ	יְקַטְּלוּ
3. *f.*	תִּקְטֹלְנָה	תִּכְבַּדְנָה		תִּקָּטַלְנָה	תְּקַטֵּלְנָה
2. *m.*	תִּקְטְלוּ	תִּכְבְּדוּ		תִּקָּֽטְלוּ	תְּקַטְּלוּ
2. *f.*	תִּקְטֹלְנָה	תִּכְבַּדְנָה		תִּקָּטַלְנָה	תְּקַטֵּלְנָה
1. *c.*	נִקְטֹל	נִכְבַּד		נִקָּטֵל	נְקַטֵּל
Part. act.	קֹטֵל	כָּבֵד,	קָטֹן	נִקְטָל	מְקַטֵּל
Part. pass.	קָטוּל				

VERB. *Cf.* §§ **14–25.**

Quṭṭal.	*Hithqaṭṭēl.*	*Hiqṭîl.*	*Hoqṭal.*
קֻטַּל	הִתְקַטֵּל	הִקְטִיל	הָקְטַל
קֻטְּלָה	הִתְקַטְּלָה	הִקְטִילָה	הָקְטְלָה
קֻטַּלְתָּ	הִתְקַטַּלְתָּ	הִקְטַלְתָּ	הָקְטַלְתָּ
קֻטַּלְתְּ	הִתְקַטַּלְתְּ	הִקְטַלְתְּ	הָקְטַלְתְּ
קֻטַּלְתִּי	הִתְקַטַּלְתִּי	הִקְטַלְתִּי	הָקְטַלְתִּי
קֻטְּלוּ	הִתְקַטְּלוּ	הִקְטִילוּ	הָקְטְלוּ
קֻטַּלְתֶּם	הִתְקַטַּלְתֶּם	הִקְטַלְתֶּם	הָקְטַלְתֶּם
קֻטַּלְתֶּן	הִתְקַטַּלְתֶּן	הִקְטַלְתֶּן	הָקְטַלְתֶּן
קֻטַּלְנוּ	הִתְקַטַּלְנוּ	הִקְטַלְנוּ	הָקְטַלְנוּ
wanting	הִתְקַטֵּל	הַקְטִיל	wanting
קֻטֹּל	הִתְקַטֵּל	הַקְטֵל	הָקְטֵל
wanting	הִתְקַטֵּל	הַקְטֵל	wanting
	הִתְקַטְּלִי	הַקְטִילִי	
	הִתְקַטְּלוּ	הַקְטִילוּ	
	הִתְקַטֵּלְנָה	הַקְטֵלְנָה	
יְקֻטַּל	יִתְקַטֵּל	יַקְטִיל, יַקְטֵל	יָקְטַל
תְּקֻטַּל	תִּתְקַטֵּל	תַּקְטִיל	תָּקְטַל
תְּקֻטַּל	תִּתְקַטֵּל	תַּקְטִיל	תָּקְטַל
תְּקֻטְּלִי	תִּתְקַטְּלִי	תַּקְטִילִי	תָּקְטְלִי
אֲקֻטַּל	אֶתְקַטֵּל	אַקְטִיל	אָקְטַל
יְקֻטְּלוּ	יִתְקַטְּלוּ	יַקְטִילוּ	יָקְטְלוּ
תְּקֻטַּלְנָה	תִּתְקַטֵּלְנָה	תַּקְטֵלְנָה	תָּקְטַלְנָה
תְּקֻטְּלוּ	תִּתְקַטְּלוּ	תַּקְטִילוּ	תָּקְטְלוּ
תְּקֻטַּלְנָה	תִּתְקַטֵּלְנָה	תַּקְטֵלְנָה	תָּקְטַלְנָה
נְקֻטַּל	נִתְקַטֵּל	נַקְטִיל	נָקְטַל
	מִתְקַטֵּל	מַקְטִיל	
מְקֻטָּל			מָקְטָל

THE WEAK VERB ע״ו

	Q.		Ni.	Hi.	Ho.
Perf. s. 3. *m.*	קָם	מֵת	נָקוֹם	הֵקִים	הוּקַם
3. *f.*	קָמָה	מֵתָה	נָקוֹמָה	הֵקִימָה	הוּקְמָה
2. *m.*	קַמְתָּ	מַתָּה	נְקוּמוֹתָ	הֲקִימוֹתָ	הוּקַמְתָּ
2. *f.*	קַמְתְּ	מַתְּ	נְקוּמוֹת	הֲקִימוֹת	הוּקַמְתְּ
1. *c.*	קַמְתִּי	מַתִּי	נְקוּמוֹתִי	הֲקִימוֹתִי	הוּקַמְתִּי
pl. 3. *c.*	קָמוּ	מֵתוּ	נָקוֹמוּ	הֵקִימוּ	הוּקְמוּ
2. *m.*	קַמְתֶּם	מַתֶּם	נְקוּמוֹתֶם	הֲקִימוֹתֶם	הוּקַמְתֶּם
2. *f.*	קַמְתֶּן	מַתֶּן	נְקוּמוֹתֶן	הֲקִימוֹתֶן	הוּקַמְתֶּן
1. *c.*	קַמְנוּ	מַתְנוּ	נְקוּמוֹנוּ	הֲקִימוֹנוּ	הוּקַמְנוּ
Inf. cstr.	קוּם		הִקּוֹם	הָקִים	הוּקַם
Inf. abs.	קוֹם		הִקּוֹם	הָקֵם	wanting
Imp. s. m.	קוּם		הִקּוֹם	הָקֵם	wanting
f.	קוּמִי		הִקּוֹמִי	הָקִימִי	
pl. m.	קוּמוּ		הִקּוֹמוּ	הָקִימוּ	
f.	קֹמְנָה		הִקֹּמְנָה	הָקֵמְנָה	
Impf. s. 3. *m.*	יָקוּם,	יָקֹם	יִקּוֹם	יָקִים, יָקֵם	יוּקַם
3. *f.*	תָּקוּם		תִּקּוֹם	תָּקִים	תּוּקַם
2. *m.*	תָּקוּם		תִּקּוֹם	תָּקִים	תּוּקַם
2. *f.*	תָּקוּמִי		תִּקּוֹמִי	תָּקִימִי	תּוּקְמִי
1. *c.*	אָקוּם		אֶקּוֹם	אָקִים	אוּקַם
pl. 3. *m.*	יָקוּמוּ		יִקּוֹמוּ	יָקִימוּ	יוּקְמוּ
3. *f.*	תְּקוּמֶינָה		(תִּקּוֹמֶינָה)	תָּקֵמְנָה	תּוּקַמְנָה
2. *m.*	תָּקוּמוּ		תִּקּוֹמוּ	תָּקִימוּ	תּוּקְמוּ
2. *f.*	תְּקוּמֶינָה		(תִּקּוֹמֶינָה)	תָּקֵמְנָה	תּוּקַמְנָה
1. *c.*	נָקוּם		נִקּוֹם	נָקִים	נוּקַם
Impf. with w.c.	וַיָּקָם			וַיָּקֶם	
Part. act.	קָם	מֵת	נָקוֹם	מֵקִים	
Part. pass.	קוּם				מוּקָם

(*or* ע״י). *See* §§ **44, 45**.

Q.		*Qôṭēṭ.*	*Qôṭaṭ.*
בָּן	בִּין	קוֹמֵם	קוֹמַם
בָּ֫נָה	בִּ֫ינָה	קֽוֹמְמָה	קֽוֹמְמָה
בַּ֫נְתָּ	בִּינ֫וֹתָ	קוֹמַ֫מְתָּ	קוֹמַ֫מְתָּ
בַּנְתְּ	בִּינוֹת	קוֹמַמְתְּ	קוֹמַמְתְּ
בַּ֫נְתִּי	בִּינ֫וֹתִי	קוֹמַ֫מְתִּי	קוֹמַ֫מְתִּי
בָּ֫נוּ	בִּ֫ינוּ	קֽוֹמְמוּ	קֽוֹמְמוּ
בַּנְתֶּם	בְּינוֹתֶם	קֽוֹמַמְתֶּם	קֽוֹמַמְתֶּם
בַּנְתֶּן	בְּינוֹתֶן	קֽוֹמַמְתֶּן	קֽוֹמַמְתֶּן
בַּ֫נּוּ	בִּינ֫וֹנוּ	קוֹמַ֫מְנוּ	קוֹמַ֫מְנוּ
בִּין		קוֹמֵם	wanting
בֹּן		wanting	wanting
בִּין		קוֹמֵם	wanting
בִּ֫ינִי		קֽוֹמְמִי	
בִּ֫ינוּ		קֽוֹמְמוּ	
wanting		קוֹמֵ֫מְנָה	
יָבִין ,יָבֵן		יְקוֹמֵם	יְקוֹמַם
תָּבִין		תְּקוֹמֵם	תְּקוֹמַם
תָּבִין		תְּקוֹמֵם	תְּקוֹמַם
תָּבִ֫ינִי		תְּקֽוֹמְמִי	תְּקֽוֹמְמִי
אָבִין		אֲקוֹמֵם	אֲקוֹמַם
יָבִ֫ינוּ		יְקֽוֹמְמוּ	יְקֽוֹמְמוּ
תְּבִינֶ֫ינָה		תְּקוֹמֵ֫מְנָה	תְּקוֹמַ֫מְנָה
תָּבִ֫ינוּ		תְּקֽוֹמְמוּ	תְּקֽוֹמְמוּ
תְּבִינֶ֫ינָה		תְּקוֹמֵ֫מְנָה	תְּקוֹמַ֫מְנָה
נָבִין		נְקוֹמֵם	נְקוֹמַם
וַיָּ֫בֶן			
בָּן		מְקוֹמֵם	
בּוֹן			מְקוֹמָם

THE WEAK VERB ע״ע. *See* § 46.

	Q.		*Ni.*	*Hi.*	*Ho.*	*Qôlēl.*	*Qôlal.*
Perf. s. 3. *m.*	סַב	קַל,	נָסַב	הֵסֵב	הוּסַב	סוֹבֵב	סוֹבַב
3. *f.*	סַבָּה		נָסַבָּה	הֵסֵבָּה	הוּסַבָּה	סוֹבְבָה	סוֹבְבָה
2. *m.*	סַבּוֹתָ		נְסַבּוֹתָ	הֲסִבּוֹתָ	הוּסַבּוֹתָ	סוֹבַבְתָּ	סוֹבַבְתָּ
2. *f.*	סַבּוֹת		נְסַבּוֹת	הֲסִבּוֹת	הוּסַבּוֹת	סוֹבַבְתְּ	סוֹבַבְתְּ
1. *c.*	סַבּוֹתִי		נְסַבּוֹתִי	הֲסִבּוֹתִי	הוּסַבּוֹתִי	סוֹבַבְתִּי	סוֹבַבְתִּי
pl. 3. *c.*	סַבּוּ		נָסַבּוּ	הֵסֵבּוּ	הוּסַבּוּ	סוֹבְבוּ	סוֹבְבוּ
2. *m.*	סַבּוֹתֶם		נְסַבּוֹתֶם	הֲסִבּוֹתֶם	הוּסַבּוֹתֶם	סוֹבַבְתֶּם	סוֹבַבְתֶּם
2. *f.*	סַבּוֹתֶן		נְסַבּוֹתֶן	הֲסִבּוֹתֶן	הוּסַבּוֹתֶן	סוֹבַבְתֶּן	סוֹבַבְתֶּן
1. *c.*	סַבּוֹנוּ		נְסַבּוֹנוּ	הֲסִבּוֹנוּ	הוּסַבּוֹנוּ	סוֹבַבְנוּ	סוֹבַבְנוּ
Inf. cstr.	סֹב		הִסֵּב	הָסֵב	wanting	סוֹבֵב	wanting
Inf. abs.	סָבוֹב		הִסּוֹב	הָסֵב	wanting	סוֹבֵב	סוֹבַב
Imp. s. m.	סֹב		הִסַּב	הָסֵב	wanting	סוֹבֵב	wanting
f.	סֹבִּי		הִסַּבִּי	הָסֵבִּי		סוֹבְבִי	
pl. m.	סֹבּוּ		הִסַּבּוּ	הָסֵבּוּ		סוֹבְבוּ	
f.	סֻבֶּינָה		הִסַּבֶּינָה	הֲסִבֶּינָה		סוֹבֵבְנָה	
Impf. s. 3. *m.*	יָסֹב	יֵקַל, יִסֹּב	יִסַּב	יַסֵּב, יָסֵב	יוּסַב	יְסוֹבֵב	יְסוֹבַב
3. *f.*	תָּסֹב	תִּסֹּב	תִּסַּב	תָּסֵב	תּוּסַב	תְּסוֹבֵב	תְּסוֹבַב
2. *m.*	תָּסֹב	תִּסֹּב	תִּסַּב	תָּסֵב	תּוּסַב	תְּסוֹבֵב	תְּסוֹבַב
2. *f.*	תָּסֹבִּי	תִּסְּבִי	תִּסַּבִּי	תָּסֵבִּי	תּוּסַבִּי	תְּסוֹבְבִי	תְּסוֹבְבִי
1. *c.*	אָסֹב	אֶסֹּב	אֶסַּב	אָסֵב	אוּסַב	אֲסוֹבֵב	אֲסוֹבַב
pl. 3. *m.*	יָסֹבּוּ	יִסְּבוּ	יִסַּבּוּ	יָסֵבּוּ	יוּסַבּוּ	יְסוֹבְבוּ	יְסוֹבְבוּ
3. *f.*	תְּסֻבֶּינָה	תִּסֹּבְנָה	תִּסַּבֶּינָה	תְּסִבֶּינָה	תּוּסַבֶּינָה	תְּסוֹבֵבְנָה	תְּסוֹבַבְנָה
2. *m.*	תָּסֹבּוּ	תִּסְּבוּ	תִּסַּבּוּ	תָּסֵבּוּ	תּוּסַבּוּ	תְּסוֹבְבוּ	תְּסוֹבְבוּ
2. *f.*	תְּסֻבֶּינָה	תִּסֹּבְנָה	תִּסַּבֶּינָה	תְּסִבֶּינָה	תּוּסַבֶּינָה	תְּסוֹבֵבְנָה	תְּסוֹבַבְנָה
1. *c.*	נָסֹב	נִסֹּב	נִסַּב	נָסֵב	נוּסַב	נְסוֹבֵב	נְסוֹבַב
Impf. with w.c.	וַיָּסָב			וַיָּסֶב			
Part. act.	סֹבֵב	קַל	נָסָב	מֵסֵב		מְסוֹבֵב	
Part. pass.	סָבוּב				מוּסָב		מְסוֹבָב

EXERCISES IN TRANSLATION.

§ 8. אָנֹכִי[1] יְהוָֹה: הִיא[2] חֶבְרוֹן[3]: אִם־אָב אֲנִי: אֲנִי
רִאשׁוֹן: כִּי קָדוֹשׁ הוּא: כִּי עָפָר אֲנָחְנוּ: אַתָּה אֲדֹנָי טוֹב:
צַדִּיק אַתָּה יְהוָֹה: לֹא[4] אֱלֹהִים הֵמָּה: אֲנִי־הוּא: אֲנִי־
אֵל שַׁדַּי[3]:

§ 9. כָּל־הָעָם: הַשָּׁמַיִם וְהָאָרֶץ[5]: אִישׁ אוֹ אִשָּׁה:
הָאֵפֶר: הֶעָפָר: הָאוֹר: הַחֹשֶׁךְ: הָעֶבֶד: רֵאשִׁית חָכְמָה:
הוּא חָכָם: הַלְּבָנוֹן[3]: הַיּוֹם לֹא־חֹדֶשׁ וְלֹא[5] שַׁבָּת[6]:
עִם־הַחֲמוֹר:

§ 10. זֶה חָדָשׁ: הֶהָמוֹן הַזֶּה: הַמִּדְבָּר הַגָּדוֹל: זֶה
חֳלִי: אִישׁ חָכָם מְאֹד: שֵׁם גָּדוֹל: הָאִישׁ הַלָּזֶה: הַיָּמִים[7]
הָהֵם[8]: אֲשֶׁר דִּבֶּר מֹשֶׁה[3]: הָאָרֶץ הַטּוֹבָה[9] הַזֹּאת: כִּסֵּא
רָם: בַּיִת חָדָשׁ: אֲשֶׁר־שָׁם הַזָּהָב[10]: שֶׁאֲנִי[11]: כִּי תְרוּמָה
הוּא:

§ 11. מִי אַתֶּם: מָה־אֱנוֹשׁ: לָמָּה זֶּה אָנֹכִי: הַאַתָּה זֶה
עֵשָׂו[3] אִם־לֹא: אִם־בֵּן אִם־בַּת: הֲלֹא־זֶה הַדָּבָר: בַּת־מִי
אַתְּ: הַבְּרָכָה הַזֹּאת: מִי־אַתָּה הַר־הַגָּדוֹל: אֵי־זֶה בַּיִת[12]:
מָה הָעֲבֹדָה הַזֹּאת: אֶת־הָאָרֶץ מַה־הִוא:

§ 12. אֵי מִזֶּה עַם[13]: מַה־בַּבָּיִת: בַּחֲלוֹם: בַּלַּיְלָה: קָרָא
אֱלֹהִים לָאוֹר יוֹם: יָד לְפֶה: בַּכֶּסֶף: כָּאֲרִי: מִי אֵל[14]
גָּדוֹל כֵּאלֹהִים[15]: מִי כַּיהוָֹה: עֶבֶד לְדָוִד[3]: לַחֹשֶׁךְ:
בַּהֵיכָל אֲשֶׁר־שָׁם אָרוֹן: בֶּעָמָל: כַּאֲשֶׁר[16] לְיִשְׂרָאֵל[3]:

---

[1] The predicate of a sentence may be a substantive or adjective, as well as a verb, and no copula is necessary to connect them with the subject. [2] It. [3] Proper name. [4] not (no). [5] וְ = and. [6] Sabbath. [7] See יוֹם. [8] *Sing.* הַהוּא; but *pl.* as here. [9] *Fem.* of טוֹב. [10] gold. [11] which I. [12] What manner of house. [13] From what people. [14] God. [15] § 5. 4. R. 1. [16] According as.

בַּמָּה הַחַטָּאת הַזֹּאת הַיּוֹם: בִּבְהֵמָה: כַּבְּהֵמָה: כְּמוֹ־
אֶבֶן[1]: לְמִי אַתָּה:

§ 13. חֶרֶב וְדֶבֶר: מִירוּשָׁלַםִ: מִבַּיִת וּמִחוּץ: מִשָּׁם:
אֲשֶׁר . . . מִשָּׁם[2]: מֵיהוּדָה: בִּיהוּדָה: מִן־הַיְאֹר: לֶחֶם וָיַיִן[3]:
אֱלֹהִים וָמֶלֶךְ[4]: כָּל־רֹאשׁ לָחֳלִי[5]: וּמִן־הָעָם: וְהוּא יָצָא:
מֵאֶרֶץ מִצְרַיִם[6]: מִזֶּה וּמִזֶּה: מִן־הַמִּקְדָּשׁ: מֵעֶרֶב:

§ 14. וְלֹא שָׁבַר[7] אֶת־הַחֲמוֹר: כֹּל אֲשֶׁר אָמַר אֱלֹהִים:
וְאָמְרוּ מִי־הָאִישׁ: כִּי־גָדַל מְאֹד: גְּדֹלָה: קָהָל גָּדוֹל:
אָמַר הַקּוֹהֶלֶת[8]: אָבְדָה מִצְרָיִם[9]: אָבָדְנוּ: חָרְבוּ הַמָּיִם:
קָדֵשׁוּ[9]: אֲשֶׁר יהוה שָׂנֵא: וְאֵת אֲמַצְיָהוּ[10] תָּפַשׂ יוֹאָשׁ[10]:
שִׂנְאָה גְדוֹלָה[11] מְאֹד: יָשְׁבוּ בְּמִצְרַיִם: בֵּין טוֹב וּבֵין[12]
רָע[13]: וְלֹא מָצָא: אֲשֶׁר־עָמַד שָׁם: אַחְאָב[10] עָבַד אֶת־
הַבַּעַל[10]: דָּרַךְ: דָּרְכָה: דָּרְכוּ: דָּרַכְתִּי: דָּרַכְתָּ:

§ 15. שְׁמֹר אֶת־הָאִישׁ הַזֶּה: שָׁמְרָה־זֹּאת: בְּמֶלֶךְ
בִּירוּשָׁלַםִ[9]: שָׁמָּה[14] קָבְרוּ אֶת־אַבְרָהָם: דְּרָשׁ[15]־נָא כַּיּוֹם[16]:
דִּרְשׁוּ יְהוָה: לִשְׁבֹּר הַדָּלֶת[9]: כֶּאֱמֹר יְהוֹשֻׁעַ[10] אֶל[17]־הָעָם:
וּפִקְדוּ אֶת־הָעָם: מַה־הַמָּשָׁל הַזֶּה: כִּי חָכְמָה מְאֹד:
כְּתֹב זֹאת:

§ 16. וְהוּא לֹא שָׂנֵא: וְאַתָּה מֹשֵׁל בַּכֹּל[18]: יִדְרְשׁוּ:
כְּכָל־הַכָּתוּב בַּסֵּפֶר: וְאַתֶּם תִּכְתְּבוּ[19] אֶת־הָאָרֶץ: כָּל־
הֶעָמָל שֶׁעָמַלְתִּי[20]: כָּל־הָאָרֶץ אֲשֶׁר תִּדְרְכוּ־בָהּ[21]: קֶצֶף
גָּדוֹל אֲנִי קֹצֵף: לָמָּה יִקְצֹף הָאֱלֹהִים: וְאַל[22] תַּעֲמֹד

---

1 Like a stone. 2 Whence. § 10. 4. 3 Bread and wine. 4 Note connective. 5 (given up) to, for. 6 Egypt. 7 had not torn. 8 Preacher. 9 in pause. § 6. 4. R. 10 p.n. 11 *Fem.* 12 Not to be translated. 13 Evil. 14 שָׁם with ָה *locative*, usually rendered "thither"; here, "there." 15 ō become o by loss of tone. 16 כ = while it is. 17 to. 18 ב = *over*, with מָשַׁל. 19 describe. 20 contracted אֲשֶׁר. § 10. 3. R. 21 § 10. 4. 22 § 15. 4.

בְּכָל־הַדָּבָר׃ כְּכֹל אֲשֶׁר־שָׁאַלְתִּי מֵעִם[1] יהוה בְּחֹרֶב׃ כִּי
גֹאֵל אָנֹכִי׃ הֲמָלֹךְ תִּמְלֹךְ עָלֵינוּ[2] אִם־מָשׁוֹל תִּמְשֹׁל
בָּנוּ[2]׃ אַל־תִּתְקַצֵּף יהוה[3]׃

§ 17. וְלֹא יָכְלוּ לַעֲמֹד׃ גָּדְלָה הָאָרֶץ׃ עַם נָבָל וְלֹא
חָכָם׃ תִּכְבַּד הָעֲבֹדָה עַל[4]־הָאֲנָשִׁים[5]׃ דָּבָר קָטֹן אוֹ
גָדוֹל׃ מִי־הָאִישׁ אֲשֶׁר בָּנָה בַּיִת־חָדָשׁ׃ כָּל־הַמִּדְבָּר
הַגָּדוֹל הַהוּא׃ וְאֶת־הַדֶּלֶת סָגָרוּ[6]׃ יָכֹלְתָּ עֲמֹד׃ קָטֹנְתִּי׃
תִּשְׁפַּלְנָה׃ אַתָּה זָקַנְתָּה[7]׃ הוּא יִגְדָּל[6]׃ וּמַה־יִּצְדַּק אֱנוֹשׁ
עִם־אֵל׃

§ 18. וְהָיָה מְגֹרָשׁ׃ וְהָיָה כָעָם כַּכֹּהֵן כַּעֶבֶד כָּאָדוֹן׃
וַיִּקְבֹּץ שָׁאוּל[8] אֶת־כָּל־יִשְׂרָאֵל׃ אִם־שָׁמוֹעַ תִּשְׁמַע[9]׃
אֵלֶּה אֶזְכְּרָה׃ שְׁמַע יִשְׂרָאֵל׃ שִׁמְעָה יהוה צֶדֶק׃ וַיִּגְדַּל
מֹשֶׁה׃ וְאֶקְבְּרָה אֶת־אָבִי[10]׃ וַיִּזְבַּח יַעֲקֹב[8] זֶבַח בָּהָר׃
כָּל־זָכָר׃ אַל־תִּקְרַב הֲלֹם[11]׃ נִזְבְּחָה לַיהוָה׃ יִשְׁמְעוּ
וְלָמְדוּ׃

§ 19. לָקַחְתִּי סֵפֶר וָאֶכְתֹּב׃ בָּגְדָה׃ בֹּגֵד׃ בָּגוֹד׃
תִּבְגּוֹדוּ[6]׃ וַיִּבְגְּדוּ׃ עֵץ אוֹ בֶגֶד אוֹ־עוֹר אוֹ שָׂק׃ וְלָכוֹד לֹא
יִלְכּוֹד׃ וְלִכְדוּ אֶת־הַמַּיִם׃ וּלְקַחְתֶּם מֵהַפְּרִי׃ הַמָּקוֹם
אֲשֶׁר שָׁכַב־שָׁם שָׁאוּל׃ וְהָיָה כִשְׁכַּב הַמֶּלֶךְ׃ שִׁכְבִי׃
שִׁכְבָה׃ אֶשְׁכְּבָה׃ וַיִּשְׁכַּב בַּמָּקוֹם הַהוּא׃ וַיֹּאמֶר[12] מֹשֶׁה
אֶל־אַהֲרֹן[8] קְרַב אֶל־הַמִּזְבֵּחַ׃

§ 20. נִכְרְתָה בְּרִית אֲנִי וְאַתָּה׃ יִגָּנֵב׃ נִכְרַת׃ נִכְרָת׃
וְנִכְרְתָה׃ הִכָּרֵת׃ וְלֹא־תִכָּרֵת הָאָרֶץ׃ יִכָּרֵתוּן[13]׃ לְעֶבֶד

---

[1] Compound *Prep.* [2] over us. [3] The vowels of certain familiar words will sometimes be left to be supplied by the pupil. [4] upon. [5] See אִישׁ. [6] in p. [7] A superfluous ה. [8] p.n. [9] § 15. 2; 5. 2. [10] My (father). [11] hither. [12] § 18. 3. [13] Older ending.

נִמְכַּר יוֹסֵף[1]: נִמְכַּרְתֶּם וְלֹא בְכֶסֶף[2] תִּגָּאֵלוּ: וַתִּקָּשֵׁר כָּל-
הַחוֹמָה[3]: בָּרוּךְ יהוה: קְלָלָה וְלֹא בְרָכָה: כַּכְּפִיר:
כִּכְפִיר: הִשָּׁמֵד תִּשָּׁמֵדוּן: פָּרַץ יהוה פֶּרֶץ בְּעֻזָּה[1]
וַיִּקְרָא לַמָּקוֹם הַהוּא פֶּרֶץ עֻזָּה: וַיֹּאמֶר הֲשָׁלוֹם יֵהוּא[1]:
הִשָּׁמֶר לְךָ[4]: לֹא תִגְנֹב:

§ 21. פֶּן[5]-תִּשְׁכַּח אֶת-יהוה: וְשָׁכַן בַּמִּדְבָּר מִשְׁפָּט:
וְנִסְתְּרָה וְהִיא נִטְמָאָה: וַיְקַדֵּשׁ אֶת-הָעָם: וְהוּא יֹשֵׁב
פֶּתַח[6]: כַּאֲשֶׁר דִּבֶּר: וְשָׁחַט אֶת-הַכֶּבֶשׂ: מָה אֲדֹנִי[7]
מְדַבֵּר: בַּיּוֹם שֶׁיְּדֻבַּר[8] בָּהּ[8]: מַה-נְּדַבֵּר וּמַה-נִּצְטַדָּק:
וְכִפֶּר אַהֲרֹן[1]: שִׁבְעַת[9] יָמִים[10] תְּכַפֵּר עַל-הַמִּזְבֵּחַ: וְטִהַר
הַכֹּהֵן אֶת-הַבַּיִת: וְלֹא נִמְלַט אִישׁ: צַדִּיק בָּאָרֶץ יְשֻׁלָּם[11]:
גֻּנֹּב גֻּנַּבְתִּי: אַל-תִּטַּמְּאוּ בְּכָל-אֵלֶּה: אֶשְׁתַּמֵּר מֵעֲוֹנִי[12]:
נָבָל נְבָלָה יְדַבֵּר:

§ 22. אֵת אֲשֶׁר-הִקְצַפְתָּ אֶת-יהוה: אֶל-שַׁדַּי[1] יִתְגַּבָּר[13]:
הַשְׁלִיכָה: מַשְׁלִיךְ: הַשְׁלֵךְ: וָאַשְׁלִיכָה: תַּשְׁלֵךְ:
הַשְׁלִיכוּ: מֻשְׁלָךְ: הָשְׁלַחְתִּי: הַסְתֵּר אַסְתִּיר פָּנַי[14]:
וְהִקְרִיב אַהֲרֹן[1] אֶת-הַפָּר: הַקְרֵב אֶת-הַמַּטֶּה: יַשְׁבִּית
הַזֶּבַח: בַּמָּה[15] אֲקַדֵּם יהוה: שֻׁלְחָן בַּמִּדְבָּר: לֹא-נָפַל דָּבָר
מִכֹּל הַדָּבָר הַטּוֹב אֲשֶׁר-דִּבֶּר יהוה: יִלְבְּשׁוּ-בֹשֶׁת:

§ 23. זְכֹר אַל-תִּשְׁכַּח: בְּשַׁלַּח מֹשֶׁה: וַיַּשְׁלֵךְ אֶת-
הָאֶבֶן: בֶּאֱמֶת וּבְלֵבָב שָׁלֵם[16]: וְאֶת-הָעָם הֶעֱבִיר: אֲשֶׁר
בְּעֵבֶר הַיַּרְדֵּן[1]: תַּעַזְבוּ אֶת-יהוה: וְנֶעֱזַרְתִּי: לֹא-מָצָא
עֹזֵר: וְהַאֲבַדְתִּי אֶת-הַנֶּפֶשׁ[17] הַהִיא: צֶדֶק צֶדֶק תִּרְדֹּף:

---

1 p.n. 2 בְּ = for (of price). 3 wall. 4 to thyself. Note retraction of tone in preceding word. § 20. 1. R. 2. 5 lest. 6 Adv. accus. 7 my lord. 8 in which. § 10. 4. 9 seven. 10 see יוֹם. 11 be rewarded. 12 from my iniquity. 13 in p. 14 my face. 15 § 12. 1. 16 Adj., whole, perfect. 17 soul, person.

אֶת־מִי תַעַבְדוּן[1]: לֹא יֵאָסְפוּ וְלֹא יִקָּבֵרוּ: לֹא הֶאֱמִינוּ
בַּיהוה: וַיֶּחֱזַק הָרָעָב[2] בָּאָרֶץ: וַיֶּחְדַּל הַנָּבִיא[3]: שְׁמַע־
אַתָּה וְהֶחָכָם[1]: לָמָּה זֶּה עֲזַבְתֶּן אֶת־הָאִישׁ:

§ 24. וְשָׁחַטְתָּ אֶת־הַפָּר: רְחַץ[4] וּטְהָר: לָמָּה זֶּה
תִּשְׁאַל: וַיְבָרֶךְ אֵת כָּל־הַקָּהָל: נִקְהֲלוּ הַיְּהוּדִים[5]:
וַיהוה בֵּרַךְ[6] אֶת־אַבְרָהָם בַּכֹּל: אֵת אֲשֶׁר־תְּבָרֵךְ מְבֹרָךְ:
אֶפְקְדָה אֶת־הָאָרֶץ אֲשֶׁר אַתָּה יֹשֵׁב בָּהּ: עֶזְרָתָה:
וּפְלִשְׁתִּים[7] נִלְחֲמוּ בְּיִשְׂרָאֵל: הַנַּעַר[8] מְשָׁרֵת אֶת־יהוה:
הִטָּהֲרוּ הַכֹּהֲנִים[9]: גָּרֵשׁ אֲגָרֵשׁ אֶתְכֶם[10] מִזֶּה: לִפְנֵי[11]
שַׁחֵת יהוה אֶת־סְדֹם[12]: וָאֶזְעַק קוֹל־גָּדוֹל: לְשָׁרֵת עֵץ
וָאָבֶן: אַל־תַּשְׁחֵת:

§ 25. לֹא יִשְׂבְּעוּ־לָחֶם: קִדַּמְתִּי לִבְרֹחַ תַּרְשִׁישָׁה[12]:
וַיִּשְׁבֹּת בַּיּוֹם הַשְּׁבִיעִי: וַיִּבָּקְעוּ הַמָּיִם: וַיִּפְשְׁעוּ יִשְׂרָאֵל
בְּבֵית[13] דָּוִד[12]: וַאֲמַרְתֶּם יְחִי[14] הַמֶּלֶךְ: כִּי־יִצְעַק וְשָׁמַעְתִּי:
כִּי לֹא יִשְׁקֹט הָאִישׁ: וַיִּמְשַׁח אֶת־הַמִּשְׁכָּן: וַיִּפְגְּעוּ אֶת־
מֹשֶׁה וְאֶת־אַהֲרֹן: לִמְדוּ לְהִשָּׁבֵעַ בַּבַּעַל[15]: אֶשְׁמְעָה:
בְּהִשָּׁמַע: שְׁלַח: שָׁבַחְתָּ: וְאֶשְׁלְחָה סֵפֶר[16] אֶל[17]־
הַמֶּלֶךְ: בֵּן חָכָם יְשַׂמַּח־אָב:

§ 26. כִּי מָרִים הֵם: אַתָּה סֵתֶר מִצָּר: שִׁיר הַשִּׁירִים
אֲשֶׁר לִשְׁלֹמֹה[12]: כֹּל הַשָּׂרִים וְהַגִּבּוֹרִים: הָהָר מָלֵא[18]
סוּסִים: מַשְׁבִּית מִלְחָמוֹת: מִן־הַחֲמֹרִים: וַיַּשְׁכֵּן מִקֶּדֶם
לְגַן־עֵדֶן[19] אֶת־הַכְּרוּבִים: שְׁבֻעוֹת: בְּאֵרֹת: גְּבוּלִים:
שְׁמוּעוֹת: פִּקּוּדִים: קוֹלוֹת: עוֹרוֹת: אוֹרִים[20]: חֲלֹמוֹת:
יְאֹרִים: טוֹבָה: רִאשֹׁנָה: שַׂר הַטַּבָּחִים:

---

1 in p. 2 famine. 3 prophet. 4 wash. 5 the Jews. 6 frequently ַ for ֵ here. 7 Philistines. 8 young man. 9 *pl.* 10 you. 11 before. 12 p.n. 13 against the house of. 14 (long) live! 15 בְּ = by. 16 letter. 17 to. 18 Verbs denoting fulness or want are followed by an accus. without a Prep. 19 of the garden of Eden. 20 Only in Ps. cxxxvi. 7.

§ 27. שָׁכַבְתִּי וְאֶשְׁקוֹט׃ אֶרֶץ הָרִים וּבְקָעֹת׃ אִישׁ
דָּמִים[1] אַתָּה׃ וּפָרַצְתָּ יָמָּה[2] וָקֵדְמָה וְצָפֹנָה׃ הָכְרַת
הַמִּנְחָה׃ אָחוּז׃ אֱחֹז׃ בֶּאֱחֹז׃ אֶחֱזוּ׃ אֹחֵז׃ הָאֳחַז׃
מֵאֲחָזִים׃ אֲחֻזָּה בָאָרֶץ׃ אֶת־הַנֵּרוֹת עַל[3]־הַמְּנֹרָה הַטְּהֹרָה׃
הַנִּשְׁאָרִים אֲשֶׁר נִשְׁאֲרוּ מִן־הַשֶּׁבִי׃ וְלֹא נִמְצָא חֶרֶב
וַחֲנִית׃ מַחֲנֵה אֱלֹהִים זֶה וַיִּקְרָא שֵׁם־הַמָּקוֹם הַהוּא
מַחֲנָיִם׃ כַּצִּפֳּרִים הָאֲחֻזוֹת׃ וְחָרְבוּ יְאֹרֵי מָצוֹר[4]׃ פְּקֻדַּת
הַמֶּלֶךְ׃ עֶזְרָה בְצָרוֹת נִמְצָא מְאֹד׃

§ 28. שְׁבוּתְךָ׃ אַתֶּם עֵדַי׃ לְדוֹרֹתֵיכֶם׃ דָּבַקְתִּי
בְעֵדְוֹתֶיךָ[5]׃ וַיִּשְׁמֹר מִצְוֹתַי וְחֻקּוֹתָי׃ שָׁמַע בְּקֹלִי[6]׃ אִישׁ
רִיב׃ חֲנִיתוֹתֵיהֶם׃ שִׁירַת דּוֹדִי׃ וַיְסַפֵּר אֶת־חֲלֹמוֹ׃ עִבְדוּ
אֶת־יהוה בְּשִׂמְחָה׃ אִמְרוֹת יהוה׃ עַל־רָאשֵׁי[7] הָעַמּוּדִים׃
יהוה אוֹרִי׃ מַלְכוּתוֹ בַּכֹּל מָשָׁלָה׃ נַעֲבֹר גְּבֻלֶךָ[5]׃ כֹּל
הַמִּשְׁפָּחוֹת הַנִּשְׁאָרוֹת׃ שִׁפְחוֹתֵיכֶם׃ אַתֵּן צֹאנִי׃ עֵדֵיהֶם
הֵמָּה׃ וּמֶה־חַטָּאתִי׃ אִשָּׁה זָקֵן׃ אִישׁ אֱלֹהִים קָדוֹשׁ׃
בַּת־צִיּוֹן כְּסֻכָּה בְכָרֶם׃

§ 29. שֹׁד וָשֶׁבֶר בִּגְבוּלָיִךְ׃ הֲגַם[8] שָׁאוּל בַּנְּבִיאִים׃
נְגִיד הַבְּרִית׃ לֹא־יַעֲזֹב אֶת־חֲסִידָיו׃ זֶה עָנִי קָרָא וַיהוה
שָׁמֵעַ׃ זְכָר־עָנְיִי׃ עִם־הַנְּדִיבִים׃ נְשִׂיא אֱלֹהִים אַתָּה׃
בְּזֹאת יְכֻפַּר עֲוֹן־יַעֲקֹב[9]׃ הַמְּאֹרֹת הַגְּדֹלִים׃ וַאֲרוֹן אֱלֹהִים
נִלְקַח׃ כְּבוֹד מַלְכוּתְךָ׃ גְּבוּרָתְךָ יְדַבֵּרוּ[5]׃ וְלֹא־נִצְפַּן
עֲוֹנָם מִנֶּגֶד עֵינָי[5]׃

§ 30. חָלָה בֶן־הָאִשָּׁה׃ הַבּוֹגֵד בּוֹגֵד וְהַשּׁוֹדֵד שׁוֹדֵד׃

---

[1] *Pl.*, generally refers to blood shed criminally. [2] יָם sea (seaward = westward). [3] On, upon. [4] Egypt. [5] in p. [6] Defectively written. Many verbs, as here, require a Prep. with the word with which they are construed. [7] See רֹאשׁ. [8] also. [9] p.n.

זְבַח לֵאלֹהִים תּוֹדָה׃ מִיַּד־מִי לָקַחְתִּי כֹפֶר׃ חֲזוֹן יְשַׁעְיָהוּ[1] בֶן־אָמוֹץ אֲשֶׁר חָזָה׃ יִשְׁפֹּט עֲנִיֵּי־הָעָם׃ עַל־מִטָּתוֹ׃ מַטֵּה לֶחֶם׃ כִּי־נָטָה אֶל־אֵל יָדוֹ׃ זָכַרְתִּי מִשְׁפָּטֶיךָ מֵעוֹלָם׃ יָכְלוּ עוֹד לַעֲמֹד לִפְנֵי[2] אוֹיְבֵיהֶם׃ דָּמוֹ נִגְרַשׁ׃ יהוה שִׁמְךָ לְעוֹלָם׃ כֹּהֲנֶיךָ יִלְבְּשׁוּ־צֶדֶק׃ בְּכֹל מוֹשְׁבֹתֵיכֶם׃ טֻמְאָתוֹ אֲשֶׁר יִטְמָא בָהּ׃ אַתָּה מָרוֹם לְעֹלָם יהוה׃

§ 31. קִרְיַת[1]־סֵפֶר[1]׃ מָלֵא רוּחַ[3] חָכְמָה כִּי־סָמַךְ מֹשֶׁה אֶת־יָדָיו׃ בְּצַוְּארֵי גְמַלֵּיהֶם׃ מַשָּׂא דְבַר יהוה׃ קוֹלִי אֶל־בְּנֵי אָדָם׃ אִישׁ[4] עֹבֵד אֲדָמָה אָנֹכִי׃ אֶת־לֵב הָאֶבֶן מִבְּשַׂרְכֶם׃ כַּנְפֵי הַכְּרוּבִים׃ נוֹטֶה[5] כְנָהָר שָׁלוֹם׃ וְכָתַב אֶת־מִשְׁנֵה הַתּוֹרָה[6] הַזֹּאת׃ כְּמִשְׁתֵּה הַמֶּלֶךְ׃ הִשְׁבַּתִּי[7] אֶת־הַמָּשָׁל הַזֶּה׃ בִּרְכוֹתֵיכֶם׃ זְקַן בֵּיתוֹ[8]׃ וַיְגָרֶשׁ אֶת־הָאָדָם׃ וְיֵאָמְנוּ דִבְרֵיכֶם׃ מְכַבְּדַי אֲכַבֵּד׃ טָבְחָה טִבְחָהּ׃ כֹּל צִפּוֹר כָּל־כָּנָף׃

§ 32. רַגְלֵי מְבַשֵּׂר מַשְׁמִיעַ שָׁלוֹם׃ בְּצֶדֶק כָּל־אִמְרֵי פִי׃ בְּדֶרֶךְ חַטָּאִים לֹא עָמָד׃ כָּל־חֵטְא אֲשֶׁר יֶחֱטָא׃ אַדְמַת־קֹדֶשׁ הוּא׃ עַד־אָבוֹא[9] אֶל־מִקְדְּשֵׁי־אֵל׃ וְהַאֲזַנְתָּ לְמִצְוֹתָיו וְשָׁמַרְתָּ כָּל־חֻקָּיו׃ בִּכֹרֵי יִשְׂרָאֵל׃ מְכָרָה אֶת־בְּכֹרָתְךָ׃ אֶת־נִדְרוֹ אֲשֶׁר נָדָר׃ מִכַּף רֶגֶל וְעַד־רֹאשׁ׃ שֶׁמֶן הַמָּאוֹר׃ שֶׁמֶשׁ צְדָקָה׃ שֹׁרֶשׁ הַדָּבָר[10]׃ מַה־פִּשְׁעִי׃ בֵּינִי וּבֵין כַּרְמִי׃ וְכִבֶּס אֶת־בְּגָדָיו הַכֹּהֵן׃ זִבְחֵי־צֶדֶק׃

§ 33. אֹזֶן שֹׁמַעַת וְעַיִן רֹאָה׃ וַיִּפְרֹשׂ אֶת־הָאֹהֶל עַל־הַמִּשְׁכָּן׃ אֶלֶף[11] כָּסֶף׃ אֲלָפֶיךָ[12]׃ שַׂמֵּחַ נֶפֶשׁ עַבְדֶּךָ׃

---

[1] p.n. [2] before. [3] spirit. [4] Note the idiom. [5] extending. [6] law. [7] Note contraction. [8] See בַּיִת. [9] I came. [10] matter. [11] *pieces*, understood, as often the case with words commonly used in measurements. [12] Kine. It is of com. gender, except in *pl*.

לְקָחוּ אִישׁ[1] חַרְבּוֹ׃ לַבֹּקֶר וְלָעֶרֶב׃ כָּרְתוּ יַעְרָהּ׃ אֶת־כָּל־נְחֻשְׁתָּם בָּבֶלָה[5]׃ יְמֵי נְעוּרֶיהָ׃ נַעֲרֵי בְנֵי יִשְׂרָאֵל׃ אַל־תִּשְׁכַּח לָנֶצַח׃ מַה־פָּעַל אֵל׃ כְּכָל־חֻקַּת הַפֶּסַח׃ אֲדַבְּרָה הַפָּעַם׃ פְּעֻלָּתוֹ אֲשֶׁר־עָבַד בָּהּ׃ וְדָרְשׁוּ[2] מֵחָרְבוֹתֵיהֶם׃ כִּסֵּא מַמְלַכְתּוֹ עַד־עוֹלָם׃ מִלְחַמְתִּי׃ עַל־דַּלְתֹתַי יוֹם יוֹם[3]׃ שָׂרָה אִשְׁתּוֹ[4]׃ מַלְכַּת־שְׁבָא[5] שֹׁמַעַת אֶת־שֵׁמַע שְׁלֹמֹה׃ וּפִתְּחוּ שְׁעָרַיִךְ תָּמִיד׃

§ 34. מִנְחָה לְעֵשָׂו[5] אָחִיו׃ וַיִּשְׁמְעוּ אֶחָיו׃ לָמָּה אָמַרְתָּ אֲחֹתִי הִוא׃ וּתְדַבֶּר־נָא אֲמָתְךָ בְּאָזְנֶיךָ׃ הַשֻּׁלְחָן וְכֵלָיו׃ וַנִּלְכֹּד אֶת־כָּל־עָרָיו׃ אֶלֶף אַמָּה׃ לֹא־יֶחְדַּל אֶבְיוֹן מִקֶּרֶב הָאָרֶץ׃ טוֹב תַּאֲוַת צַדִּיקִים׃ יַעֲזָב־אִישׁ אֶת־אָבִיו וְאֶת־אִמּוֹ וְדָבַק בְּאִשְׁתּוֹ׃ יהוה רֹאֶה כְלָיוֹת וָלֵב׃ רוּת[5] כַּלָּתָהּ׃ אֱלֹהִים אֲחֵרִים׃ חֹדֶשׁ מָחָר׃ אַחֲרִית לְאִישׁ שָׁלוֹם׃ אֶת[6]־אַחֲרֹנִים אֲנִי־הוּא׃ וְהָשְׁלוּ אָחוֹר׃ וְלֹא־אָבָה יהוה לְהַשְׁחִית אֶת־בֵּית דָּוִד׃

§ 35. שְׁנֵי נְעָרָיו׃ שְׁתֵּי בָנוֹת׃ שְׁנֵיהֶם׃ אַרְבַּע בְּאַמָּה[7]׃ שִׁבְעָה שְׁבֻעֹת תִּסְפֹּר׃ בֶּן שְׁמֹנֶה שָׁנָה׃ עֲשֶׂרֶת בְּנֵי הָמָן[5]׃ מִסְפָּרָם עֶשְׂרִים וּשְׁנַיִם אֶלֶף וְשֵׁשׁ מֵאוֹת׃ בְּיוֹם עֶשְׂרִים וְאַרְבָּעָה לְעַשְׁתֵּי־עָשָׂר חֹדֶשׁ׃ וְאִלּוּ[8] חָיָה אֶלֶף שָׁנִים׃ שֵׁשֶׁת יָמִים תַּעֲבֹד׃ בַּשָּׁנָה הַשִּׁשִּׁית׃

§ 36. מוֹצָא[9] שְׂפָתֶיךָ תִּשְׁמֹר׃ פַּלְּטָה נַפְשִׁי׃ פַּחַד פָּחַדְתִּי[10]׃ הַפַּח נִשְׁבָּר וַאֲנַחְנוּ נִמְלָטְנוּ׃ גִּדֶּלְךָ בְּעֵינֵי כָל־יִשְׂרָאֵל׃ בְּזָבְחוֹ אֶת־הַזְּבָחִים׃ בְּקֻצְרְכֶם אֶת־קְצִיר אַרְצְכֶם׃ רֹכֶבֶת עַל־הַחֲמוֹר׃ לִשְׁמָרְךָ בַּדָּרֶךְ׃ אָנֹכִי לֹא

---

[1] every man. [2] *their bread*, understood. [3] day by day. [4] See אִשָּׁה. [5] p.n. [6] with. [7] Note construction. [8] if. [9] From יצא. Note final vowel. [10] Numerous verbs are followed by a cognate accus.

שִׁלַּחְתִּים׃ רְחֹבוֹת הָעִיר יִמָּלְאוּ יְלָדִים וִילָדוֹת׃ יָצָאתִי
לְהַשְׂכִּילְךָ בִינָה[1]׃ חֲמִשִּׁים אַמָּה רָחְבָּהּ׃ פָּחֲדוּ וְרָגְזוּ׃
הִשְׁבִּיעֶךָ׃ הִשְׁבַּעְתָּנוּ׃ לְשָׁרְתוֹ׃ בְּעָבְרְכֶם אֶת־הַיַּרְדֵּן[2]׃

§ 37. תִּפְשׂוּם חַיִּים׃ לֹא בִקַּשְׁתֶּהוּ בְּכָל־זֹאת׃ טוֹב
וָחֶסֶד יִרְדְּפוּנִי׃ תִּשְׂרְפֻנוּ׃ אֲשֶׁר לִמְּדוּם אֲבוֹתָם׃ כַּבֵּס
בַּיַּיִן לְבֻשׁוֹ׃ בָּקַע יָם וַיַּעֲבִירֵם׃ סְלַח־נָא לַעֲוֹן הָעָם
הַזֶּה׃ וּצְרַפְתִּים כִּצְרֹף אֶת־הַכֶּסֶף׃ מֵאָה שֶׁקֶל־כֶּסֶף׃
לֹא הָיָה מִשְׁקָל לַנְּחֹשֶׁת׃ וַיַּבְדֵּל אלהים בֵּין הָאוֹר
וּבֵין הַחֹשֶׁךְ׃ וַיִּשְׁלַח ישראל אֶת־יְמִינוֹ׃ תִּשְׁפְּכֻנוּ כַּמַּיִם׃
הַרְחֶב־פִּיךָ וַאֲמַלְאֵהוּ׃ וַיְקַטֵּר הַקְּטֹרֶת׃ כָּל־נֵבֶל יִמָּלֵא
יָיִן׃

§ 38. יֵשׁ יהוה בַּמָּקוֹם הַזֶּה׃ אַיּוֹ מֶלֶךְ־חֲמָת[2]׃ הִנְּנִי
בְנִי׃ אֵינֶנִּי בְּקִרְבְּכֶם׃ אֵינְכֶם מַאֲמִינִם ביהוה׃ הֲזָקֵן
אֲשֶׁר אֲמַרְתֶּם הַעוֹדֶנּוּ חָי[3]׃ אָז יַבְדִּיל מֹשֶׁה שָׁלֹשׁ עָרִים
בְּעֵבֶר הַיַּרְדֵּן׃ יַחְדָּו כֻּלָּם[4]׃ אֵין־קָדוֹשׁ כיהוה כִּי אֵין
בִּלְתֶּךָ׃ לֹא־טוֹב הֱיוֹת[5] הָאָדָם לְבַדּוֹ׃

§ 39. בִּלְתִּי אֲחִיכֶם אִתְּכֶם׃ הֵן הָאָדָם הָיָה כְּאַחַד
מִמֶּנּוּ׃ בְּעוֹד שַׁדַּי עִמָּדִי[6] סְבִיבוֹתַי נְעָרָי׃ כָּל־אֲשֶׁר
יֶשׁ־לוֹ׃ אִם־יֶשְׁךָ מְשַׁלֵּחַ אֶת־אָחִינוּ אִתָּנוּ׃ אֵין אִישׁ
עִמָּנוּ[6]׃ אֵינֶנּוּ אֵלַי כִּתְמוֹל[7] שִׁלְשֹׁם[7]׃ שֵׁן תַּחַת שֵׁן׃
עוֹדָם מְדַבְּרִים עִמּוֹ׃ זֶה הָאִשֶּׁה אשר תַּקְרִיבוּ ליהוה׃
אֶרֶץ אשר אֲבָנֶיהָ בַרְזֶל׃ הָרְסוּ חוֹמוֹתַיִךְ׃ כֹּהֵן לְאֵל
עֶלְיוֹן׃ עוֹלָה וְחַטָּאָה לֹא שָׁאָלְתָּ׃ חָמֵשׁ עֶשְׂרֵה אַמָּה
מִלְמַעְלָה גָּבְרוּ הַמָּיִם׃ שֵׁשׁ מַעֲלוֹת לַכִּסֵּא׃ כִּי־שְׁלֹמֹה

[1] Make thee skilful in understanding. [2] p.n. [3] in p. [4] Note change of ō (o) in a sharpened syllable. [5] *Inf. cstr.* of הָיָה. [6] Note use of strengthened form of עִם (with 1st Pers. *sing.* and *pl.*). [7] Adverbial expression for *heretofore*.

בִּנְךָ יִמְלֹךְ אַחֲרַי׃ וּשְׂרָפָהּ בָּאֵשׁ׃ יִלָּכְדוּ בְּחַבְלֵי־עֹנִי[1]׃
לְךָ לְבַדְּךָ חָטָאתִי׃ וַיַּרְכֵּב אֹתוֹ בְּמִרְכֶּבֶת הַמִּשְׁנֶה׃
קָרוֹב לָנוּ הִיא׃ הֲבֵל הֲבָלִים אָמַר קֹהֶלֶת׃

§ 40. אָרוּר[2] אַתָּה מִכָּל־בְּהֵמָה׃ וְאֵין אִישׁ מִבְּנֵי יִשְׂרָאֵל
טוֹב מִמֶּנּוּ׃ תַּחַת לְשׁוֹנֶךָ׃ כַּאֲלָפַיִם אַמָּה בַּמִּדָּה׃ תָּמִיד
יִגְדַּל אֱלֹהִים׃ הֶן־אֵלֶּה קְצוֹת דְּרָכָיו׃ מִקְצֵה הארץ וְעַד־
קְצֵה הארץ׃ קֶשֶׁת יְשַׁבֵּר׃ בְּעוֹד רָשָׁע לְנֶגְדִּי׃ לֹא טוֹב אָנֹכִי
מֵאֲבֹתָי׃ שֵׁם הַגְּדֹלָה לֵאָה[3]׃ הוּא אֱלֹהֵי הָאֱלֹהִים׃ וְדָוִד
הוּא הַקָּטָן׃ נִמְלָא בָתֵּינוּ[4] שָׁלָל׃ זֶבַח רְשָׁעִים תּוֹעֲבַת
יהוה׃ בְּתוֹךְ עַם־טְמֵא שְׂפָתַיִם אָנֹכִי יֹשֵׁב׃ הַאֲזִינָה עַמִּי
תּוֹרָתִי׃ יָבֵשׁ רֹאשׁ הַכַּרְמֶל[3]׃ עָשָׂה[5] אֶת־הַיָּם וְאֶת־
הַיַּבָּשָׁה׃ חָטָאנוּ רָשָׁעְנוּ׃ תּוֹעֲבַת שִׂפְתֵי רָשָׁע׃ אָנֹכִי
שָׁלוּחַ אֵלֶיךָ קָשָׁה[6]׃ וְתוֹרָה יְבַקְשׁוּ מִפִּיהוּ׃ דְּבַשׁ עַל־פְּנֵי[7]
הַשָּׂדֶה׃

§ 41. שְׁלֹשׁ מֵאוֹת אַמָּה אֹרֶךְ הַתֵּבָה[8] חֲמִשִּׁים אַמָּה
רָחְבָּהּ וּשְׁלֹשִׁים אַמָּה קוֹמָתָהּ׃ כָּל־הַמִּשְׁכָּב אֲשֶׁר
יִשְׁכַּב עָלָיו יִטְמָא׃ וַיֹּאמֶר לָהֶם יְהוֹשֻׁעַ[3]׃ לָכֶם אִישׁ אֶבֶן
אַחַת עַל־שִׁכְמוֹ׃ וְזָבַחְתָּ עָלָיו אֶת־עֹלֹתֶיךָ וְאֶת־שְׁלָמֶיךָ׃
וַיֶּאֱסֹף שְׁלֹמֹה[3] רֶכֶב וּפָרָשִׁים׃ אֱכֹל בְּשִׂמְחָה לַחְמֶךָ׃
לֹא תֹאכְלוּ מִמֶּנּוּ׃ מָה אֹמַר אֱלֹהֶם׃ וְיֹאחֵז[9] צַדִּיק דַּרְכּוֹ׃
שַׂר הָאֹפִים׃ יִפְתַּח יהוה לְךָ אֶת־אוֹצָרוֹ הַטּוֹב׃ כָּל־אֹכֶל
תְּתַעֵב[10] נַפְשָׁם׃ מִכָּל־מַאֲכָל אֲשֶׁר יֵאָכֵל׃ וְאָפָה לָהֶם׃
וַיַּקְטֵר מֹשֶׁה אֶת־כָּל־הָאַיִל׃ אֹרַח לְחַיִּים׃ יַאֲרִיךְ יָמִים׃
הַשְׁלִיכוּ אֹתוֹ אֶל־הַבּוֹר הַזֶּה׃ בַּחֲרוּ לָכֶם[11] הַיּוֹם׃ שְׁמַע

---

[1] Affliction = עֳנִי in p. [2] Cursed. [3] p.n. [4] See p. 9, foot-note. [5] He made. [6] hard (tidings). [7] face, surface of. [8] the ark. [9] hold (on). [10] R. of תּוֹעֵבָה. [11] § 39. 1. R. 4.

יְהוָה קוֹל בְּכִי: עוֹד הָעָם מְזַבְּחִים וּמְקַטְּרִים בַּבָּמוֹת:
יֹאבַד: יֹאבֵד: תֹּאבֵדוּן: תֹּאבְדוּ: נֹאבְדָה: הַבַּחוּרִים
כָּשֹׁל יִכָּשֵׁלוּ:

§ 42. וְעָשָׂה[1] קָצִיר כְּמוֹ־נָטַע: נְאֻם־אֲדֹנָי יֱהוִֹה[2]: נֻגְּבָה:
לִנְגֹּעַ[3]: כְּגַעַת: וְגַע בְּכָל־אֲשֶׁר־לוֹ: יִגַּע: נְגַע: שֶׁמַּגִּיעַ:
יַגִּיעֶנָּה: נֹגֵעַ: וַיִּתֵּן יהוה דֶּבֶר וַיִּפֹּל שִׁבְעִים אֶלֶף אִישׁ:
יהוה נֹגֵף מַגֵּפָה גְדוֹלָה: וּבְתוֹךְ[4] בְּנֵי ישׂראל לֹא יִנָּחֲלוּ
נַחֲלָה: עַל־שְׂפַת־הַנַּחַל: נִחַם: וַיִּנָּחֶם: לְנַחֲמוֹ: מִתְנַחֵם:
הֲנֹטַע אֹזֶן הֲלֹא יִשְׁמָע: וְיַעֲקֹב[5] נָסַע סֻכֹּתָה: וַיַּצֵּב יַעֲקֹב
מַצֵּבָה וַיַּסֵּךְ עָלֶיהָ נֶסֶךְ: נִצַּל: נִצֵּל: הַמֶּלֶךְ הִצִּילָנוּ מִכַּף
אֹיְבֵנוּ: תִּצְּרֶנּוּ מִן הַדּוֹר זוּ[6] לְעוֹלָם: נֹצֵר פִּיו שֹׁמֵר
נַפְשׁוֹ: וַיִּסַּע מִשָּׁם אַרְצָה[7] הַנֶּגֶב: האלהים נִסָּה אֶת־
אברהם: וַיְטַמֵּא אֶת־הַבָּמוֹת אֲשֶׁר קִטְּרוּ שָׁמָּה[8]: נִגַּשׁ:
גַּשׁ פְּגַע בּוֹ:

§ 43. וְאִם לֹא תֵיטִיב לַפֶּתַח חַטָּאת רֹבֵץ[9]: אָנֹכִי לֹא
אוּכַל לְהִמָּלֵט הָהָרָה: וְיָדַעְתָּ: יֹדֵעַ: לָדַעַת: יָדֹעַ: דְּעוּ:
וְאֵדְעָה: יֵדָעֶנּוּ: יִוָּדַע: הוֹדִיעוּ: הִוָּסְרוּ שֹׁפְטֵי אָרֶץ:
אֱמֶת קְנֵה[10] וְאַל תִּמְכֹּר: חָכְמָה וּמוּסָר וּבִינָה: וַיִּירְאוּ
מִגֶּשֶׁת אֵלָיו: נוֹסַף: הוֹסִיף: אֹסִיף: לֹא אֹסִף לְקַלֵּל עוֹד
אֶת־הָאֲדָמָה: לְבִלְתִּי לֶכֶת אַחֲרֵי הַבַּחוּרִים: בְּלֶכְתּוֹ
לִדְרוֹשׁ אלהים: לְכוּ וְנֵלְכָה: לְכָה וְנִוָּעֲדָה יַחְדָּו: וַיֵּצְאוּ
כָּל־בְּנֵי ישׂראל וַתִּקָּהֵל הָעֵדָה: לְכִי אִיעָצֵךְ נָא עֵצָה:
וַיִּצֹק שֶׁמֶן עַל־רֹאשָׁהּ: הֲיִצַּר עַיִן הֲלֹא יַבִּיט: יָרְדָה:
בְּרֶדֶת הַמֶּלֶךְ אֵלָיו: רֵד: רְדָה: הוֹרִיד: וְיוֹסֵף[5] הוּרַד

---

[1] make. [2] Note vowels. [3] § **3**. 4. foot-note. [4] תָּוֶךְ. [5] p.n. [6] § **10**. 1. R. 4.
[7] Note ה *locative* with *cstr*. [8] אֲשֶׁר . . . שָׁמָּה, usually *whither*, here *where*.
[9] croucheth. [10] Buy.

מִצְרַיְמָה׃ בַּמָּה אֵדַע כִּי אִירָשֶׁנָּה׃ לְרִשְׁתָּהּ׃ הוֹבִישׁ תִּירוֹשׁ׃ וַתֹּסֶף[1] לָלֶדֶת אֶת־אָחִיו׃ הָלְכוּ בַיַּבָּשָׁה בְּתוֹךְ הַיָּם׃ פֶּתַח מִשְׁכַּן אֹהֶל־מוֹעֵד׃

§ 44. לְכָה אִתָּנוּ וְהֵטַבְנוּ[2] לָךְ[3]׃ רָמָה׃ הָרָמָה׃ כְּרֹם׃ וַתָּרָם׃ וַיָּרֶם׃ הוּרַם׃ בְּקוּם לַמִּשְׁפָּט אלהים׃ קוּמָה יהוה הוֹשִׁיעֵנִי׃ אַל־אֵבוֹשׁ׃ בּוֹשָׁה אִמְּכֶם מְאֹד׃ וּפָתַח וְאֵין סֹגֵר׃ מִי גֶבֶר יִחְיֶה וְלֹא יִרְאֶה[4] מָוֶת׃ לְכָל־יָבוֹא... גְּבוּרָתֶךָ׃ קֵץ כָּל־בָּשָׂר בָּא׃ מְבוֹא הַשֶּׁמֶשׁ׃ תְּבוּאַת רָשָׁע לְחַטָּאת׃ אֵשׁ לְהָאִיר לָיְלָה׃ וּבָא וְלָן וְשָׁכַב אָרְצָה[3]׃ מוּת׃ מֵת׃ מוֹת׃ וַיָּמֹת׃ וַיָּמָת׃ וַיָּמֶת׃ וַתּוּמַת׃ וַהֲמִיתִיו׃ נָחָה שָׁקְטָה כָּל־הארץ׃ כַּאֲשֶׁר יָנִיחַ יָדוֹ וְגָבַר עֲמָלֵק[5]׃ וְהִנִּיחַ[6] מִחוּץ לַמַּחֲנֶה׃ מְמִתִים יָדְךָ יהוה׃ וַיִּפְתַּח הַדֶּלֶת וַיָּנֹס׃ וְנוֹעַ יָנוּעוּ בָנָיו׃ אֲשֶׁר הֵנִיף תְּנוּפַת[7] זָהָב[8] ליהוה׃ נָסוּ וְאֵין־רֹדֵף רָשָׁע׃ וְהִקְרַבְתֶּם עוֹלָה ליהוה רֵיחַ[9] נִיחֹחַ

§ 45. אֵין נִשְׁפָּט בֶּאֱמוּנָה׃ עֶבְרָתוֹ שְׁמָרָה[10] נֶצַח׃ אֲשֶׁר־גָּר־שָׁם אברהם׃ גֵּר אנכי עִמָּךְ׃ נָבוֹן׃ בּוֹנֵן׃ הָבֵן׃ בִּינוּ׃ עַמִּי לֹא הִתְבּוֹנֵן[11]׃ בְּנֵי צִיּוֹן גִּילוּ וְשִׂמְחוּ ביהוה׃ חָלָה[12] גַּם[13]־יָלְדָה צִיּוֹן׃ לִבִּי יָחִיל בְּקִרְבִּי׃ וַיָּחֶל עוֹד שִׁבְעַת יָמִים׃ יֵלְכוּ מֵחַיִל אֶל־חָיִל׃ כְּחוֹל אשר עַל־שְׂפַת־הַיָּם׃ קוּם בְּתוּלַת ישראל׃ שָׁתוּ בַשָּׁמַיִם פִּיהֶם׃ אַל־תָּשֶׁת יָדְךָ עִם־רָשָׁע׃ שָׂמַנִי אלהים לְאָדוֹן׃ שִׂים־נָא כָבוֹד ליהוה׃ שִׂימָה־לָּנוּ[14] מֶלֶךְ׃ וַיָּשֶׂם כַּצֹּאן מִשְׁפָּחוֹת׃

---

[1] Note change of vowel from ֵי to ֵ, to ֶ; also the idiom. [2] טוֹב. [3] in p. [4] lives and shall not see. [5] p.n. [6] *them*, to be understood. [7] offered an offering. [8] gold. [9] odor. [10] For שָׁמְרָה with tone retracted. [11] consider. [12] חוּל. [13] also. [14] D. forte *conjunctive*.

לֹֽא־תַעֲזֹב נַפְשִׁי לִשְׁאוֹל לֹא תִתֵּן חֲסִידְךָ[1] לִרְאוֹת[2]
שָׁחַת׃ וְצַרְתָּ הַכֶּסֶף בְּיָדְךָ׃ אָחוֹר וָקֶדֶם צַרְתָּנִי׃ שָׁפְטֵנִי
אלהים וְרִיבָה רִיבִי׃ שִׁירוּ־לוֹ שִׁיר חָדָשׁ׃ וְחֵילוֹ יָרָה
בַיָּם׃

§ 46. בְּשׁוּב אלהים שְׁבוּת עַמּוֹ יָגֵל יַעֲקֹב יִשְׂמַח
יִשְׂרָאֵל׃ לְךָ יוֹם אַף־לְךָ לָיְלָה׃ עַד־שׁוּב אַף־אָחִיךָ
מִמְּךָ׃ וַתִּפֹּל עַל־אַפֶּיהָ אַרְצָה׃ עַל־לְבוּשִׁי יַפִּילוּ גוֹרָל׃
בְּיִרְאַת יהוה סוּר מֵרָע׃ וְנָסוֹרָה׃ הֲסִירֹתָ׃ הָסֵר׃ וַיָּסַר׃
וְיָסֵר׃ וַיְסִרֵהוּ׃ יְשְׁבֵיהֶן קִצְרֵי־יָד[3]׃ חַתּוּ וַיֵּבֹשׁוּ׃ בְּרֹב
חַסְדְּךָ אָבוֹא בֵיתֶךָ׃ רַבָּה רָעַת הָאָדָם בארץ׃ מְרֵעִים
יִכָּרֵתוּן׃ לְהָרֵעַ׃ וַיֵּרַע בְּעֵינֵי יהוה׃ רַבַּת[4] צְרָרוּנִי מִנְּעוּרָי׃
וַתָּבוֹא הָעִיר בַּמָּצוֹר׃ דָּבַקְתִּי בְעֵדְוֹתֶיךָ יהוה אַל־
תְּבִישֵׁנִי׃ וְהָיָה לְעֵד בֵּינִי וּבֵינֶךָ׃ יהוה מֶלֶךְ עוֹלָם וָעֶד[5]׃
סֹבּוּ וְהֵמִיתוּ כֹּהֲנֵי יהוה׃ אֲשֶׁר לֹא־יִמַּד וְלֹא יִסָּפֵר׃

§ 47. כָּל־מִשְׁכָּבוֹ הָפַכְתָּ בְחָלְיוֹ׃ טוֹב־לִי תוֹרַת־פִּיךָ
מֵאַלְפֵי זָהָב וָכָסֶף[6]׃ בְּקָרְאִי עֲנֵנִי אֱלֹהֵי צִדְקִי׃ וְעַתָּה
הָשֵׁב אֵשֶׁת־הָאִישׁ׃ לְמַעַן הָבִיא יהוה עַל־אברהם את
אשר־דִּבֶּר עָלָיו׃ יַעַן אֲשֶׁר הָיְתָה זֹאת עִם־לְבָבֶךָ׃ עֵת
לָטַעַת׃ עֵת לִבְנוֹת׃ חֶרֶב עוּרִי עַל־רֹעִי׃ וַיֹּאמְרוּ אִישׁ
אֶל־רֵעֵהוּ[7]׃ חַסְדְּכֶם כַּעֲנַן בֹּקֶר׃ הוֹדִינוּ לְךָ אלהים׃
מוֹדֶה׃ אוֹדֶנּוּ׃ אֲשֶׁר קָרְךָ בַּדֶּרֶךְ׃ אַךְ־הֶבֶל[8] יֶהֱמָיוּן[6]׃
לֵאמוֹר מַה־נִּשְׁתֶּה׃ עָלִיתָ לַמָּרוֹם שָׁבִיתָ שֶּׁבִי[6]׃ לַמְנַצֵּחַ׃
הֶעֱוִינוּ הִרְשָׁעְנוּ׃ כָּל־הַיּוֹם הִתְאַוָּה תַאֲוָה׃

---

1 Kᵉthibh. 2 to see. 3 i.e., moved exceedingly. 4 much (adverbial). 5 עֶד changed for euphonic reasons after וָ. 6 in p. 7 Note the idiom = said among themselves, to one another. 8 in vain.

§ 48. וַיְכַס הֶעָנָן אֶת־אֹהֶל מוֹעֵד׃ וַיֵּבְךְּ יוֹסֵף בְּדַבְּרָם
אֵלָיו׃ הֶרֶף[1] מֵאַף׃ הַחֲזֵק בַּמּוּסָר אַל־תֶּרֶף׃ וַיְצַף אֶת־
הַכְּרוּבִים זָהָב[2]׃ עָשׂוּ אֵת כָּל־אֲשֶׁר צִוִּיתִךָ׃ הִכָּה בְּכוֹרֵי
מִצְרַיִם׃ לְהַצִּיל אֶת־אִישָׁהּ מִיַּד מַכֵּהוּ׃ וְהַךְ כַּף אֶל־כַּף׃
מָה הַמַּכּוֹת הָאֵלֶּה בֵּין יָדֶיךָ׃ אֲשֶׁר־הִכִּיתָ בָּעֵמֶק׃
לַעֲשֹׂתוֹ׃ הַטּוֹב בְּעֵינֶיךָ עֲשֵׂה׃ וַיַּעַשׂ לָהּ אֶת־נִדְרוֹ׃ אֵת
פֹּעַל יהוה לֹא יַבִּיטוּ וּמַעֲשֵׂה יָדָיו לֹא רָאוּ׃ קוּמָה
עֶזְרָתָה לָּנוּ וּפְדֵנוּ לְמַעַן חַסְדֶּךָ׃ וַיִּפֶן אלהים לְמַעַן
בְּרִיתוֹ׃ פַּנּוּ דֶּרֶךְ יהוה׃ הִיא הָיְתָה לְרֹאשׁ פִּנָּה׃ שֹׂבַע[3]
שְׂמָחוֹת אֶת־פָּנֶיךָ׃ לְפָנַי׃ לִפְנֵיהֶם׃ וַיִּתֵּן אֶת־הַכְּרוּבִים
בְּתוֹךְ הַבַּיִת הַפְּנִימִי׃ בֹּאוּ נִשְׁתַּחֲוֶה וְנִכְרָעָה[4]׃ הַגִּידָה־נָּא
לָנוּ בַּאֲשֶׁר לְמִי[5]־הָרָעָה׃ יהוה בּוֹרֵא הַשָּׁמַיִם וְנוֹטֵיהֶם[6]׃
נְטוֹת׃ נְטֵה׃ וַיֵּט־שָׁם אָהֳלוֹ׃ נֹטֶה׃ נָטָה׃ כִּי־הִטָּה אָזְנוֹ
לִי׃ הַטֵּה׃ הַט׃ וְאַט׃ וָאַט׃ עָמַד וַיְמֹדֶד אֶרֶץ[7]׃ הוֹדִיעֵנִי
יהוה קִצִּי וּמִדַּת יָמַי מַה־הִיא׃ פֶּן־תְּמֻתוּן׃

§ 49. אִם־צָמֵא שֹׂנַאֲךָ הַשְׁקֵהוּ מָיִם׃ אִם־תַּחֲנֶה עָלַי
מַחֲנֶה לֹא־יִירָא לִבִּי׃ וַיַּרְא אלהים אֶת־הָאוֹר כִּי־טוֹב׃
יֵרָאֶה׃ וַתֵּרֶא הָאִשָּׁה כִּי טוֹב׃ אֵל שַׁדַּי נִרְאָה־אֵלַי׃ וַיֵּרָא
יהוה׃ וַיִּבֶן שָׁם מִזְבֵּחַ׃ וַנֵּפֶן וַנִּסַּע הַמִּדְבָּרָה׃ וַיֵּפֶן׃
מִי־אֵל כָּמוֹךָ נֹשֵׂא עָוֹן וְעֹבֵר עַל־פֶּשַׁע׃ לֹא־אוּכַל לְבַדִּי
שְׂאֵת אֶתְכֶם׃ נְשֹׂא׃ לָשֵׂאת אֶת־הָאָרוֹן׃ שָׂא עֵינֶיךָ׃
וְעַתָּה[8] אָמוּת בַּצָּמָא׃ לִבִּי חָלַל[9] בְּקִרְבִּי׃ חִלֵּל[10] יְהוּדָה
קֹדֶשׁ יהוה׃ וַיְהִי כִּי־הֵחֵל[11] הָאָדָם לָרֹב[12]׃ תְּחִלַּת חָכְמָה

---

[1] רפה. [2] Adv. accus. [3] Fulness. [4] bow down. [5] on whose account. [6] *Sing.* The old ending *ay* being contracted to ê before an afformative beginning with a consonant. [7] poetic, and so without the art. [8] Question without an inter. particle. [9] wounded. [10] polluted. [11] began. [12] to multiply (רבב).

יִרְאַת יהוה׃ אֲבָרְכָה אֶת־יהוה בְּכָל־עֵת תָּמִיד תְּהִלָּתוֹ
בְּפִי׃ וְאֶבְכֶּה יוֹמָם וָלַיְלָה אֵת חַלְלֵי בַת־עַמִּי׃ אַל־
תִּתְהַלֵּל בְּיוֹם מָחָר׃ וַאֲהַלְלָה שִׁמְךָ לְעוֹלָם וָעֶד׃ תִּקְעוּ
בַחֹדֶשׁ שׁוֹפָר׃ יָדַע שׁוֹר קֹנֵהוּ׃ עַד־תֹּם אַנְשֵׁי הַמִּלְחָמָה
הַיֹּצְאִים מִמִּצְרָיִם׃ תּוֹרַת יהוה תְּמִימָה מְשִׁיבַת נָפֶשׁ׃
שְׁמָר־תָּם[1]׃ עִם־נְבִיאִים נִבָּא׃ תָּמִים תִּהְיֶה עִם יהוה
אֱלֹהֶיךָ׃ וַיְהִי מַבְדִּיל בֵּין מַיִם לָמָיִם׃ כִּי הוּא אָמַר
וַיֶּהִי[2]׃ הָיָה (הָיוֹ)׃ הֱיוֹת׃ הֱיֵה אַתָּה לָעָם׃ וֶהְיֵה בְּרָכָה׃
וְאָכַל וָחַי לְעוֹלָם׃ יְחִי הַמֶּלֶךְ׃ וַיְחִי׃ וְנִחְיֶה וְלֹא נָמוּת׃
אֲנִי יהוה לֹא שָׁנִיתִי׃ וַיִּשְׁמֹר מִשְׁמַרְתִּי׃ עֲלוּ וְרַגְּלוּ אֶת־
הָאָרֶץ׃ נִקְרָא לַנַּעֲרָ[3] וְנִשְׁאֲלָה אֶת־פִּיהָ׃ וַיִּשְׁתַּחוּ אַרְצָה
שֶׁבַע פְּעָמִים׃ כָּלָה לְבָבִי׃ וַיְהִי כְּכַלּוֹת מֹשֶׁה לִכְתֹּב
אֶת־דִּבְרֵי הַתּוֹרָה הַזֹּאת עַל־סֵפֶר עַד־תֻּמָּם׃ יהוה
צְבָאוֹת עִמָּנוּ׃

---

[1] the perfect (man). [2] in p. [3] Note dropping of ה (in Pent.).

NOTE. — A few words in the preceding exercises have been used, by oversight, in advance of their occurrence in the vocabularies. In such cases the following alphabetical list of words should be consulted. The word נֵבֶל, in the sense of "bottle," and שָׁבוּעַ *week* (*pl.* שָׁבֻעוֹת), there used, are not to be found in the vocabularies; while יָשַׁע *save* is found only in the following one. Further, while the words צָמֵא, פָּנִים, שָׁלוֹם, appear in the following alphabetical list twice, חָדָשׁ, מָלֵא, נָדַר, נַחַל, and עָוָה have been unintentionally omitted, and אֵל *God*, אֶל *to*, עָלַם *be strong*, עַלְמָה *maiden*, have been unnecessarily inserted.

WORDS OF THE VOCABULARIES (*Alphabetically arranged*).

אָב 8
אָבַד 34
אָבָה 34
אֶבְיוֹן 34
אֶבֶן 23
אָדוֹן 2
אֲדֹנָי 2
אָדָם 31
אֲדָמָה 31
אֹהֶל 33
אָוָה 34
אוֹ 2
אוֹצָר 41
אוֹר 8
אוֹר 8
אָז 38
אֹזֶן 32
אָזַן 32
אָח 34
אֶחָד 35
אָחוֹר 34
אָחוֹת 34
אָחַז 27
אֲחֻזָּה 27
אַחַר 34
אַחֵר 34
אַחֲרוֹן 34
אַחֲרִית 34
אַי 38
אֹיֵב 30
אַיִל 41
אַיִן 38
אִישׁ 9
אֲנָשִׁים 9
אָבַל 41
אֵבֶל 41
אֵל 15

אַל
אֶל
אֱלֹהִים 2
אֱלוֹהַּ 2
אֶלֶף 3
אִם 34
אֵם 2
אָמָה 34
אַמָּה 34
אֱמוּנָה 23
אָמֵן 23
אָמַר 5
אֹמֶר 5
אִמְרָה 5
אֱמֶת 23
אֱנוֹשׁ 11
אָסַף 23
אַף 46
אַף 46
אָפָה 41
אֵפֶר 8
אַרְבַּע 35
אָרוֹן 12
אֹרַח 41
אֲרִי 12
אָרַךְ 41
אֹרֶךְ 41
אֶרֶץ 9
אֵשׁ 39
אִשָּׁה 39
אִשָּׁה 9
אֲשֶׁר 10
אֵת 2
אֶת 2
בְּאֵר 25
בָּגַד 19
בֶּגֶד 19

בַּד 38
בָּדַל 37
בְּהֵמָה 12
בּוֹא 44
בּוֹר 41
בּוֹשׁ 17
בָּחוּר 41
בָּחַר 41
בִּין 14
בֵּין 14
בִּינָה 14
בַּיִת 3
בָּכָה 41
בְּכִי 41
בְּכֹר 32
בְּכֹרָה 32
בִּלְתִּי 38
בָּמָה 41
בֵּן 11
בָּנָה 11
בָּקַע 25
בִּקְעָה 25
בָּקָר 31
בֹּקֶר 31
בָּקַשׁ 37
בָּרָא 45
בַּרְזֶל 39
בָּרַח 25
בְּרִיחַ 25
בְּרִית 20
בָּרַךְ 6
בְּרָכָה 6
בָּשָׂר 31
בָּשַׂר 31
בֹּשֶׁת 17
בַּת 11
בְּתוּלָה 45
גָּאַל 5

גִּבּוֹר 22
גְּבוּל 22
גְּבוּרָה 22
גָּבַר 22
גֶּבֶר 22
גָּדוֹל 10
גָּדַל 10
גּוֹל *v.* גִּיל
גּוֹלָה 14
גּוּר 45
גּוֹרָל 46
גִּיל 45
גָּלָה 14
גָּמַל 3
גָּמָל 3
גָּנַב 20
גֵּר 45
גָּרַשׁ 16
דָּבַק 22
דָּבַר 6
דָּבָר 6
דֶּבֶר 6
דְּבַשׁ 37
דּוֹד 28
דּוֹר 28
דֶּלֶת 2
דָּם 26
דַּעַת 43
דֶּרֶךְ 12
דָּרַךְ 12
דָּרַשׁ 15
הֶבֶל 39
הָיָה 11
הֵיכָל 9
הָלַךְ *v.* יָלַךְ
הָלַל 49
הֵמָּה 9
הָמוֹן 9

הֵן 38
הִנֵּה 38
הָפַךְ 47
הַר 9
הָרַס 39
זָבַח 18
זֶבַח 18
זָהָב 47
זָכַר 18
זָכָר 18
זָעַק 24
זָקֵן 17
זָקַן 17
חֶבֶל 39
חָדַל 15, 23
חָדָשׁ 9
חֹדֶשׁ 9
חֵיל 45
חוֹל 45
חוֹמָה 39
חוּץ 2
חָזָה 30
חֹזֶה 30
חָזוֹן 30
חָזַק 23
חָזָק 23
חָטָא 5
חֵטְא 5
חַטָּאת 5
חַי 11
חָיָה 11
חַיָּה 11
חִיל *v.* חוּל
חַיִל 45
חָכַם 3
חָכָם 3
חָכְמָה 3
חָלָה 2

חֳלִי 2
חֲלוֹם 3
חָלַל 49
חָלָל 49
חֲמוֹר 11
חָמֵשׁ 35
חָנָה 27
חֲנִית 27
חֶסֶד 29
חָסִיד 29
חֹק 2
חֻקָּה 2
חָרַב 8
חָרֵב 8
חֹרֶב 8
חָרְבָּה 8
חֹשֶׁךְ 5
חָתַת 46
טָבַח 18
טֶבַח 18
טַבָּח 18
טָהוֹר 21
טָהֵר 21
טוֹב 10
טוֹב 10
טוּב 10
טָמֵא 21
טָמֵא 21
טֻמְאָה 21
יְאֹר 3
יַבָּשָׁה 40
יָבֵשׁ 40
יָד 3
יָרַד 3
יָדַע 43
יוֹם 10
יוֹמָם 10
יַחְדָּו 38

יַחְדָּיו 38
יָטַב 10
יַיִן 37
יָכֹל 9
יָלַד 32
יֶלֶד 32
יֵלֵךְ 43
יָם 37
יָמִין 37
יָסַף 41
יָסַר 43
יָעַד 43
יַעַן 47
יָעַץ 43
יַעַר 33
יָצָא 5
יָצַב 42
יָצַק 43
יָצַר 43
יָרֵא 17
יָרֵא 17
יִרְאָה 17
יָרַד 43
יָרָה 40
יָרַשׁ 43
יֵשׁ 38
יָשַׁב 14
כָּבֵד 11
כָּבֵד 11
כָּבוֹד 11
כָּבַס 21
כָּבַשׁ 21
כִּי 2
כִּכַּר 4
כֹּל 2
כָּלָה 34
כְּלִי 34
כִּלְיָה 34
כַּלָּה 34
כָּנָף 31

כִּסֵּא 4
כָּסָה 4
כֶּסֶף 12
כַּף 3
כְּפִיר 20
כָּפַר 20
כִּפֶּר 20
כַּפֹּרֶת 20
כְּרוּב 24
כֶּרֶם 24
כָּרַת 20
כָּשַׁל 22
כָּתַב 4
לֹא (לוֹא) 11
לֵב (לֵבָב) 23
לְבַד v. בַּד
לְבוּשׁ 22
לָבַשׁ 22
לוּן 44
לָחַם 24
לֶחֶם 24
לַיִל (לַיְלָה) 44
לִין v. לוּן
לָכַד 19
לָמַד 18
לָמָּה 11
לְמַעַן v. מַעַן
לִפְנֵי v. פָּנֶה
לָקַח 19
לָשׁוֹן 40
מְאֹד 2
מֵאָה 35
מָאוֹר 8
מַאֲכָל 41
מָבוֹא 44
מִגְדָּל 10
מַגֵּפָה 42
מִגְרָשׁ 16
מִדְבָּר 6

מָדַד 40
מִדָּה 40
מָה 11
מוּסָר 43
מוֹעֵד 43
מוֹצָא 5
מוֹשָׁב 14
מוּת 44
מָוֶת 44
מִזְבֵּחַ 18
מַחֲנֶה 27
מָחָר 34
מָחֳרָת 34
מַטֶּה 30
מִטָּה 30
מַיִם 3
מַכָּה 48
מָכַר 20
מָלֵא 17
מָלֵא 17
מִלְחָמָה 24
מָלַט 16
מָלַךְ 13
מֶלֶךְ 13
מַלְכָּה 13
מַלְכוּת 13
מַמְלָכָה 13
מַמְלֶכֶת 13
מִן 13
מְנוֹרָה 27
מִנְחָה 27
מִסְפָּר 12
מְעִיל 30
מַעֲלָה 30
מַעֲלָה 39
מַעַן 47
מַעֲשֶׂה 48
מָצָא 14
מִצְוָה 28
מָצוֹר 25

מַצֵּבָה 42
מִקְדָּשׁ 6
מָקוֹם 19
מִקְוֶה 30
מַר 21
מַרְאֶה 47
מָרוֹם 10
מֶרְכָּבָה 36
מַשָּׂא 29
מָשַׁח 25
מָשִׁיחַ 25
מִשְׁכָּב 19
מִשְׁכָּן 21
מָשַׁל 15
מָשָׁל 15
מִשְׁמֶרֶת 15
מִשְׁנֶה 31
מִשְׁפָּחָה 26
מִשְׁפָּט 30
מִשְׁקָל 37
מִשְׁתֶּה 26
מֵתִים 44
נָא 3
נְאֻם 42
נִבָּא 20
נָבַט 20
נָבִיא 29
נָבֵל 17
נָבָל 17
נֵבֶל 17
נְבֵלָה 17
נְבָלָה 17
נֶגֶב 42
נֶגֶד 29
נָגַד 20
נָגִיד 29
נָגַע 42
נֶגַע 42
נָגַף 42
נָגַשׁ 14

נָדִיב 29
נֶדֶר 32
נָהָר 31
נוּחַ 44
נוּם 44
נוּעַ 44
נוּף 44
נַחַל 42
נַחֲלָה 42
נִחַם 42
נְחֹשֶׁת 33
נָטָה 30
נָטַע 42
נִיחֹחַ 44
נָכָה 48
נָסָה 42
נָסַךְ 42
נֶסֶךְ 42
נָסַע 42
נְעוּרִים 33
נַעַר 33
נַעֲרָה 33
נָפַל 22
נֶפֶשׁ 32
נָצַב 42
נָצַח 33
נֵצַח 33
נָצַל 42
נָצַר 42
נֵר 27
נָשָׂא 29
נָשִׂיא 29
נָתַן 42
סָבַב 38
סָבִיב 38
סָגַר 16
סוּס 26
סוּר 40
סֻכָּה 28
סָלַח 37
סָמַךְ 3

סָפַר 12
סֵפֶר 12
סָתַר 21
סֵתֶר 21
עָבַד 8
עֶבֶד 8
עֲבוֹדָה 8
עָבַר 23
עֵבֶר 23
עֶבְרָה 23
עַד 28
עַד 28
עֵד 28
עֵדָה 43
עֵדוּת 28
עוֹד 28
עוּר 28
עוֹלָם 30
עָוֹן 29
עוּר 34
עוֹר 8
עָזַב 23
עָזַר 23
עֵזֶר 23
עַיִן 3
עִיר 34
עַל 30
עָלָה 30
עֹלָה 39
עֶלְיוֹן 39
עֶלֶם
עַלְמָה
עַם 9
עִם 9
עָמַד 5
עָמָל 9
עַמּוּד 5
עֵמֶק 48
עָנָה 47
עָנָה 29
עָנִי 29

עֵזֶר 29
עָזַז 47
עָפָר 8
עֵץ 13
עֵצָה 43
עֶרֶב 9
עָשָׂה 48
עֹשֶׁר 35
עֲשָׂרָה 35
עֵת 47
עַתָּה 47
פָּדָה 48
פָּגַע 25
פֶּה 3
פַּח 36
פַּחַד 36
פָּחַד 36
פָּלַט 16
פָּלִיט 16
פְּלֵיטָה 16
פָּנָה 48
פָּנִים 48
פֶּן 48
פְּנִים 48
פְּנִימִי 48
פִּנָּה 48
פֶּסַח 33
פָּסִיל 33
פֶּסֶל 33
פְּסִלִים 33
פָּקַד 15
פְּקֻדָּה 15
פִּקּוּדִים 15
פַּר (פָּר) 9
פָּרָה 9
פְּרִי 9
פָּרַץ 20
פֶּרֶץ 20
פָּרַשׁ 20
פָּרָשׁ 20
פָּשַׁע 25
פֶּשַׁע 25
פָּתַח 21
פֶּתַח 21
צֹאן 2
צָבָא 49
צְבָאוֹת 49
צַדִּיק 13
צָדַק 13
צֶדֶק 13
צְדָקָה 13
צָוָה 28
צַוָּאר 26
צוּר 26
צוּר 26
צָמֵא 49
צָמָא 49
צָמֵא 49
צָעַק 24
צָפָה 40
צָפוֹן 16
צָפַן 16
צִפּוֹר 27
צַר (צָר) 26
צָרָה 26
צָרַף 37
צָרַר 26
קָבַץ 8
קָבַר 15
קֶבֶר 15
קָדוֹשׁ 6
קָדִים 13
קָדַם 13
קֶדֶם 13
קֵדְמָה 13
קָדַשׁ 6
קֹדֶשׁ 6
קָהָל 9
קָהַל 9
קוֹל 9
קוּם 19
קוֹמָה 19
קָטַל 14
קָטֹן 17
קָטָן 17
קָטַר 37
קְטֹרֶת 37
קָלַל 19
קְלָלָה 19
קָוָה 30
קָנָה 30
קֵץ 40
קָצָה 40
קָצִיר 36
קָצַף 16
קֶצֶף 16
קָצַר 36
קָרָא 4
קָרָא 4
קָרַב 18
קֶרֶב 18
קָרְבָּן 18
קָרָה 4
קָרוֹב 18
קִרְיָה 4
קָשָׁה 40
קָשַׁר 16
קֶשֶׁת 40
רָאָה 30
רֹאשׁ 3
רִאשׁוֹן 3
רֵאשִׁית 3
רַב 46
רֹב 46
רְבָבָה 35
רִבּוֹ 35
רָבָה 46
רֶגַע 36
רֶגֶל 32
רָגַל 32
רָדַף 21
רָם 10
רוּם 10
רָחָב 36
רֹחַב 36
רְחוֹב 36
רָחַץ 36
רִיב 28
רִיב 28
רָכַב 36
רֶכֶב 36
רֵעַ 47
רָצָה 47
רָעַע 46
רַע (רָע) 46
רָפָא 4
רָפָה 4
רָשַׁע 40
רָשָׁע 40
רֶשַׁע 40
שָׂבַע 25
שָׂדֶה 40
שׂוּם 45
שִׂים v. שׂוּם
שָׂכַל 36
שָׂמַח 3
שִׂמְחָה 3
שָׂנֵא 2
שִׂנְאָה 2
שָׂפָה 31
שַׂק 4
שַׂר (שָׂר) 26
שָׂרַף 24
שְׁאוֹל 12
שָׁאַל 12
שָׁאַר 27
שְׁאָר 27
שְׁאֵרִית 27
שָׁבָה 27
שְׁבִי 27
שְׁבוּעָה 25
שְׁבוּת 27
שָׁבַע 25
שֶׁבַע 25
שִׁבְעָה 25
שָׁבַר 14
שֶׁבֶר 14
שָׁבַת 16
שַׁבָּת 16
שַׁד 2
שָׁדַד 2
שׁוּב 46
שׁוֹפָר 49
שׁוֹר 49
שָׁחָה 48
שָׁחַט 24
שָׁחַת 24
שַׁחַת 24
שִׁיר 26
שִׁיר 26
שִׁית 45
שָׁכַב 19
שָׁכַח 21
שָׁכַם 19
שְׁכֶם 19
שָׁכַן 21
שָׁלוֹם 22
שָׁלוֹשׁ 35
שָׁלַח 22
שֻׁלְחָן 22
שָׁלַךְ 22
שָׁלָל 40
שָׁלוֹם 20
שָׁלֵם 20
שָׁלַם 20
שֵׁם 10
שָׁם 10
שָׁמַד 20
שְׁמוּעָה 18
שָׁמַיִם 10
שֶׁמֶן 32
שְׁמֹנָה 35
שָׁמַע 18
שָׁמַר 15
שֶׁמֶשׁ 32
שֵׁן 3
שָׁנָה 31
שָׁנָה 31
שֵׁנִי 31
שְׁנַיִם 31
שַׁעַר 33
שִׁפְחָה 28
שָׁפַט 30
שָׁפַךְ 36
שָׁפֵל 17
שְׁפֵלָה 17
שָׁקָה 26
שָׁקַט 24
שָׁקַל 37
שֹׁרֶשׁ 32
שָׁרַת 24
שֵׁשׁ 35
שָׁתָה 26
תַּאֲוָה 34
תְּבוּאָה 44
תְּבוּנָה 14
תְּהִלָּה 49
תּוֹדָה 3
תָּוֶךְ 40
תּוֹעֵבָה 40
תּוֹרָה 40
תְּחִלָּה 40
תַּחַת 39
תִּירוֹשׁ 43
תֹּם 49
תָּמִיד 40
תָּמִים 49
תָּמַם 49
תְּנוּפָה 44
תָּפַשׂ 2
תָּקַע 25
תְּרוּמָה 10
תֵּשַׁע 35

ABSTRACT OF NOTES TO VOCABULARIES.

§ **2.** O-r. with. coot. cholera. Coke. whole. mў oath. zone. an initial hissing letter. Šadday. topaz.

§ **3.** א. ב. ג. ד. י. כ. מ. ס. ע. פ. ר. ש. Camel (etymological meaning). Ḥokhmāh. hal-lucination. ye oar. joy supports.

§ **4.** Car. case. K^ethîbh. Q^erê. Raphe. Rephaim. sack (article of dress).

§ **5.** Emir. gaol. hate. חשך and שכח. yachts. מַה־.

§ **6.** Baruch. Deborah. Qādhēš.

§ **8.** Abba. Abaddon. ore. Horeb. Obed. ָ.

§ **9.** Hum. Hor. קדש and חדש. deriv. of עמם. Moil. *Erebus.* Ephraim (berry, pear). Qōheleth.

§ **10.** Migdol. Tobias. Yom. Abram. Shem.

§ **11.** Derivatives of בנה. היה and חיה. Hamor. Ichabod. ל and מה.

§ **12.** Aaron. Ariel. behemoth. t(d)rack. Kohen. Meaning of כסף? Sheol.

§ **13.** Melchizedek. Κάδμος.

§ **14.** בין and בין. בן and בן. Goliath. Sabbath (ישב). יצא and מצא. נג.

§ **15.** Midrash. חדל and חלל. marshal. פקד (r. meaning). cover. שמר and שבר.

§ **16.** Sansc. *gras* (Eng. *grass*). מדבר and מגרש. מלט (r. meaning). *seguro* (secure). צפן (r. meaning and derivative). קין (r. meaning and deriv.). קיש (*ibid.*). Sabbath.

§ **17.** Ishbosheth. cane (קן and ן). wary (י = ו). Millo. Nabal. Joktan. Shephelah.

§ **18.** זבח and טבח. Zechariah. Talmud. corban. Ishmael.

§ **19.** *Rob* and *robe* (בגד). לכד and לקח. ταλειθά κούμ. Qal. שבב and שבה.

§ **20.** כרת and ברית. nab. כפר and קבר. *mercator.* Perez. Pharisee. Salaam. שמר and consonants of *smite.*

§ **21.** טהר and טמא. כבס (r. meaning). מסתר and "mystery." Páthaḥ. sounding like a hoof-beat. שכח and חשך. Shekinah.

§ **22.** גב. כשל and נפל. lavish. Siloam (John ix. 7). שלח and שלך.

§ **23.** Ebenezer. Asaph. amen. Hezekiah. חדל and עזב. *laving.* Hebrew. למה עזבת (Ps. xxii. 2).

§ **24.** זעק (mimetic). Carmel. Bethlehem. שח (r. meaning and deriv.). שקט and שחט. משרת and עבד.

§ **25.** Beersheba. beka. ברה and ברך. Messiah. πάγω. Pasha. שבע and שבע. Tekoa.

§ **26.** דם and אדום. Marah. Tyre. Tsar. Sarah. heading of a number of Psalms (שיר). שקה and שתה (Rabshakeh).

§ **27.** Ahaz. Mahanaim. חנית (r. meaning). minḥāh. Ner. Zipporah. Shear-jashub. Tishbeh.

§ **28.** David. door. Succoth. add. Zion (ציה and צוה). reeve. שפח (r. meaning and derivatives).

§ **29.** חסידה (r. meaning and derivatives). נבא and נבט (Nebat). נגד (r. meaning and deriv.). נכה and נשא. awa. Anna (A.D. 1730–1740).

§ **30.** Word used 280 times as Part. (enemy). syn. of נביא and ראה (seer). *nata-re.* cane[2] (*cf.* § **17**). all the letters weak and the first "vibrating" (see). Jehosaphat.

§ **31.** אדם and אדמה. בקר (idea of r. and its derivatives). בשר (noun and verb). כן (idea of r. and word for wing). שפה (idea of r. and word for lip). Mishna (change, year, etc.).

§ **32.** ὠσίν. בכר (firstborn) and בקר. *yeledh.* Nazirite. רן (idea of r. and deriv.). Gethsemane. Beth-shemesh. שרש and קדש.

§ **33.** Oholiab. Jearim. Necho *and* Seth. gnār or snarl (young man). מנצח. Niph'al (r. and its meaning). πάσχα. פִּים. share.

§ **34.** Ebionite. אח. Acheron. *Amme* (*mamma*). כלה (idea of r. and its deriv.). עיר or ער (idea of r.).

§ **36.** פח (idea of r. and its deriv.). קן (*ibid.* See § **16**). רנן and רגל (רן). Rehob. רח (idea of r. and its deriv.). Rechabite. Maschil. שפך and דם.

§ **37.** כר (idea of r. and its deriv.). backshish. *dibs.* יין (ן for י). yam. Benjamin. סלח and שלך. צרף and שרף. Keturah. Shekel.

§ **38.** אן (demon. ן, etc.). אי (Ichabod, § **11**). אין and עין. negative from כלה. הנה and הִנֵּה. אחד and יחדו. לבד and בד (see § **37**). ס (סבב) form of letter suggests meaning.

§ **39.** אשה and אשה. אש and איש. Barzillai. Abel. harass. הבל and חבל. χῶμα. על (idea of r. and deriv.).

§ **40.** Jabesh (Gilead). לשון (r. meaning and form of first letter). *Mād* (mete). Mizpeh. קץ. קצה and קצה (idea of r. and deriv. See § **16**). קשה and קשת (idea of r.). rash. שלל and שאל. תוך and קרב. תועבת יהוה.

§ **41.** Oats are. Aijalon. ארך and ארח. bore. בחר, בכר and בקר. Baca. Bema (βῆμα). Joseph.

§ **42.** איב and נאם. Negeb. נג (r. meaning and deriv.). נהל and נחל. Nahum. נטה, נטע and נסע. Massah. sack (נסך. See § **43**). נצב and צוה (Zion). נצל and נצר. Nathan.

§ **43.** εἴδω (οἶδα). Get thee (point לך לך). אהל מועד. עצה and עצה. sack (pour). צרר and יצר. Jordan. רש with ד, נ, or י prefixed.

§ **44.** בוא and יצא. לין and ליל. מות and מתים. words for offerings (תנופה, etc.).

§ **45.** בתולה and בדל. Abigail. גיל and חיל. שים and שית.

§ **46.** אף and אף. coral. Hittite. turn aside (about, return). Rabbi. רעע (idea of r. and deriv.).

§ **47.** Mᵉhuppākh. ענה and ענה (see § **29**). ראה, רעה and רעע.

§ **48.** Knock. Peniel. שח (idea of r. and deriv.).

§ **49.** Hallelujah. הלל and חלל. צמא and מצא. Sabaoth. שופר (idea of r.). שור and שה. Thummim.

APPENDIX I.

ADDITIONAL EXERCISES IN TRANSLATION.

§§ 14-25.[a] וְהָרָה עָמָל וְיָלַד שָׁקֶר: הָפֵק[1] עֶבְרוֹת אַפֶּךָ: וְהָיָה בְלִבִּי
כְּאֵשׁ בֹּעֶרֶת עָצֻר בְּעַצְמֹתָי: וָאֹמַר אַךְ טָרֹף טֹרָף: לֹא תְכַלֶּה פְּאַת שָׂדְךָ
לִקְצוֹר וְלֶקֶט קְצִירְךָ לֹא תְלַקֵּט: אָרוּר הָאִישׁ אֲשֶׁר יַעֲשֶׂה פֶסֶל: פֶּן־
יְקַלֶּלְךָ וְאָשָׁמְתָּ: מָאֲסוּ אֵת תּוֹרַת יהוה צְבָאוֹת וְאֵת אִמְרַת קְדוֹשׁ־
יִשְׂרָאֵל נִאֵצוּ: יִבְצֹר רוּחַ נְגִידִים: כִּי־גָבְהוּ שָׁמַיִם מֵאֶרֶץ כֵּן גָּבְהוּ דְרָכַי
מִדַּרְכֵיכֶם: וְתָמִיד לַהֲרֹג גּוֹיִם לֹא יַחְמוֹל: כִּי־טוֹב אֱלֹהֵינוּ זַמְּרָה[2]: מִזְמוֹר
לְדָוִד: כָּל־יֹשֵׁב זֹרֵעַ זֶרַע: אָכְלוּ זָרִים כֹּחוֹ וְהוּא לֹא יָדָע גַּם שֵׂיבָה[3] זָרְקָה
בּוֹ: שְׁבֹר זְרוֹעַ רָשָׁע: חִגְרוּ שַׂקִּים: וְהַחֲלִיפוּ שִׂמְלֹתֵיכֶם: וַאֲחַלְּצָה צוֹרְרִי
רֵיקָם: אֹהֵב חָמָס שָׂנְאָה נַפְשׁוֹ: יְהוֹנָתָן[4] חָפֵץ בְּדָוִד מְאֹד: אֶת־מִי חֵרַפְתָּ:
אַשְׁרֵי־אָדָם לֹא יַחְשֹׁב יהוה לוֹ עָוֹן: אַל־תִּבְטְחוּ בְעֹשֶׁק[5]: גַּם־תְּמוֹל
גַּם־הַיּוֹם: יַעַן קָרָאתִי וַתְּמָאֵנוּ נָטִיתִי יָדִי וְאֵין מַקְשִׁיב: אָז יִבָּקַע[6] כַּשַּׁחַר
אוֹרֶךָ: אֶת־מִי עָשַׁקְתִּי: גַּם־בְּעֵינַי יִפָּלֵא נְאֻם־יהוה: כְּאֶרֶז בַּלְּבָנוֹן[4]:
אֶצְבַּע אֱלֹהִים הוּא: חֲזַק וֶאֱמַץ מְאֹד: וְהוּא רֹכֵב עַל אֲתֹנוֹ: מִי בֶחָצֵר:
פֶּתִי יַאֲמִין לְכָל־דָּבָר: אִסְרוּ־חַג[7]: אַל־תְּבַהֵל בְּרוּחֲךָ לִכְעוֹס כִּי כַעַס
בְּחֵיק[8] כְּסִילִים יָנוּחַ: הָאִישׁ קַטֵּר יַקְטִירוּן כַּיּוֹם[9] הַחֵלֶב: לֹוֶה רָשָׁע וְלֹא
יְשַׁלֵּם: בְּעֶצֶם[10] הַיּוֹם הַזֶּה: עֵשָׂו[4] אִישׁ יֹדֵעַ צַיִד אִישׁ שָׂדֶה: וְשָׂמַחְתָּ בְּחַגֶּךָ:

§§ 26-40. דֶּרֶךְ אֱוִיל יָשָׁר בְּעֵינָיו: אַהֲבַת עוֹלָם אֲהַבְתִּיךְ: אִוֶּלֶת כְּסִילִים
מִרְמָה: אֵצֶל עַצְמֹתָיו הַנִּיחוּ[11] אֶת־עַצְמֹתָי: וּבְחַנְתִּים כִּבְחֹן אֶת־הַזָּהָב:
חֹרְשֵׁי אָוֶן יִקְצְרֻהוּ: שָׂכַר עָלֶיךָ אֶת־בִּלְעָם[4]: וְאֶת־אֲסִירָיו[12] לֹא בָזָה: עַל־מִי
בָטַחְתָּ כִּי מָרַדְתָּ בִּי: בְּשָׂרִי יִשְׁכֹּן לָבֶטַח: זֹרוּ[13] רְשָׁעִים מֵרָחֶם תָּעוּ מִבֶּטֶן
דֹּבְרֵי כָזָב: בָּלַל יהוה שְׂפַת כָּל־הָאָרֶץ: בָּבֶל: מִבְּצָרֵיהֶם תְּשַׁלַּח[14]

---

[a] The sections (of the Grammar) named are simply *more especially* illustrated than others.

[1] Disting. from חָפֵץ. [2] Qi. Inf. with *fem.* termination. [3] gray hair. [4] p.n. [5] oppression. [6] break forth. [7] Here *sacrifice*, usually *feast*. Art. omitted in poetry. [8] bosom. [9] during the (same) day. [10] Note the idiom. [11] § **44**. 1. R. 8. [12] prisoners. [13] Otherwise זָרוּ from זוּר. [14] idiomatic, *set on fire*.

בָּאֵשׁ׃ לִפְנֵי־שֶׁבֶר גָּאוֹן׃ לֹא־גָבַהּ לִבִּי׃ עֵינֵי גְבֹהִים תַּשְׁפִּלְנָה׃ שׁוֹעֵר
הָעִיר׃ גַּן עֵדֶן׃ פַּלְטוּ־דַל וְאֶבְיוֹן׃ וְעָמְדוּ רַגְלָיו בַּיּוֹם הַהוּא עַל־הַר הַזֵּיתִים׃
מִמִּזְרַח־שֶׁמֶשׁ יִקְרָא בִשְׁמִי׃ חֲגוֹר חַרְבְּךָ עַל־יָרֵךְ גִּבּוֹר׃ חֵלֶק יהוה עַמּוֹ׃
מַחְלְקוֹת הַכֹּהֲנִים׃ חֲמַת־מֶלֶךְ מַלְאֲכֵי־מָוֶת׃ חִנָּם טָמְנוּ לִי רִשְׁתָּם[1]׃
תָּבוֹא תְּחִנָּתִי לְפָנֶיךָ׃ אַשְׁרֵי כָּל־חוֹסֵי בוֹ׃ חֵפֶץ יהוה בְּיָדוֹ יִצְלָח׃ הַחֵרֵם
הַחֲרִים אֹתָם׃ חֵרֶם בְּקִרְבְּךָ יִשְׂרָאֵל׃ הַפֶּסֶל נָסַךְ[2] חָרָשׁ׃ אִישׁ תְּבוּנוֹת יַחֲרִישׁ׃
לֹא מַחְשְׁבוֹתַי מַחְשְׁבוֹתֵיכֶם׃ הִשְׁבַּתִּי קוֹל חָתָן וְקוֹל כַּלָּה׃ לֶחֶם לְפִי
הַטַּף׃ וְיָנַקְתְּ חֲלֵב[3] גּוֹיִם׃ כֵּן יִסַּד הַמֶּלֶךְ׃ דְּבַר יהוה הָיָה יָקָר׃ יָרֵחַ
יָקָר[4] הֹלֵךְ׃ תִּצְפְּנֵהוּ שְׁלֹשָׁה יְרָחִים׃ אֲרוֹן בְּרִית־יהוה תַּחַת יְרִיעוֹת׃
אַל־תְּחַבֵּב בְּשִׁפְחָתֶךָ׃ פָּשַׁטְתִּי אֶת־כֻּתָּנְתִּי׃ חֲרוּשָׁה עַל־לוּחַ לִבָּם׃ עֵץ
פְּרִי עֹשֶׂה פְּרִי לְמִינוֹ׃ מַה־מְּלַאכְתֶּךָ׃ לֹא יִמְנַע־טוֹב לַהֹלְכִים בְּתָמִים׃
יַשְּׁרוּ בָּעֲרָבָה מְסִלָּה לֵאלֹהֵינוּ׃ מֶה־הַמַּעַל הַזֶּה אֲשֶׁר מְעַלְתֶּם בֵּאלֹהִים׃
וַיִּמָּלֵט אֶל־מְעָרַת עֲדֻלָּם[5]׃ לֹא־תִנְאָף׃ כָּל־הַנְּחָלִים הֹלְכִים אֶל־הַיָּם׃
צֶדֶק וְשָׁלוֹם נָשָׁקוּ׃ כְּצֵל סֶלַע־כָּבֵד׃ עֶגְלֵי הַזָּהָב אֲשֶׁר בֵּית־אֵל[5]׃ בְּרָעָה
עֶדְרוֹ יִרְעֶה׃ עִזִּים מָאתַיִם׃ מַה עַז מֵאֲרִי׃ עָצְמַתְּ מִמֶּנּוּ מְאֹד׃ וְאֶת[6]
עֲצוּמִים יְחַלֵּק שָׁלָל׃ וַיַּעֲרֹךְ עָלָיו עֵרֶךְ לֶחֶם׃ עַם־קְשֵׁה־עֹרֶף הוּא׃ הִנְנִי
מִתְפַּלֵּל יהוה׃ יִפְרַח בְּיָמָיו צַדִּיק׃ יהוה סַלְעִי וּמְצוּדָתִי׃ מֵאֲדָמָה לֹא־
יִצְמַח עָמָל׃ יָצָא קַוָּם וּבִקְצֵה תֵבֵל מִלֵּיהֶם׃ מִמֶּנּוּ תִקְוָתִי׃ קִנְאַת בֵּיתְךָ
אֲכָלָתְנִי׃ קִרְעוּ לְבַבְכֶם וְאַל־בִּגְדֵיכֶם[7]׃ לַפֶּתַח חַטָּאת רֹבֵץ׃ אֶזְבְּחָה בְּאָהֳלוֹ
זִבְחֵי תְרוּעָה׃ טֶרֶף בְּבֵיתִי׃ הַבּוֹר רֵק׃ בְּחֶסֶד עוֹלָם רִחַמְתִּיךְ׃ אֵל רַחוּם
וְחַנּוּן אֶרֶךְ אַפַּיִם וְרַב־חֶסֶד וֶאֱמֶת׃ רֵיחַ בְּנִי כְּרֵיחַ שָׂדֶה׃ וְהִרְעַשְׁתִּי
אֶת־כָּל־הַגּוֹיִם׃ אַחַר הָרוּחַ רַעַשׁ׃ תְּפִלַּת יְשָׁרִים רְצוֹנוֹ׃ לֹא תִרְצָח׃
קָנֶה רָצוּץ לֹא יִשְׁבֹּר׃ אַיֵּה[8] הַשֶּׂה לְעֹלָה׃ וַיִּקְרַע יַעֲקֹב שִׂמְלֹתָיו׃ הֵן
עֵשָׂו[5] אָחִי אִישׁ שָׂעִר[9]׃ אִישׁ בַּעַל שֵׂעָר[10]׃ כַּאֲשֶׁר שָׁמְמוּ[11] עָלֶיךָ רַבִּים׃
אַחֲרָיו מִדְבַּר שְׁמָמָה׃ לְשַׁמָּה וְלִקְלָלָה׃ חֹשֶׁךְ עַל־פְּנֵי תְהוֹם׃ עֹז וְתִפְאֶרֶת
בְּמִקְדָּשׁוֹ׃ אַרְזֵי לְבָנוֹן אֲשֶׁר נָטָע׃

§§ 41–49. כָּל־אַלְמָנָה וְיָתוֹם לֹא תְעַנּוּן׃ הָבוּ שְׂכָרִי׃ עֵד בְּלִיַּעַל יָלִיץ
מִשְׁפָּט וּפִי רְשָׁעִים יְבַלַּע־אָוֶן׃ וְהָיִיתָ־נָּקִי מֵאָלָתִי׃ אֶרֶץ זָבַת[12] חָלָב

---

[1] רֶשֶׁת net. [2] Here *melteth.* [3] *cstr.* of חָלָב. [4] brightness. [5] p.n. [6] with.
[7] Note half-open syllable by special exception. [8] where. [9] defectively written.
[10] i.e., Elijah. [11] *astonished,* usually *desolate.* [12] זָב (Part. *cstr.*).

וּדְבַשׁ׃ וַיִּתֵּן יהוה אֹתֹת וּמֹפְתִים גְּדֹלִים׃ אִם־תָּשִׂים אָשָׁם נַפְשׁוֹ יִרְאֶה
זֶרַע׃ כָּל־בֹּזְזַיִךְ אֶתֵּן לָבַז׃ וַיֵּשְׁבוּ אִישׁ תַּחַת גַּפְנוֹ׃ זָנִית מֵעַל אֱלֹהֶיךָ׃
עַל כָּל־גָּרְנוֹת דָּגָן׃ גִּשְׁמֵי בְרָכָה יִהְיוּ׃ וַיְהִי כִּזְרֹחַ הַשֶּׁמֶשׁ וַיְמַן אלהים
רוּחַ קָדִים׃ וַיֵּלֶךְ גֵּיא הַמֶּלַח׃ אַשִּׂיג אֲחַלֵּק שָׁלָל׃ חֵן וְכָבוֹד יִתֵּן יהוה׃
פְּנֵה אֵלַי וְחָנֵּנִי׃ תְּנָה עֻזְּךָ לְעַבְדֶּךָ׃ מֵחֵץ יָעוּף יוֹמָם׃ וַיְהִי בַּחֲצִי הַלַּיְלָה׃
וַיִּחַר לְקַיִן[1] מְאֹד׃ חֲרוֹן אַפְּךָ יַשִּׂיגֵם׃ אַל־תִּירְאוּ חֶרְפַּת אֱנוֹשׁ׃ וַיָּסַר
פַּרְעֹה אֶת־טַבַּעְתּוֹ׃ אֶהְיֶה כַטַּל לְישראל׃ טֶרֶם יִקְרָאוּ וַאֲנִי אֶעֱנֶה׃
הֲתָצוּד לְלָבִיא[2] טָרֶף׃ יָרוּצוּ וְלֹא יִיגָעוּ׃ יַחֵל ישראל אל־יהוה׃ אוֹכִיחֲךָ
וְאֶעֶרְכָה לְעֵינֶיךָ[3]׃ הֵילִילוּ כָּל־שֹׁתֵי יָיִן׃ סוֹד יהוה לִירֵאָיו׃ יְפֵה מַרְאֶה׃
אֶל־שְׁאוֹל תּוּרַד אֶל־יַרְכְּתֵי־בוֹר׃ פֶּן־אִישַׁן הַמָּוֶת׃ נָדְדָה שְׁנַת הַמֶּלֶךְ׃
מוֹשִׁיעַ יִשְׁרֵי־לֵב׃ אָגִילָה באלהים יִשְׁעִי׃ יְשׁוּעָה יָשִׁית חוֹמוֹת׃ וַיַּעַשׂ
יהוה תְּשׁוּעָה גְדוֹלָה׃ בְּכָל־דְּרָכֶיךָ דָעֵהוּ וְהוּא יְיַשֵּׁר אֹרְחֹתֶיךָ׃ כּוֹנְנוּ
חִצָּם עַל־יֶתֶר׃ לְבִלְתִּי הוֹתִיר לָכֶם שְׁאֵרִית׃ אנכי אֲכַלְכֵּל אֶתְכֶם וְאֶת
טַפְּכֶם׃ בּוֹשׁוּ וְגַם־נִכְלְמוּ כֻּלָּם[4]׃ כִּסְּתָה כְלִמָּה פָּנָי׃ וַיַּכְנַע בֶּעָמָל לִבָּם׃
יִשָּׂאֻהוּ עַל־כָּתֵף׃ אוֹדְךָ בָעַמִּים אֲדֹנָי אֲזַמֶּרְךָ בַּלְאֻמִּים׃ וְלָצֵאת לְבַדְּךָ
תִּשָּׂא׃ וַיַּעַשׂ לוֹ לִשְׁכָּה גְדוֹלָה׃ וְאֵין בְּיָדוֹ מְאוּמָה׃ שָׂרֵי הַמְּדִינוֹת׃ הָיִיתִי
עַד מְמַהֵר׃ אַל־תֵּצֵא לָרִב[5] מַהֵר׃ לְעוֹלָם לֹא־יִמּוֹט׃ הִמַּלְוֵי יהוה[6]׃
הֱיֵה אַתָּה לָעָם מוּל אלהים׃ חֶרְפָּתוֹ לֹא תִמָּחֶה׃ הַשְׁקִינִי־נָא מְעַט־מַיִם׃
כַּמָּה יַמְרוּהוּ[7] בַמִּדְבָּר׃ בְּכָל־הַגּוֹיִם אשר הִדַּחְתִּיךָ שָׁמָּה׃ נְחֵנִי בְּדֶרֶךְ
עוֹלָם׃ וַיְהִי לְנָחָשׁ[8]׃ וַיַּרְא יוֹסֵף אֶת־אֶחָיו וַיַּכִּרֵם וַיִּתְנַכֵּר[9] אֲלֵיהֶם׃ הָסִירוּ
אֶת־אֱלֹהֵי הַנֵּכָר׃ שְׁלֹמֹה אָהַב נָשִׁים נָכְרִיּוֹת׃ וּבָא בְכַפּוֹ וּנְקָבָהּ׃ זָכָר
וּנְקֵבָה׃ כִּי שִׁבְעָתַיִם[10] יֻקַּם־קָיִן[1]׃ וְנִתַּצְתֶּם אֶת־מִזְבְּחֹתָם׃ מִשָּׁם אֶתְּקֶנְךָּ[11]׃
סֹלֶת יִהְיֶה קָרְבָּנוֹ׃ סְרִיס פַּרְעֹה׃ מִי־אֵלֶּה כָּעָב תְּעוּפֶינָה׃ כָּעוֹף
יִתְעוֹפֵף כְּבוֹדָם׃ לָעוּז בְּמָעוֹז פַּרְעֹה׃ טוֹב לַגֶּבֶר כִּי יִשָּׂא עֹל בִּנְעוּרָיו׃
אנכי אֶעֶרְבֶנּוּ׃ לִרְאוֹת עֶרְוַת הארץ בָּאתֶם׃ לֹא יוֹסִיף[12] יָבֹא־בָךְ עוֹד
עָרֵל וְטָמֵא׃ אֶת־בְּרִיתִי הֵפַר׃ בְּנִי אִם־יְפַתּוּךָ חַטָּאִים אַל־תֹּבֵא׃ וַיִּקַּח
אַחַת מִצַּלְעֹתָיו וַיִּסְגֹּר בָּשָׂר תַּחְתֶּנָּה׃ הִנְנִי מֵבִיא אֶת־עַבְדִּי צֶמַח׃ קַוֵּה
קִוִּיתִי יהוה׃ כְּקִיר נָטוּי׃ קַנֹּא קִנֵּאתִי לַיהוה אֱלֹהֵי צְבָאוֹת׃ אַיִל אַחַת

---

[1] p.n. [2] lion. [3] ל before. [4] כֻּל. [5] defectively written. [6] To (the Lord).
[7] How often they rebelled against. [8] Note use of לְ. [9] Made himself strange.
[10] sevenfold. § **35**. 6. R. [11] נתק. [12] Note the idiom.

נֶאֱחַז בַּסְּבַךְ [1] בְּקַרְנָיו׃ תִּקְעוּ־כַף הָרִיעוּ לאלהים׃ וַהֲרִיקֹתִי לָכֶם
בְּרָכָה׃ לְאֻמִּים יֶהְגּוּ־רִיק׃ אֵל שַׁדַּי יִתֵּן לָכֶם רַחֲמִים׃ בְּרָן[2]־יַחַד כּוֹכְבֵי
בֹקֶר׃ וּבָאוּ צִיּוֹן בְּרִנָּה וְשִׂמְחַת עוֹלָם עַל־רֹאשָׁם׃ עוֹלָה לֹא תֵרָצֶה׃
אַל־תֵּט יָמִין וּשְׂמֹאול הָסֵר רַגְלְךָ מֵרָע׃ הֵמָּה בָּאוּ בֵּית [3] לֶחֶם [3] בִּתְחִלַּת
קְצִיר שְׂעֹרִים׃ וְקָם שֵׁבֶט מִיִּשְׂרָאֵל׃ לֹא תִשָּׂא אֶת־שֵׁם־יהוה אלהיך
לַשָּׁוְא׃ וַיָּשֶׂם עַל־שִׁכְמוֹ׃ הֵמָּה שֶׁבֶר׃ וַיֵּשְׁתְּ וַיִּשְׁכָּרֵהוּ׃ אֵת שַׂר הָאֹפִים
תָּלָה׃

VOCABULARY.

אָהַב (breathe after) love. *אַהֲבָה a loving, love. Mimetic.

*אֱוִיל foolish, fool. *אִוֶּלֶת *f.* folly, godlessness. Mn. "Evil."

אָוֶן (*cstr.* אוֹן) *m.* travail, nothingness. אַיִן is from same r.

אוֹת *f.* sign. Discrim. from אֵת sign of accus. which takes suffixes (אֹתִי).

אַךְ surely, only, yet.

*אָלָה *f.* oath. R. syn. of אָרַר.

אַלְמָנָה *f.* widow. Suggests "almoner."

*אָמֵץ be strong, of good courage. Mn. "Amoz," (אָמוֹץ) father of Isaiah.

אָסַר bind.

*אֶצְבַּע *f.* finger.

אָצֶל (*cstr.* אֵצֶל) *m.* side; *Prep.* beside.

אֶרֶז *m.* cedar. Discrim. from אֶרֶץ.

אָרַר curse. Syn. קָלַל, אָלָה.

*אָשֵׁם trespass. *אָשָׁם *m.* trespass offering, guilt.

*אַשְׁרֵי (*pl. cstr.* of אֶשֶׁר) Hail! Happy!

*אָתוֹן *m.* she-ass. Syn. חֲמוֹר.

*בָּהַל be troubled, in consternation.

*בָּזָה despise; *intrans.* be despicable.

בָּזַז plunder, strip. בַּז *m.* booty.

בָּחַן try, prove. *Cf.* בָּחַר.

בָּטַח trust, confide. בֶּטַח *m.* trust.

בֶּטֶן *f.* belly. R. בט = empty.

בְּלִיַּעַל uselessness. Mn. "Belial."

*בָּלַל mix, confound.

בָּלַע swallow up.

בַּעַל lord, husband, Baal.

בָּעַר burn, extirpate.

*בָּצַר cut off, separate. *מִבְצָר *c.* fortress. (Idea ?)

גָּאוֹן *m.* majesty, pride. From גּוה. *Cf.* גּוֹי, etc.

*גָּבַהּ be high. גָּבֹהַּ high. R. גב. גב = be rounded up, *gibbous.*

גּוֹי *m.* people, nation (rounded together).

גַּיְא valley. R. גוה (rounded out).

*גִּלּוּלִים *m.* idols (r. גלל roll), stocks.

גַּם also (both — and). R. גמם = bind.

*גַּן *c.* garden.

גֶּפֶן *m.* vine (crooked; גב = גף).

*גֹּרֶן *m.* threshing-floor.

*גֶּשֶׁם (i) *m.* shower.

*דָּגָן *m.* grain. R. דָּגָה multiply. Deriv. דָּג† fish; דָּגוֹן (fish-god) "Dagon."

---

[1] thicket. [2] רנן. [3] p.n.

דַּל* feeble, poor. R. דלל languish. Mn. and deriv. "Delilah," the languishing.

הָגָה* meditate, "imagine."

הָרַג murder, kill.

הָרָה* conceive. Disting. חָרָה.

זוּב* flow. Part. זָב, זָבָה.

זוּר be strange. Part. זָר.

זַיִת (cstr. זֵית) m. olive.

זָמַר* sing, etc. מִזְמוֹר m. psalm. Mimetic.

זָנָה play the harlot, be idolatrous.

זָרַח† shine forth (of sun), sprout. מִזְרָח m. dawn, east. R. = scatter.

זָרַע sow. זְרוֹעַ c. arm. זֶרַע m. seed. Associate ideas together. R. akin to preceding and following.

זָרַק* scatter, (espec.) sprinkle.

חַג or חָג (r. חגג) m. feast.

חָגַר* gird. Note last two radicals and form of first.

חָלָב* m. milk (sweet). Assoc. with next.

חֵלֶב fat. Mn. "Helbon" (חֶלְבּוֹן), celebrated for its wine: Ezek. xxvii. 18.

חָלַף* change, exchange. Mn. "Caliph," vicar of Mohammed.

חָלַץ* draw out, off (clothing, etc.), deliver.

חָלַק divide, apportion. חֵלֶק m., חֶלְקָה* f. portion, smoothness, flattery. מַחֲלֹקֶת* f. divisions, classes. Mn. "Hilkiah" = Jehovah's portion.

חֵמָה f. heat, rage. R. יחם, akin to חמם. Mn. "Ham."

חָמַל* pity, spare. Cf. ἁμαλός.

חָמָס m. violence, wrong. R. (חם) = be hot.

חָנַן incline, be gracious to. Cf. חָנָה. חֵן m. grace, favor. חִנָּם* in vain, gratis. תְּחִנָּה† f. favor, supplication. Mn. חַנָּה mother of Samuel.

חָסָה* find refuge in, trust. R. = hasten (to).

חָפֵץ be pleased with. חֵפֶץ* m. delight. Mn. "Hephzibah": 2 Ki. xxi. 1.

חֵץ (i) m. arrow. חֲצִי* half. R. = divide.

חָצֵר m. court, hedge. R. allied to last.

חָרַד* tremble. Syn. רָגַז, etc.

חָרָה be hot, angry. חָרוֹן* heat, anger. R. חר suggests char.

חָרַם devote, destroy. חֵרֶם m. curse, set apart (to destruction). Cf. "Harem."

חָרַף reproach, despise. חֶרְפָּה f. ibid.

חָרַשׁ* engrave, plough. חָרָשׁ* m. engraver, artisan.

חָרַשׁ* be silent, dumb.

חָשַׁב desire, impute, reckon. מַחֲשָׁבָה thought, purpose.

חָתַן* join. Part. father-in-law. חָתָן† m. bridegroom.

טַבַּעַת* f. seal, seal ring, ring.

טַל* m. dew. R. akin to דל hang (stream) down.

טָמַן* secrete (Moses — body of Egyptian).

טַף m. little one. R. טפף = trip, spring.

טֶרֶם not yet, before (gen. with Impf. and Inf.). Mn. term.

טָרַף* pluck, tear. טֶרֶף* m. fresh leaf, prey, food.

יָגַע* be weary, labor (to weariness).

יָהַב* give; only Imp. הַב, הָבָה.

יָחַל* wait. Akin to חול.

יָכַח adjudicate, correct. R. = stamp level.

יָלַל* complain, howl, yell.

יָנַק* (Hi.) give suck. Cf. עָנַק be long-necked. Mn. "Anak."

יָסַד* found, sit together. סוֹד † *m.* secret, mutual counsel.

יָפֶה* beautiful. Mn. and deriv. "Joppa" (Jaffa).

יָקָר* precious. Syn. כָּבֵד.

יָרֵחַ* *m.* moon. R. akin to אָרַח wander.

יֶרַח † *m.* month. Syn. חֹדֶשׁ.

יְרִיעָה *f.* curtain (from its motion).

יָרֵךְ* *f.* side, loin.

יַרְכָה* *f.* side, loin.

יָשֵׁן † sleep. שֵׁנָה † *f.* sleep.

יָשַׁע save. יֵשַׁע* (i) *m.* salvation. תְּשׁוּעָה, יְשׁוּעָה *ibid.* Mn. "Joshua," "Jesus."

יָשַׁר* be upright. יָשָׁר upright. Mn. "Jasher."

יָתוֹם* *m.* orphan.

יָתַר remain over. יֶתֶר (i) *m.* what is left, string of bow. R. = stretch out.

כֹּה thus, so = כָּה (כָּכָה).

כּוּל* contain, sustain. R. akin to כלל (כֹּל).

כּוּן place, prepare. Mn. "Jachin" (יָכִין), pillar of the temple: 1 Ki. vii. 21.

כָּזַב † deceive, lie. כָּזָב* liar. Mn. "Cozbi" (כָּזְבִּי).

כֹּחַ *m.* strength. R. akin to יכח.

כָּלַם* be ashamed. כְּלִמָּה* *f.* shame.

כֵּן thus (upright, place, base).

כָּנַע* (and כרע) bow. Mn. "Canaan," i.e. lowland.

כְּסִיל *m.* fool. R. = heavy, stupid.

כָּעַס vex, provoke. כַּעַס † *m.* vexation.

כֻּתֹּנֶת* (כְּתֹנֶת) *f.* tunic, shirt, χιτών.

כָּתֵף *f.* shoulder. R. press. *Cf.* כתב.

לְאֹם *m.* people. Syn. עַם, גּוֹי.

לָוָה* (r. join) borrow, (Hi.) lend. Mn. "Levi" (לֵוִי).

לוּחַ* (r. shine) *m.* tablet. *Cf.* λύχνος.

לוּץ* (r. stammer) mock, scorn.

לָקַט* glean. *Cf.* לקח; לקק lick up.

לִשְׁכָּה* *f.* chamber, cell (of temple).

מְאוּמָה* anything (whatever), from מְאוּם fleck, spot.

מָאֵן* (Qi.) refuse.

מָאַס despise, reject. Syn. of last.

מְדִינָה* (r. דִּין rule) *f.* province.

מָהַר (Qi.) hasten. מַהֵר* (מְהֵרָה *f.*) quickly.

מוֹט* move, totter. Mn. "mote."

מוּל* cut off (foreskin), circumcise.

מוּל* (מוֹל) (what is) before, over against.

מוֹפֵת* (r. אפת distort) *m.* wonder.

מָחָה* wipe out, destroy.

מִין* (r. divide) *m.* kind, species.

מַלְאָךְ (r. לאך send) *m.* angel, messenger.

מְלָאכָה *f.* business.

מִלָּה* *f.* word (poetic).

מֶלַח* *m.* salt.

מָנָה* count, apportion, prepare. *Cf.* next.

מָנַע* withhold. *Cf.* r. מן (divide) elsewhere.

מְסִלָּה* (r. סלל elevate) highway.

מְעַט little, short.

מָעַל* act treacherously, sin. מַעַל* *m.* sin.

מְעָרָה* (r. עָרַר be deep) *f.* cave. *Cf.* עִוֵּר* blind.

מָרַד revolt. Mn. "Nimrod" (נִמְרֹד).

מָרָה* (r. akin to last) rebel.

מִרְמָה* (r. רמה) *f.* deception.

נָאַף* commit adultery.

נָאַץ* despise. Syn. מָאַס.

נָדַד* wander. נִדָּה* separation, uncleanness.

נָדַח drive away.
נָחָה* lead, direct.
נַחַל wady, valley (with a brook).
נָחָשׁ* *m.* serpent.
נָכַר be strange; Hi. recognize. נֵכָר,* נָכְרִי* foreigner.
נָקַב* pierce, bore. נְקֵבָה† female.
נָקָה be innocent. נָקִי* innocent.
נָקַם avenge.
נָשַׂג overtake.
נָשַׁק* kiss, arm (put on weapons), obey.
נָתַץ* tear down (altars, houses, etc.).
נָתַק* tear away, out, down, etc.

סֶלַע *m.* (cleft) rock. *Cf.* צוּר.
סֹלֶת* *c.* (fine) flour (as well bolted, סלל).
סָרִיס* *m.* eunuch, officer.

עָב* (r. עוּב be thick) *c.* cloud. Syn. עָנָן.
עֵגֶל* *m.* (*f.* עֶגְלָה) calf (r. = roll), so called as frolicsome.
עֵדֶר* *m.* flock. R. = order, set in rows.
עוּף* cover. עוֹף *m.* bird.
עֵז (r. עזז bow) *f.* she-goat.
עָזַז† be strong. עֹז* *f.*, עֹז *m.* מָעוֹז* *m.* strength.
עֹל* *m.* yoke.
עָצַם† be strong. עָצוּם* strong. עֶצֶם *f.* bone (selfsame).
עָצַר* restrain. עֲצָרָה† (עֲצֶרֶת) holy day.
עָרַב* give security, exchange.
עֲרָבָה *f.* plain, "Arabah."
עֶרְוָה* *f.* nakedness.
עָרַךְ put in order. עֵרֶךְ* *m.* preparation, appraisal.
עָרֵל* (foreskin) uncircumcised.
עֹרֶף* (r. separate) *m.* neck (back side).
עֵשֶׂב* *m.* herb, plant.
עָשַׁק* oppress.

פֵּאָה *f.* corner. R. open, yawn. Deriv. פֶּה.
פּוּץ scatter.
פָּלָא be wonderful.
פָּלַל smooth over, set right, intercede. R. separate.
פֶּסֶל* (i) *m.* (hewn) image.
פָּרַח* sprout, bloom.
פָּרַר break, make void. R. פר divide.
פָּשַׁט* strip, put off.
פָּתָה* entice. פְּתִי simple(ton). *Cf.* פתח.

צוּד* hunt, fish. מְצוּדָה† *f.* fortress, etc. צַיִד† game, provision.
צֵל* *m.* shadow. Mn. "Zillah" (צִלָּה).
צָלַח prosper.
צֵלָע* *f.* side, rib.
צָמַח* sprout. צֶמַח† = Messiah: Zech. iii. 8.

קָוָה (r. be stretched) wait, hope. קַו† *m.* line. תִּקְוָה* *f.* hope.
קִיר (r. encircle) *m.* wall.
קָנָא† (r. be red) be jealous. קִנְאָה* *f.* jealousy.
קֶרֶן *f.* horn.
קָרַע rend (the garment), tear away.
קָשַׁב* attend. R. stiffen, point (the ear, etc.).

רָבַץ* lie down, crouch.
רוּחַ *c.* breath, spirit.
רוּעַ* shout. תְּרוּעָה *f.* shout, *hurrah*.
רוּץ run. Suggests in sound and (distantly in) sense *roots*.
רוּק† be empty. רִיק† *adj.*, רֵיק† *adj.*, רֵיקָם† *adv.* vain, without cause. Mn. "Raca": Matt. v. 22.
רָחַם (r. be soft) show mercy. רַחוּם† merciful. רֶחֶם* *m.* womb. רַחֲמִים mercy.
רֵיחַ *m.* savor, odor. *Cf.* רוּחַ of same r.

רָנַן rejoice, shout. רִנָּה* *f. ibid.* Mn. "Arnon" (אַרְנֹן).

רָעַשׁ* tremble, quake. רַעַשׁ† *m.* earthquake.

רָצָה be pleased with. רָצוֹן *m.* acceptance.

רָצַח kill. R. רץ = touch: רוּץ the earth, in running; רָצָה *adhere* to one; רָצַח and רָצַץ touch hard, kill, crush.

רָצַץ* break, crush.

שֶׂה* *c.* one sheep. Related to צֹאן as שׁוֹר is to בָּקָר.

שָׂכַר† serve for hire. שָׂכָר* wages, hire.

שַׂלְמָה† *f.* robe, garment; or שִׂמְלָה* *f. ibid.*

שְׂמֹאל (א inserted) *m.* the left side (as the שִׂמְלָה was worn there).

שָׂעִיר hairy; goat.

שֵׂעָר* *m.* hair.

שְׂעֹרָה* *f.* barley (as bearded).

שֵׁבֶט *c.* rod, sceptre, tribe.

שָׁוְא (r. perish) *m.* vanity. Suggests *show.*

שׁוֹעֵר* *m.* gatekeeper. *Cf.* שַׁעַר.

שַׁחַר* *m.* morning (gray). R. overspread.

שְׁכֶם* *m.* shoulder. Mn. "Shechem."

שָׁכַר† drink (oneself full). שֵׁכָר† *m.* strong drink.

שָׁמֵם (r. be stiff) be waste, astonished. שַׁמָּה* *f.* astonishment, waste. שְׁמָמָה *f. ibid.*

שֶׁקֶר *m.* falsehood; *adv.* falsely.

תֵּבֵל* (r. יבל flow) *f.* world (inhabited).

תְּהוֹם* *m.* the (great) Deep. Mimetic.

תָּלָה* hang (impale). *Cf.* תלל, דלל.

תְּמוֹל* (= אֶתְמוֹל = אֵת, מוּל) *adv.* over against, yesterday. See מוּל.

תָּעָה wander.

תִּפְאָרָה (תִּפְאֶרֶת) *f.* beauty, glory.

חֶמְדָּה *f.* desire.

יָסַד confer, found.

מָטָר *m.* rain.

נָזַר separate.

פִּילֶגֶשׁ *c.* concubine.

פָּרַד separate.

APPENDIX II.

(A). — LIST OF SYNONYMS.[1]

1. אָבַד, נָפַל, כָּשַׁל.

2. אָבָה, אָהַב, אָוָה, בָּחַר, חָפֵץ, רָצָה.

3. אָדוֹן, בַּעַל, מֶלֶךְ, נָגִיד, נָדִיב, נָשִׂיא, סָרִיס, שַׂר.

4. אָדָם, אִישׁ, אֱנוֹשׁ, גֶּבֶר, זָכָר, מְתִים ; אִשָּׁה, נְקֵבָה.

5. אֲדָמָה, אֶרֶץ, גְּבוּל, חֶבֶל (rarely), חָרָבָה, יַבָּשָׁה, מְדִינָה, עָפָר, שָׂדֶה, תֵּבֵל.

6. אֹהֶל, בַּיִת, גּוּר, הֵיכָל, חָנָה, יָשַׁב, לִין, סֻכָּה, שָׁכַן.

7. אֱוִיל, הָלַל (sometimes), כְּסִיל, נָבָל, פְּתִי.

8. אָוֶן, אָשָׁם, חָטָא, מַעַל, עָוֹן, פֶּשַׁע, רַע, רָשָׁע.

9. אוֹר, בֹּקֶר, נֵר, שַׁחַר.

10. אוֹת, מוֹפֵת, מַרְאֶה, פֶּלֶא.

11. אֹזֶן, עָנָה (answer), קָשַׁב, שָׁמַע.

12. אֶחָד, פַּעַם.

13. אָחַז, חָזַק (Hi.), תָּפַשׂ.

14. אֹיֵב, צָר, רָדַף, שָׂנֵא.

15. אַיִל, כֶּבֶשׂ, עֵז, צֹאן, שֶׂה, שָׂעִיר.

16. אַיִן, אַל, בִּלְתִּי, לֹא.

17. אָכַל, בָּעַר, טֶרֶף, לָחַם (Q.), צַיִד.

18. אֲדֹנָי, אֵל, אֱלֹהִים, אֱלוֹהַּ, יְהֹוָה, עֶלְיוֹן, שַׁדַּי.

19. אָלָה, אָרַר, בָּרַךְ (rarely), קָלַל.

20. אֶלֶף, בְּהֵמָה, בָּקָר, חַיָּה, עֵגֶל, פַּר, שׁוֹר.

21. אָמֵן, חָסִיד, יָשָׁר, צֶדֶק, תָּם.

22. אָמַר, בָּשַׂר, דִּבֶּר, מִלָּה, נְאֻם, נָגַד, סָפַר, עָנָה (cf. 11).

23. אָסַף, לָקַט, קָבַץ, קָהַל, קָוָה (rarely).

24. אָסַר, צוּר, צָרַר (last two rarely), קָשַׁר.

25. אֹרַח, דֶּרֶךְ, מְסִלָּה.

26. אֲרִי, כְּפִיר.

27. אָרַךְ, יָסַף.

28. אִשֶּׁה, אָשָׁם (cf. 8), זָבַח, חָטָא (cf. 8), מִנְחָה, נֶסֶךְ, עֹלָה, קָרְבָּן, קָטַר, שָׁחַט, שֶׁלֶם, תְּנוּפָה, תְּרוּמָה.

29. אָתוֹן, חֲמוֹר.

30. בְּאֵר, בּוֹר, מוֹצָא, עַיִן.

31. בָּגַד, כָּזָב, פִּתָּה, מִרְמָה, שֶׁקֶר.

32. בֶּגֶד, לְבוּשׁ, כֻּתֹּנֶת, שִׂמְלָה (שַׂלְמָה), שַׂק.

33. בָּדַל, בָּקַע, חָלַק, מָנָה, פָּרַד, פָּרַר.

34. בָּהַל, חָרַד, חָתַת, יָרֵא, פָּחַד, רָגַז, רָעַשׁ.

35. בּוֹא, בָּרַח, דָּרַךְ, הָלַךְ, יָצָא, יָרַד, נוּס, נָסַע, נָשַׂג, סָבַב, סוּר, עָבַר, רָגַל, עָלָה, רוּץ, שׁוּב. (These verbs

---

[1] The term is here used with some latitude; the object being to associate together as many of the words *used in this Grammar*, having a *kindred meaning*, as possible. Nouns and adjectives as well as verbs, are taken, if necessary, as representing roots and, generally, but one representative of a root is used, unless it be as expressing a different shade of meaning.

of motion are put together for convenience.)

36. בּוֹשׁ, בָּזָה, חָרַף, בָּלַם.

37. בָּזַז, טָרַף, שָׁלַל.

38. בָּחוּר, בְּכֹר, יֶלֶד, נַעַר.

39. בָּחַן, בָּחַר, נָסָה, צָרַף.

40. בָּטַח, אָמַן (Hi.), חָסָה, יָחַל (Qi.), תִּקְוָה.

41. בֶּטֶן, רֶחֶם.

42. בִּין, חָכַם, יָדַע, שָׂכַל.

43. בָּמָה, גָּבַהּ, גִּבְעָה, הַר, מָרוֹם.

44. בָּנָה, בָּרָא, חָרַשׁ, יָצַר, פָּעַל, עָשָׂה.

45. בָּצַר, קָצָה, קָצַר.

46. בִּקְעָה, גַּיְא, נַחַל, עֵמֶק, שְׁפֵלָה.

47. בָּקַשׁ, דָּרַשׁ, רָגַל (spy out; *cf.* 35).

48. בָּשַׂר (*cf.* 22), מַלְאָךְ, שְׁמוּעָה.

49. בָּשָׂר, עוֹר.

50. בַּת, אָמָה, בְּתוּלָה, כַּלָּה, נַעֲרָה, שִׁפְחָה.

51. גָּאוֹן, רוּם, נִשָּׂא.

52. גָּאַל, כָּפַר, פָּדָה.

53. גִּבּוֹר, אַנְשֵׁי מִלְחָמָה (חַיִל).

54. גָּבַר, אָמֵץ, חָזַק, יָכֹל.

55. גּוֹי, עַם, לְאֹם.

56. גּוֹלָה, שְׁאֵרִית, שָׁבָה.

57. גִּיל, רוּעַ, רָנַן, שָׂמַח.

58. גָּמַל, כָּלָה (Qi.), שָׁלַם (Qi.).

59. גָּרַשׁ, יָרַשׁ (Hi.), נָדַח.

60. גֶּשֶׁם, יָרָה (rarely), מָטָר.

61. דָּבַק, רָדַף (*cf.* 14).

62. דָּבָר, בְּרִית, חֹק, מִצְוָה, מִשְׁמֶרֶת, מִשְׁפָּט, עֵדוּת, פִּקּוּדִים, תּוֹרָה.

63. דּוֹר, זֶרַע, מִשְׁפָּחָה.

64. דַּל, אֶבְיוֹן, עָנִי.

65. הֶבֶל, אָוֶן (*cf.* 8), שָׁוְא, רוּחַ, רֵיקָם, חִנָּם.

66. הָלַל (*cf.* 7), בֵּרַךְ, זָמַר, יָדָה, שִׁיר.

67. הָמוֹן, רֹב.

68. הָרַג, בָּלַע, חָלָל, חָרַם, טָבַח, כָּרַת, מוּת (Hi.), מָחָה, קָטַל, שָׁחַט (*cf.* 28), שָׁחַת, שָׁמֵם. See 1.

69. הָרַס, הָפַךְ, טָרַף (*cf.* 17), נָתַץ, נָתַק, פָּרַץ, פָּרַר (*cf.* 33), קָרַע, שָׁבַר.

70. זוּב, יְאוֹר, נָהָר, נַחַל (*cf.* 46).

71. זוּר, גּוּר (*cf.* 6), נָכַר.

72. זָעַק (צָעַק), יָלַל, קָרָא.

73. זָרַח, זָרַע, פּוּץ, פָּרַשׂ.

74. זָרַע, נָטַע.

75. זָרַק, יָצַק, נָסַךְ, רוּק, שָׁפַךְ.

76. חֶבֶל, קַו, תִּקְוָה (*cf.* 40).

77. חַג, מוֹעֵד, מִשְׁתֶּה, עֲצָרָה.

78. חָדַל, כָּלָה, עָזַב, שָׁבַת, שָׁלַם (*cf.* 58), תָּמַם.

79. חֹדֶשׁ, יֶרַח.

80. חוּל, דָּבָה, חָלָה, יָחַל (*cf.* 40), יָגַע, עָמַל, צַר (*cf.* 14), רַע (*cf.* 8).

81. חוֹמָה, קִיר.

82. חָזָה, נָבָא.

83. הָיָה, חָיָה.

84. חֲלוֹם, חָזוֹן (*cf.* 82), מַשָּׂא.

85. חָלַף, חָדַשׁ, שָׁנָה.

86. חָלַץ, פָּשַׁט.

87. חֵמָה, אַף, חָרָה, כַּעַס, עֶבְרָה, קָצַף.

88. חָמַל, חָנַן, חֶסֶד, טוֹב, נִחַם, רִחַם. See 2.

89. חָמָס, עָשַׁק, שָׁדַד.

90. טָהֵר, נָקָה (Q., Ni.), קָדַשׁ. See 21.

91. טַף, יֶלֶד (*cf.* 38).

92. יָד, כַּף.

93. יָהַב, נָתַן.

94. יַיִן, תִּירוֹשׁ, שֵׁכָר.

95. יָכַח, יָסַר, יָרָה (Hi.), לָמַד (Qi.), נָקַם, עָנָה, פָּקַד.

96. יָלַד (הָרָה), חִיל (*cf.* 80).

97. יָם, תְּהוֹם.
98. יָסַד (Qi.), יָעַד.
99. יָעַץ, יָסַד (Ni.).
100. יְקָר, חֶמְדָּה, כָּבֵד, תִּפְאֶרֶת.
101. יָשַׁע, מָלַט (פָּלַט), נָצַל, נָצַר,
עָזַר, שָׁמַר.
102. יָתַר, שָׁאַר.
103. כָּבַס, רָחַץ.
104. בּוּל, סָמַךְ.
105. כּוּן, נָצַב (יָצַב), עָמַד, קוּם
(Hi.).
106. כֹּחַ, עֹז, עָצוּם. See 54.
107. כֵּן, כֹּה.
108. כָּסָה, טָמַן, כָּפַר (cf. 52),
סָכָה (cf. 6), סָתַר, צָפַן.
109. כָּתַב, חָרַשׁ (cf. 44), סָפַר
(cf. 22).
110. כָּתֵף, זְרוֹעַ, עֹרֶף, צַוָּאר,
שְׁכֶם.
111. לֵב, נֶפֶשׁ, כְּלָיוֹת, קֶרֶב.
112. לָוָה, מָכַר, עָרַב, קָנָה.
113. לוּחַ, שֻׁלְחָן.
114. לַיְלָה, חֹשֶׁךְ, עֶרֶב.
115. לָכַד, לָקַח. See 13.
116. מָאֵן, לוּן, מָאַס, מָנַע, נָאַץ.
See 36.
117. מִבְצָר, מִגְדָּל, מָעוֹז, מְצוּדָה,
מָצוֹר.
118. מִגְרָשׁ, מִדְבָּר, רָעָה.
119. מוּל, נֶגֶד.
120. מוֹעֵד (אֹהֶל), מִקְדָּשׁ, מִשְׁכָּן.
121. מִזְבֵּחַ, גִּלּוּלִים, מַצֵּבָה, פֶּסֶל.
122. מִזְמוֹר, שִׁיר. See 66.
123. מִזְרָח, קֶדֶם, מוֹצָא (with
שֶׁמֶשׁ).
124. מַטֶּה, שֵׁבֶט, קָנֶה.
125. מִטָּה, מִשְׁכָּב.
126. מְלָאכָה, מַעֲשֶׂה, עֲבוֹדָה, פֹּעַל.
127. מְעַט, קָטֹן.
128. מָצָא, קָרָה.

129. מִקְנֶה, הָמוֹן (cf. 67), כָּבֵד
(cf. 100).
130. מָרַד, מָרָה, סוּר (cf. 35).
131. מָשַׁל, מָלַךְ.
132. נָאַף, זָנָה, פִּילֶגֶשׁ.
133. נָבַט, חָזָה (cf. 82), צָפָה, רָאָה.
134. נָגַשׁ, קָרַב.
135. נוּחַ, שָׁקַט.
136. נָדַד, מוֹט, נוּעַ, תָּעָה.
137. נַחֲלָה, אֲחֻזָּה, גּוֹרָל, חֵלֶק.
See 33.
138. נָטָה, שָׁלַח.
139. נֶצַח, עַד, עוֹלָם.
140. נָשָׂא (cf. 51), כָּפַר (cf. 52),
סָלַח.
141. סָגַר, עָצַר.
142. סֶלַע, אֶבֶן, צוּר.
143. עָב, עָנָן.
144. עָבַד, שָׁרַת.
145. עֵדָה, מוֹעֵד, עֲצָרָה, קָהָל.
146. עֵדֶר, צֹאן (cf. 15).
147. עוֹף, צִפּוֹר.
148. עַם, אֻמָּה.
149. פָּלַל, חָנַן (Hithq.), שָׁאַל,
תְּחִנָּה, תְּפִלָּה.
150. פָּרָה, פָּרַח, צָמַח.
151. פָּתָה (cf. 7), דֶּלֶת, פָּתַח,
שַׁעַר.
152. צָבָא, חַיִל (cf. 53).
153. צֵלָע, אֵצֶל, יַרְכָּה.
154. קִנֵּא, צָרַר (cf. 24).
155. קֶרֶב (cf. 111), בֶּטֶן (cf. 41),
תָּוֶךְ.
156. קִרְיָה, עִיר.
157. רָבַץ, שָׁכַב.
158. רוּם (cf. 51), נָשָׂא (cf. 51,
140). See 43.
159. רְחֹב, חוּץ.
160. רֶכֶב, פָּרָשׁ.
161. רֵעַ, אָח, קָרוֹב.
162. רָפָא, רָפָה.

163. שבע, מלא.
164. שרף, בער (*cf.* 17).
165. שבר, דגן.
166. שחה, כנע, שפל (*cf.* 46).
167. שית, נתן (sometimes), שים.
168. שכב, קום (*cf.* 105).
169. שלך, נפל (Hi.).
170. שקה, שתה.
171. תודה, תהלה. See 66.
172. תחלה, ראשית.
173. תקע (tent-pin, trumpet), נגע, נגף, נכה, שמד. See 68, 69.

(*B*). — WORDS TO BE DISTINGUISHED.

אב, עב : אבד, עבד : אבה, אוה,
אפה : אבן, אגן : און (*cstr.*), עון (*cstr.*) :
אור, עור : את, אך : אחר, אחר :
איל, חיל : אין, עין : אל, על : אלה,
עלה : אם, עם : אמי (אם), עמי :
אמה, אמה : עמה, אסף : עזב, אסר,
עזר : אפר, עפר : ארבע, ארבה :
ארון, אהרון, אחרון : ארז, ארץ :
ארח, ארך : ארך, ערך : איש, אש :
אשה, אשה : את, את : אתה, עתה.

באר, בער : בד, בת : בוא, בו :
בחר, בכר (בכר), בקר : בין, בן :
בכה, בקע : בלה (בלתי), בלע :
בלל, פלל : ברח, ברך.

גוי, גיא : גנב, כנף.

דם, תם.

הבל, חבל : היה, חיה : הלך,
חלק : הלל, חלל, קלל : המה, חמה :
הן, חן : הגה, הגה : הרה, חרה :
הרס, חרש.

זה, שה : זור, צור : זכר, שכר :
זר, צר, שר : זרח, זרע, זרק.

חדש, קדש : חדש, קדש : חול,
כול : חול, כל, קול : חומה, קומה :
חוה, חסה, כסה : חלה, כלה : חנה,
כנע, קנה, קנא : חפץ, חפץ (פוץ) :
חן, קן : חצר, קצר : חרב, קרב :
חרה, קרא, קרה, קרע : חרם, כרם :
חשב, קשב.

ים, יום : ירה, ידה : ידע, ידה
(plurals ימים, ימים) : ימין :
יסר, ישר : ירא, ראה (in some
forms) : ירח, ירך : ישע, ישר.

כה, כח : כון, קום : כפר, קבר.

לא, לו (לה).

מהר, מחר, מכר : מות, מוט :
מחה, מכה, מטה : מטה, מלא,
מלה : מלח, מלך : מן, מין : מנה,
מנע : מעל (*prep.*), מעל (*subs.*) :
מעלה (ה locative), מעלה : מצא,
משא : מחנה, מקנה.

נאף, אנף : נבל, נבל : נבלה,
נבלה : נוח, נוע : נער, נצר : נחה,
נכה, נכה : נחל, נחל : נחם, נקם :
נטה, נטע : נסה, נסע, נשא.

סלה, סלע, צלע : סלח, שלח.
שלך : סמך, שמח.

עד (*prep.*), עד (*adv.*) : עד, עת :
עדה (עד), עדה (יעד) : עוד, אות :
עזר, עצר : עמל, חמל : עני (*adj.*),
עני (*subs.*) : ענה, ענה : עצה (עץ),
עצה (יעץ).

פחד, פקד : פרה, פרה : פרש,
פרש : פתה, פתח.

צמא, צמח : צרה, צרר : צפה,
צפן : צרף, שרף.

ראה, רעה, רעע : רוח, רוע :
רהב, רכב : ריח, ריק : רפא, רפה.

שבע, שבה, שבע : שדה, צ :
שנא, זנה : שכל, שקל : שאר, שער :
שחה, שקה : שקט, שחט : שחר,
שבר : שכב, שכם : שמה, שמע.

תהלה, תחלה : תודה, תורה :
תמיד, תמים.

www.ingramcontent.com/pod-product-compliance
Lightning Source LLC
Chambersburg PA
CBHW030351170426
43202CB00010B/1340
9783337317171